Benjaya's Gifts

Benjaya's Gifts

by

M'haletta
and
Carmella B'Hahn

 Hazelwood Press

First Published
October 1996
by

Hazelwood Press

Hazelwood House
Loddiswell, Nr Kingsbridge, Devon TQ7 4EB, England.
Tel: 01548 821232

Book Design: House of Hahn

Cover Photographs: Robert Jackson Mee

Stained Glass Memorial: Rod Friend

Birth Photograph: Persh Sassoon

Printed by: Kingfisher Print & Design, Totnes, Devon.

ISBN 1901272 00 1

To the Fathers

Abel and Derek

who gave us the gift of motherhood

and

To the Source of the Fathers' seed

I am the Mother of all, bearer of the seed – Creator.
In me are borne all things. From me is born all life.
Yeah, even do I hold death and make it life again.

M·R·

An Archetype

On 31st October I was quite late for work and rushed downstairs towards the front door. The free newspaper was spread out on the mat in front of me. There, face upwards, was the picture.

There was an incredible impact, incredible! It was the same sensation as when I saw the first image of the Earth photographed from the moon, the miracle, the whole sense of an expansion of consciousness, a new frame of reference, a higher perspective of life.

This was not just the personal story of Abel and Carmella any more than the journey to the moon was just an incident in the life of an astronaut. It was an archetypal experience.

The people involved in this birth had, for me, in that moment, a much wider meaning connected with the whole of the cosmos. It was intangible, and yet there was an inner certainty that the birth of this child was also representing the birth of a new dimension of consciousness for us all.

Tony Devany

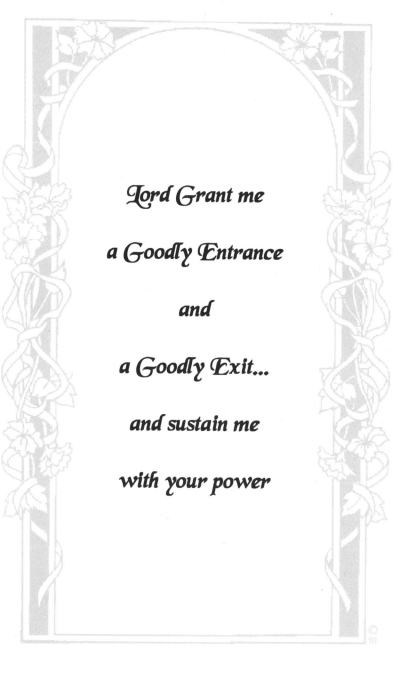

Lord Grant me

a Goodly Entrance

and

a Goodly Exit...

and sustain me

with your power

Contents

Dramatis Personae

Carmella - co-author & mother of Benjaya
M'haletta - co-author & mother of Carmella
Abel - Carmella's partner, Benjaya's father.

Derek - Carmella's father
Sandra - Carmella's elder sister
Marc - Carmella's younger brother
Charlotte - Carmella's younger sister
Wendy - Marc's girfriend at the time of Benjaya's birth.
                                          A social worker.
Peter - Charlotte's boyfriend at the time of Benjaya's birth.
                                          A carpenter.
Patricia - MetaCentre participant, teacher, & friend of M'haletta.
David - MetaCentre lodger. An electrician.
Tony - Carmella's acupuncturist
Persh - Carmella's rebirther, friend, & ex-partner of Tony.
Maggie and Sheila - The National Health midwives

Introduction

Normally, we expect a human being to go from ashes to ashes, dust to dust. This is the story of one who went from water to water leaving a tidal wave of learning in his wake.

The world's media captured and portrayed the powerful images from our story as it happened, accompanied by the usual fragments of information aimed at teasing the emotions. At creating a response. But as we move into the new millennium, sweeping changes are occurring in the way people perceive reality, and there is an increasing need to see beyond the surface of things - *to understand.*

The world in which we live and breathe is not flat. It is not viewed from a single perspective, nor it is perceived through a single sense. There are as many dimensions to life as there are creatures in the world.

Yet life is One. Indivisible. Complete.

In *Benjaya's Gifts* we have taken the scenes which lay behind those headlines and have crafted a holographic image of the reality by sharing not only our own stories, but also the accounts of many of the players - or 'witnesses', as we have come to call them. We will take you on a journey into the heart of a family - our family - and will invite you to share the impact on our lives of Benjaya's birth and life and the learning we gained from the extraordinary drama played out within our midst.

It is a story which cannot help but challenge the taboos and traditions surrounding the ageless mysteries of birth and death leaving us with an expanded awareness of the nature of reality, the strange magic of synchronicity, and the phenomenal power of the human spirit.

You will, at times, find it *beyond* belief.

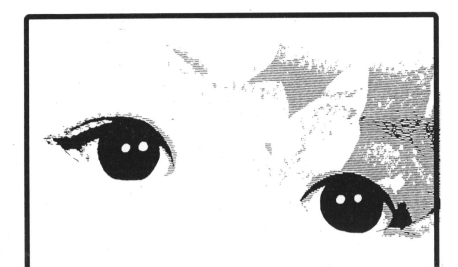

A

Goodly

Entrance

CHAPTER ONE

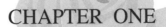

A Family on a Hill

M'haletta

In the beginning there was no Benjaya. His gifts were yet to be visited upon an unsuspecting family - my family - the heart of which has been broken open, and yet enlarged beyond measure.

The beginning of our story is set in a house called 'Adam', a name steeped in mystery and mythology. A name created by God. It is the name both of the house which is our family home and of the hill on which it stands. You may know the hill, many do. It is a beacon in the West Midlands of England, the high point of Clent Country Park, on a clear day offering the eye a vista of eight counties. Draw a line towards the east and you will find no higher point exists before you reach the Ural mountains of Russia; whilst to the west, on an ever-changing skyline, are etched the Black Mountains of Wales. There is beauty in the natural world as far as the eye can see, offering space to breathe and to open to life's natural harmonious rhythms. Glance down from the top of the hill and the village of Clent lies spread out in the valley - clusters of houses great and small, seven pubs, two restaurants, the Church of St. Leonard's, and a village post office serving its three thousand inhabitants and the millions who have, through the years, streamed here on high days and holidays bent on a green country pilgrimage.

At the turn of the century Adam House provided water for the people on the hill from a well that tapped the living spring which still flows through its cellar. In the twenty-five years of our family's life here it is people who have streamed through the house for many different reasons. The house is Victorian, built in 1886 for a bailiff of the Hagley Hall estate. It changed ownership through the years to become a Guest House and Tea Gardens, when Mrs Moses took charge and became a village institution in her own right. After her death the house stood empty, falling into disrepair, gas mantles hanging from their brackets and windows tied to rusted bath taps with string. What was the magic ingredient there that spoke to us one February day when not a blade of grass showed through the snow-crusted gardens that rose lazily upwards through seven terraces to merge with the parent hills behind? I simply fell in love with the energy of this place and we determined to transfer 'home' from a small semi-detatched edge of town house and lead a quiet village family life. We brought with us three children (soon to be four), and next to nothing in the way of finance or furniture to fill the fourteen gaping rooms carpeted with autumn leaves.

As soon as the lights went on people began to arrive in the expectation of a bed and the warmth of welcome Mrs Moses had provided. So, although we had not intended to open the house to strangers, we did our best. We purchased second-hand beds and began to serve a variety of people, many of whom were also in various states of disrepair! That was the beginning of an adventure in which Adam House has been both anchor and umbrella, sheltering, stabilising and uplifting our family as it has grown in size and number, and many hundreds of travellers who have passed through in search of a bed or of themselves.

From that young woman who made a leap into village life I have become, with the passage of time, the old-one, the grandmother. Born under the sun sign of Cancer, I have always been a home and family-lover, and my four children - Sandra, Carmella, Marc and Charlotte - are the core of my life. Carmella, my second daughter, is the mother of Benjaya[1], the youngest of four grandchildren. The generations have sprung from a relationship over the last forty-two years with one man, my husband Derek. In retrospect it seems unbelievable that we have never lived in a partnership alone - always there have been family, lodgers, guests or students in the household, only a whisper away. I feel that I might have missed out on something but, never having had it, I am not quite sure what it is! Though

---

[1] A derivative of his full name, Benjamin Jaya, pronounced Benj-eye-a

Derek is now retired, we have shared, amongst other things, the same profession in the Probation Service, an enduring love of the Greek Islands, all our money and a determination to survive the rigours of marriage. Much has passed between us which has presented challenge after challenge not only to each other, but at times to our children. There were those aspects in our characters which have had to be stripped bare, and when the pain of it all seemed endless I buried myself in my work.

In 1977 I was in India, working in prisons, when I contracted poliarthritis. I returned home in a wheelchair and the physical life closed in on me. It was there, in India, that the philosophy of holistic thinking first made its impact, when an Indian Probation Officer revealed to me that I had brought the illness upon myself due to the disharmony she sensed in my life. She was too polite to suggest that I was bitter and twisted, but as my limbs corkscrewed and the bile in my throat choked me to the point where food no longer nourished, I realised the greatest lessons of my life were upon me and it was time for a major reappraisal and reconstruction if I was going to survive. The physical and attendant emotional challenges were inescapable and substantially affected my mental attitudes, then a succession of events occurred which had an indelible effect upon my life.

First, I found myself drawn towards people who were channelling the most exquisite and instructive wisdoms. I understood nothing of this phenomenon and had not consciously sought it out. It was both disturbing and awe-inspiring and it was from this source that I learnt of the coming of a new age or era; the synchronicity and holistic patterning of all life; that all that exists is energy in ceaseless motion; that love is the great bonding force; that it is possible to co-create with the Source of all creation, and so much more. There are tapes and transcripts of these teachings collected over ten years. Though they have their own individually expressive style I have since read similar content appearing in the works of the last decade or so, but there is nothing to compare with the dynamic and riveting power of the human voice speaking with the resonance and quality of spirit. All my life I had expressed my love of God in the more traditional ways through the Christian religion, but this new input was neither preaching nor teaching in the conventional sense; it was a healing, challenging, all-knowing force which uplifted in every breath and prised open the windows of consciousness, turning my eyes inward and outward in a multi-dimensional perspective of reality. There was no question but that I should apply this benevolent guidance and the concepts which had been freely given and learn how to apply them within my own life and monitor the results.

Results were immediate. After the long illness I was able to return to work. The research in India stood me in good stead for securing a new post; that of Ethnic Advisor to West Midlands Probation Service, which was the first of its kind in the country. An amazing five years followed in which, though I worked hard, lecturing, writing[2] and training, it felt as if whatever I needed to draw upon was already there, in my mind. And so it continued that my life evolved in tandem, developing spiritually and in a successful career, until one day the knowing was simply there - that it was time to release the work in the Probation Service... to do what? There was no definitive inner answer other than 'Open a Centre'.

Carmella, who was studying in America at that time, knew simultaneously that it was time to return and convert the family home into a Centre. It was a time of amazing trust and laughter and the beginning of a new phase in our relationship as Carmella and I realised we had both changed so greatly during recent years that the old mother/child roles had been superseded and we saw ourselves uniting as partners in a task that would take us forwards into new realms of service and personal growth. Nothing could have prepared us totally for the ensuing two years. From 1984 to 1986 around two thousand people streamed through our home. We needed to call on every member of the family to assist us at different times, and each in their own way made their contributions from driving the Centre bus and peeling loads of vegetables to running slots on workshops. We did not need to advertise, people seemed to arrive by word of mouth, nor did we need to struggle greatly with decisions on what to do, it was enough to be open to the endless creative ways in which we could brings groups of people together, of a multiplicity of faiths and cultures, in a spirit of sharing and learning from each other. Derek was equally clear. He knew it was his time to remain at work to maintain us all, and yet he was also there in every sense of the word during his weekends and spare moments, playing a variety of roles. From this family triangle we founded MetaCentre[3] which initially began as a Centre for the development of human potential and holistic education. It was to be our home university as we learnt how to apply holistic principles in our everyday living and within diverse groups of people. It was a phenomenally testing time.

---

[2]*Probation and After-Care in a Multi-Racial Society* - published 1981 by the Commission for Racial Equality.

[3]*The Evolution of MetaCentre - A Light Centre Handbook* published 1986 by MetaPublications. See page 240.

In the Centre, my Probation Officer and family name, Wendy Taylor, was replaced with M'haletta, an uncommon name which I came by in an unusual way. It was given to me in a vision by my spiritual mentor at that time, Grace Lewis. As she described seeing it written above my head, I sensed that it was familiar to me as if it was floating back from some distant time. There was a need in me then to express the essential freedom of spirit that had felt so trapped in the conventional world around me, and this name invoked a sense of the deeper mysteries of life. It has remained with me. Now, with the passage of time, my names seem to have been significant in that they represent for me a merging of the practical professional who operates within a visibly structured world which seeks to contain, re-form and control, and the willing mystic who experiences and hence acknowledges dimensions of reality beyond the immediately visible.

A sense of order, harmony and balance exists in all things, even when chaos rages, and it became my consistent aim to stand at the still centre even when moving through the turbulence. But it has not always been that way. Within me I hold a vibrant sense of the drama and power of life which, in younger years, ignited the touchpapers of deep unfathomable emotions. Sixty years of living find me now well tempered by the richness of a wide variety of life's experiences, but the passion to be fully involved in the flow of life remains undimmed.

During the years of our personal development Carmella and I began the discipline of writing. It became a natural process to record events and what we felt we had learnt from them, also to write down a question on anything on which we felt we needed advice, or a higher perspective than we were reaching, and usually we found ourselves penning something helpful. There were times, too, when teachings simply came directly through to us unbidden, mostly written or in diagrammatic form, but sometimes spoken. On the workshops we ran, or when engaged in healing work, we felt that we were in a heightened state of awareness in which it was easier to communicate on a more telepathic level.

For two years we invested all our energies in the MetaCentre project, then Carmella and I simply knew that this phase was complete. We closed the Centre and for a while went on tour around the country sharing the highlights of our experiences, and when that, too, was over we entered into a void whilst we waited to discover what lay ahead. It had felt to me rather like the end of a successful long running play with no other script in sight. But a script was there, and this is it. We have called it *Benjaya's Gifts*.

CHAPTER TWO

Virginia Carmella

Carmella

oday I am known as Carmella but I was once an entirely different character bearing an entirely different name. My name at birth was Virginia Anne and I was happy with that for twenty-five years despite adolescent taunts of 'virgin for short but not for long'. I was born in my parents' bed, in a little semi-detached house in the centre of England, in the depths of the freezing cold winter of 1958. My arrival was three weeks premature and all 5lbs of me stubbornly rejected my mother's Christmas pudding-rich milk. I was blue in colour for days and blue in temperament for most of the next two decades. To this day I suffer dreadfully from extremes of cold or heat, cannot avoid being early for everything, and still hate Christmas pudding!

I was somewhat of a mystery child, living in my own internal sad and silent space, sucking on two fingers behind a blanket for comfort as I scrutinised the world about me. My big blue eyes were brimming with tears more often than not and throughout my school years passers-by would stop me in the street to enquire as to my welfare. I scarcely spoke until I was six, remaining silent during the first year of school life. The only memory I have of early school days is of an incident in class when I desperately needed to go to the toilet and struggled helplessly to express my need to the teacher. As usual my throat felt as if it were caught in a vice, and not even a frog-like sound would come out. I sat wetting myself and dripping tears onto my sums.

One of our long-standing family jokes is about Virginia and the salt. More than once I sat crying at the dinner table, deeply upset that no-one would pass me the salt. It was not surprising really as I had failed to ask for it! I assumed that people knew what I was thinking, and it came as quite a shock to discover that they did not have telepathic tendencies like my own. I was a delicate flower, an endangered species - afraid of being damaged and urgent to live in a sheltered, sensitive world. As an adult I did discover why I didn't speak, but that is the subject of another story that would take us into the contentious realm of reincarnation.

It was my mother's faith in me as a useful, whole and intelligent being that was my saving grace. Her love for me was rarely expressed physically or verbally but was shown by her unceasing interest and support in both my inner and outer life. A powerful woman is she and I have both aspired to her heights and been buffeted by her depths, her rich emotional life acting as my roller coaster in my early, impressionable days. Watching her succeed in taming and channelling the raw power with which we then lived and using it for the good of others has been one of my greatest joys.

When I think of my father I think of birdwatching, mountains, rugby, petty criticisms, good humour and lazy pints at the local public house. It is difficult not to love this charming, bear-sized man, and I doubt if he has any enemies. My only regret about his parenting role is that he did not make more effort to be present in his children's life. My mother held almost all of the responsibility for our welfare.

My parents struggled valiantly to find harmony in their relationship, casting many an uncomfortable shadow over the house in the process. The bumpy issues were never shared with the children, and the children probably never shared their intense pride in them as parents. Our teenage friends were jealous of the trust and freedom we were given on a plate - our boundaries were wide, our adventures were many and our curfews were non-existent. Whilst other mothers would ban their offspring's association with the most unruly of the local lads, my mother would invite a drunken midnight caller in, wag her finger a little and tuck him up in bed with a teddy! Adam House and its occupants gained a reputation for doing things differently and, as I recall, anyone who passed the threshold was treated with respect.

My elder sister, Sandra, two and a half years older than me, was generally easy going, although she could not resist taunting me at times for my afflictions. We whiled away many hours playing dollies side by side with little friction between us. My brother Marc, who is two and a half years younger than me, was an entirely different kettle of fish. I christened him 'that boy' and found fault in almost everything he did for many years to come. The boisterous, jolly boy and the silent violet clashed more often than not until the passage of time tempered us into recognition of each other's value.

Charlotte, who joined the fray at Adam House when my childhood was almost done, was somewhat of an only child who needed no-one except horses for friends and a pink 'golly' blanket for comfort. I paid this independent, curly-haired red head little attention and suppressed my feelings of jealously at her easy life with the now more mature parents with increased material wealth.

The emergence from my silent cocoon was very gradual and it was my stirring adolescent interest in boys that drew me out to function as if I was normal. 'As if' because my insides still crumbled whilst my now attractive, make-up enhanced exterior fooled even me with its air of fashionable confidence. And the boys were certainly stirred by me; whether because of my pretty face and long, brown, flowing tresses, my air of knowing things beyond my years, or my well endowed figure, I'm not too sure.

My virginity went to the wind at a blushingly early age in a fairly boring encounter with a local scooter-riding youth sporting the fashion of the day - red socks, stay-pressed trousers and a checkered shirt with a button down collar. The most interesting thing I remember about it is that my fractured left arm was encased in plaster and was sticking rigidly out of the bedcovers.

Halesowen Grammar School was a mixed school, and how I managed to pass six 'O' levels I'll never know considering the amount of mixing I did. Despite a supportive home life I yearned for depth and connection with people, and at Art College, fired by this need and an urge to discover something meaningful in life, I threw myself into an exploration of men!

Aged seventeen, after a year of artistic study, I left home to work in seaside hotels with my sister, Sandra, to save up for my next step in life - a two year photographic course. It was an eventful summer in which I served Margaret Thatcher breakfast in bed and was raped by the depraved head waiter in the same week. Neither event seems to have left me scarred.

At photographic college my self-worth crept up and my shrinking violet blossomed into a sunflower. I loved the work, passed my exams with flying colours and basked in the misplaced glamour of the dangling camera around my neck. With shocking confidence 'Sunflower' announced the intention to fly off to Israel for the summer to live and work on a kibbutz.

When my feet touched Israeli soil I wept. I felt choked by an inexplicable sense of relief at my homecoming . I am not Jewish and have no known Jewish connections - in this life at least - but I felt completely at home in this strangely familiar land. I also fell in love with Marty, a Canadian Jew with a wicked sense of humour and spectacular legs, and I would write to him for years to come sharing the horrors of his compulsory training course for his stint in the country's army. The following year I was to return but in the meantime an inner revolution was taking place in me.

I had always felt connected to a force greater than myself - my own private God - but it wasn't until this year, aged nineteen, that I became immovably convinced that the essential essence of a human being lives on after death. It took one outing with my mother to a Spiritualist church to make this life-changing leap in belief, and from that day on I have been committed to self-improvement and to enhancing the spiritual element in my life. My burning question has been 'How can I best live my life now in the knowledge that I will continue to evolve after death?' I consumed books on philosophy, mysticism, psychology, life after death, reincarnation, and the like and found the most common theme in all my reading material to be 'Life is a school, and it is in the best interest of humanity to accept everything upon our path as learning material, to pass the tests on offer consciously and move on to the higher grades'. I took on board this overview of life's purpose and, be it truth or fiction, it has stood me in good stead.

After finalising my college education, well equipped now to enter professional life as an assistant photographer, I returned for a few months to the promised land and the love of my life. This time I backpacked via Greece and it was here that I experienced the first of two astounding incidents that intensified my sense of connection to God.

On my last day in Greece I had run out of Greek money and was very hungry with only dry bread and cheese to last me until the following morning. Also my shoes had given up the ghost and braving the sizzling streets barefoot had blistered the soles of my feet. At least I had a bed for the night, albeit on a rooftop, on which I sat day-dreaming about the power of positive thought. I was thinking that if I could manifest two things with my thoughts right now they would be a few juicy tomatoes to go with the bread and cheese and a pair of sandals - pink ones to match my limited wardrobe. God only knows what prompted me to get on my hands and knees and look under the bed, but I did and the shock nearly felled me. There side by side were a bag of juicy tomatoes and a perfect fitting pair of pink sandals.

The second momentous event is described in Chapter four.

On arrival at the kibbutz I discovered that Marty had been investing energy in another romantic relationship with a Jewish woman from Germany. An interesting trio we made sitting together in the community dining room discussing which one of the women would be best for his marital life. He loved me passionately but, all things considered, I was not of the right religion to bear him Jewish children and so, sadly but graciously, I returned home.

London lured me, and after a couple of jobs in the photographic world I became disillusioned with the glamour and fed up with retouching wrinkles on portraits of the famous. Remembering the pink shoe episode, I sat and pictured clearly the kind of job I wanted - something that touched on the more mystical side of life which would also help further my understanding of life and people. My flatmate wandered into the room with a newspaper in her hand - *The Psychic News* - and asked me if I wanted to read it. I flicked it open and noticed instantly an advert for a job as advertising assistant on the paper. At 9.30 the next morning I was accepted on the spot for the job!

It proved to be a fascinating couple of years, which not only educated me about the psychic and healing capacities of humankind but also boggled my mind at times and taught me many a lesson in the art of discernment. It was part of my task to act as guinea pig for new advertisers for them to prove their talents as mediums and/or healers before being accepted as bona fide by the paper. It was not an easy task. I was spoken to by many a spirit guide, given messages galore and healed until I should have been a specimen of prime health - which I was not. Most of the applicants seemed genuine and good hearted but many were obviously, to say the least, misguided. At other events I witnessed instantaneous healings, witnessed a table lurching in mid-air and even saw a bunch of flowers slowly materialising out of a mist-like substance in a darkened room. It was an unusual educative venture into the hidden worlds but I was lonely in London.

Next stop, now living back at Adam House, was a post in publishing where I rose quickly to the position of assistant editor on a magazine and thrived on the work. It was here in the slack period between issues that I spent many an hour sitting with pen to paper addressing questions about my personal growth to a higher source and allowing streams of advice to pour through me. I think that the source of the wisdom was my own higher self or 'in-tuition' but, whatever it was, it was - and still is - extremely useful. This personal work was supported by incredibly inspiring teachings which were channelled through two of my mother's friends. I would sit for hours listening to these erudite teachers from other planes of existence speaking with startling accuracy and loving sensitivity about my life, my mind, my downfalls and my spiritual path. Always I was moved to tears.

In 1982, aged twenty-four, I left company car, steady income and a job I loved to fly out to the USA for a seven month living workshop in accelerated self-growth. My base was The Fellowship of the Inner Light, Virginia. I studied a variety of disciplines there including meditation, healing, effective communication, emotions management, dream analysis, the Kabbalah, astrology, Tai Chi, and the I Ching. I completed the Teacher- Training program in order to share what I had learnt in a structured way with others and really felt as if this was my calling. By the end of my stay Virginia the violet was unrecognisable and I felt so far removed from my old personality that I underwent a full immersion baptism by my teacher and emerged from the water with the new name of Carmella.

I returned to England with a bubbling enthusiasm for life - now glowing more pink than blue - and a vision for a new career. Whilst I had been away my parents had also been growing apace and we felt it was time to work together as a trio in the co-creation of a Centre for Holistic Education in our family home. The name we were given - MetaCentre - means the point of perfect balance (on a ship). 'Meta' also means changing or going beyond a fixed point. We certainly went beyond my wildest imaginings working flat out in a way that made our hearts sing and tested us to our limits.

The most vivid memories from this time include 'The Grill' and a hairdressers salon. The Grill was an exercise on a challenging four-day course for the brave called 'MetaPeople'. In our sanctuary we placed one arm chair under a spotlight and the rest of the room was dark. All the participants sat around the walls in the dark and one at a time we sat in the hot-seat and had to answer all the questions that were put to us - truthfully. Most people were terrified before the exercise and exhilarated afterwards, as if they had really absorbed the knowing that 'the truth will set you free'. The hairdressers salon in a mining town in Yorkshire was a venue for one of our talks on New Age Culture and I shall never forget sitting under a hairdryer waxing lyrical about the potential of humanity to a group of down-to-earth northerners.

At last my insides had stopped crumbling and my inner life was progressing well, but my sexual life had moved from one extreme to the other and celibacy was not a path I wanted to take indefinitely. I felt lonely for romantic loving and at twenty-seven I was beginning to consider myself to be on the shelf - not helped at all by my sister teasingly calling me 'spinster'. There was hope. I had hoarded quite a collection of predictive readings (astrological, auric, I Ching, Tarot) which had been freely given over the years, and three of these had been very specific about meeting 'the one' in my life by the end of 1985. I had also been shown a picture of a young, dark, bearded man who it was said would play a vital part in my life.

December 1985 came and almost went with no 'one' in sight, then on 27th December, as a last minute decision, I went with a friend, Annie, to a course called 'Playworld' held at Grimstone Manor in Devon. The course was for adults to release inhibitions and express their inner, spontaneous, fun-loving child.

My heart sank as I looked around the circle of participants. 'Unlikely looking marriage prospects' I thought, disappointed that the predictions were wrong, then I let go and relaxed. The second day we had a group hug which we all enjoyed so much that we agreed to repeat the experience later. However, at the appointed time no-one turned up except me and a tall, dark, bearded building contractor. We looked at each other shyly, I started to massage his feet and we proceeded to talk for hours into the night.

It felt safe with this man, there was no male/female game-playing and so I shared with him my feelings about the predictions being wrong.

To the amazement of us both, after humorously suggesting other members of the course as life partners, he said **"Maybe it's me"**. I laughed tactlessly as he puzzled as to where the words had come from, but we were both intrigued enough with the idea that we met in every available break to share further.

I learned that this Bristol-born man with a rocky marriage and a growing interest in alternative therapies had recently attended a Macrobiotic Summer Camp where he had made some sweeping decisions about his life. He had discovered the breathing technique of Rebirthing, renowned for creating clarity of vision, and after one session had decided to leave his wife, sell his house and fold up his building business, believing that he was holding on to all three for the wrong reasons. On hearing of his intention to leave, his wife had absconded abroad with almost all his wordly goods leaving him in a somewhat shocked state to complete the house sale alone. Now he was living at his parents newly bought house in the New Forest - essentially a building site - which he and his men were in the process of transforming into a high class bed and breakfast establishment. It was to be his last building contract.

Our long hours of sharing revealed that we held similar visions for the future and, both being Aquarian, had many similar character traits, the main ones being our idealism and desire to be catalysts for positive change in society. This in-depth process of checking each other out was an extraordinary beginning to a relationship which felt more like the initial explorations before an arranged marriage than a free western couple following any kind of chemical attraction. There was no raging passion growing between us, no whirlwind romance in the air, simply a feeling of intrigue and anticipation.

We left in his car as a couple and headed for MetaCentre to introduce him to my parents. An adventure had begun and my sense was that the script had been written already and we were merely living out the first scene according to the director's requirements.

CHAPTER THREE

The Creative Force

Carmella

On the last leg of our journey to the Midlands I predicted that my mother would be in tune with the director's requirements and would be eagerly awaiting our arrival in total trust of the speed of the current movements and that my father would give an affable welcome, would be completely unruffled and continue about his business. This was exactly as it proved to be and after my father had withdrawn to watch the rugby match the three of us sat in a cocoon of excitement awaiting the inevitable connections at a deeper level than the initial pleasantries.

There I was sitting, on the settee in a triangle with my mother, a mystery man, and a shared sense of destiny. He was a man with no belongings, no home and, at that point, no name as he had stated that he was keen to change his name to one with a softer sound. I felt as if I were sitting with a blank canvas which was awaiting the first stroke of a master-piece. The potential for creating together was almost tangible, as if it hung in the air ready to be absorbed and acted upon.

It was in the triangle of that first evening at MetaCentre that 'Don' found a new first name - Abel, by testing out the sounds of different names for himself until he settled on one with which he felt comfortable. He listened to our responses and we both agreed that it suited him well and felt a good strong name. Before the night was out he had also committed to a new last name which was not his conscious intent. This came to him in a somewhat different way.

To my surprise my mother felt moved to share with Abel that for some years we had been conscious of a group name under which the spiritual teachings and guidance had been given to us. The name was B'Hahn, which we understood to mean of the Brotherhood of Hahn. I heard Abel reply **"B'Hahn...I think that could be my name."** I gasped, as I knew it would be an honour to carry that name and I was also slightly jealous as I would have loved to have adopted it myself. We had been told that this group or brotherhood of discarnate and incarnate beings are primarily engaged in the task of education for the coming of the new era. For Abel to hold this vibration, I believed would mean that he would be expected to work along the same lines, and on some level I felt that he knew this and was aware of the significance of what he was suggesting. "Would it be permitted?" he asked. After a few moments of silence my mother answered "Yes, it is permitted". It was by this means that the mystery man symbolically accepted an unusual spiritual path and joined us on our journey.

Abel had already made an appointment to meet with his solicitor on other matters, and a few days later used that opportunity to change his name by statutory declaration to Abel B'Hahn, by which time he had asked me to marry him! The proposal was made on the seventh day after our first meeting at Playworld. It was not a romantic moment. I was sitting on the floor in a pool of tears telling him about my last intense relationship with a Dutch man which had caused me tremendous pain, and I was worrying out loud about this relationship ending up the same way. His response was to reassure me by saying "As soon as my divorce comes through I will marry you, if you will have me". I needed time to reply. I was blank, unable to feel a response in my heart, but what I did feel was a sense of destiny and of purpose together. Love, however, was blossoming by now in his heart.

Love for this man, and certainly respect, may have been growing within me, but I was not 'in love' in the way one would expect to be in order to accept a proposal of marriage. Nevertheless, a few hours later, with the increasingly familiar feeling of being prompted to act in a specific way because of its vital importance in my life script, I accepted the proposal and the announcement was made to my parents and sister

Charlotte at dinner. Charlotte was dumbstruck and filled with the emotion I wanted to feel myself; my mother was glowing with an air of knowing which lacked any sense of surprise; and my father humorously verbalised all the right responses, welcomed Abel into the family clan and toasted our happy future. We drank wine and made merry with hilarious jokes about the possibilities for an alternative type of wedding, and all was rosy with the world.

In the weeks that followed, Abel completed his building contract and then moved into the Centre to live and to partake in all of the forthcoming workshops. I had 'fallen' for this man in such a strange way that our unfolding relationship and his vacillating character traits were a never-ending source of fascination and challenge to me. He was at that time like two beings rolled into one, both of which I respected; but I knew that I would never in a million years be compatible with a fair few of his 'Don' characteristics. It was his Abel that captivated me, and it was he to whom I felt I had committed myself. Abel was like a new-born being, revelling in a world that he had just discovered - a world in which I had been living for quite some while. His visions for alternative ways of living complimented my own and excited me. One trend-setter had found another, and it was a relief to us both to have found such comprehension and support. He was potential personified to me and I was in the privileged position of being asked to guide him to become the most effective, attractive, well-dressed and wise man he could be. What a task! I was in effect being asked to create a new man to suit my tastes.

Don had little interest in his appearance and his dress sense clashed somewhat with my own, which, to my shame, caused me embarrassment and made me itch to transform him into my image of the strikingly hand-some man he could be. He was generally a fine, upstanding young man with sky-high principles and a good safe family background with three siblings and with parents who were proud of his amazing practical and mental abilities. He had been university educated and had a degree in physiology, a distinct lack of flow about his body and his speech, a sharp and critical mind, and a good dose of arrogance and scepticism thrown in. Of course, I wanted all the fine aspects of Don to merge with his new self, and all of the characteristics with which my personality clashed to drop away post-haste. The saving grace of our relationship was his mastery of the art of change and the headway we both made was fast and furious, but I could see that there was a very long way to go before we made a comfortable couple and life was intense, to say the least, in the early days.

It was into this intensity, in the seventh week after our first meeting, that our son chose to break through our contraceptive barriers and make his presence known. I was stunned and excited with a sense that destiny was taking its course, albeit rather rapidly. The Don in Abel was shocked and peeved that he had not been in control of the decision, but his softer part was intrigued with the idea of parenthood and willing to throw himself into creating the most beautiful pregnancy and birth experience he could. My mother's response was almost par for the course. In her journal in the week of her introduction to Abel she had written a prediction about a child that I would bear:

> *And so it is, the one you call Carmella shall bear a child and s/he shall be called 'wondrous one'. Let then the body now prepare to take the seed and take no heed of the planting... the child comes to work from the moment of birth.*

She had kept this to herself and now could release the excitement and anticipation she had been feeling for some time. None of us had any notion as to why the child might be called 'wondrous one' or what work could possibly begin at the moment of birth. These were mysteries yet to unfold.

Now I was not only co-creating a new man and a new relationship, but also a tiny new body which was growing daily within me. It was tough and I felt sick. The wedding was postponed as being a rotund bride with a passenger was not something in keeping with my vision. Instead we focussed on educating ourselves about pregnancy and birth and on seeking to understand more deeply the meaning of 'holistic birth' which, we were agreed, we wanted for our baby's entry to the world.

We were striving to create a more holistic lifestyle at that time which could be defined as living with a conscious awareness of the effect of mind, emotions, body, spirit and environment on daily living, and were attempting to bring them into harmony. This gave us a starting place for our questions about the pregnancy and birthing process, and we asked ourselves 'How will our thoughts, knowledge (or lack of it), emotional state, fitness, diet (including all input into our senses such as television, reading material, smoky atmospheres), source of inspiration, and our environment affect our ability to create a whole and healthy being and a trauma-free birth experience?'

We read many books on the subject of birth, one of which contained some educative chapters on waterbirth which was at that time almost unheard of in Britain. The book was entitled *Ideal Birth* by Sondra Ray and it was Abel who became inspired by the water idea and asked me if I would consider giving birth in water. My initial response was **"No way!"** It seemed like an added complication that I could well do without, considering that the home birth we wanted would be severely frowned upon for a first baby. However, I still wanted to read the book.

I was about four months pregnant at the time and had felt only the barest movements from the baby; but whilst I was reading those chapters about waterbirth I felt strong stirrings inside my womb. I put the book down and the stirrings stopped. I picked it up again to read and, low and behold, the flurries of movement returned. It was uncanny. Was the baby trying to tell me something? I decided to do a test, and so I sat cross-legged on the bed quietly for a few minutes and then asked the being within my womb **"If you want a waterbirth please give me a very definite kick"**. The response was immediate - a forceful kick on my left side caused me to jump so high that I recall nearly falling off the bed. What choice did I have but to put all my energies towards researching the feasibility of creating a waterbirth for this assertive being?

Abel and I attended a one-day conference in London at which the French expert in waterbirth - Michel Odent - was speaking. We heard about the work of Igor Charkovsky who had been delivering babies into water in Russia for over twenty-five years. We saw videos of waterbirths and even managed to obtain copies of two American videos on the subject. The more I learned, the more my fears and thoughts of complication dropped away. Once I had ascertained that the baby would not drown as s/he would still be receiving oxygen through the umbilical cord whilst under water, and would not take a breath until a part of the body contacted air, I could not imagine a more beautiful way of giving birth than relaxing in warm water with my baby coming from one watery womb-like space into another. I was becoming excited and crystal clear that I wanted to give birth to my baby in this way, no matter what obstacles I might encounter in the process.

My G.P.'s receptionist laughed outright when, in answer to her question as to the choice of hospital for my 'confinement', I responded "I'm planning a home birth". It took me a month and a good dose of courage to inform my G.P. that it was actually a home waterbirth we were planning. She was great, her gulp was hardly visible, and, to her credit, she proceeded to do her homework on the subject before making any pronouncement on her part in it. We provided her with some information but, as could have been predicted, she found next to no information on waterbirth in Britain and concluded that she could not support this 'untested birth method' but would remain on call in case of emergency. This felt fine, as by law we did not need a doctor present and didn't particularly want one.

We were aware of causing a major stir amongst local N.H.S. midwives as, not having been allocated a midwife due to our unusual choice of birth method, we were actively seeking communication with midwives. There was widespread interest in the idea of our planned waterbirth, but complex political issues behind the scenes prevented any midwife openly supporting us. It seemed that management were upset by the fear that if our home waterbirth was openly supported they would have a queue of pregnant mums seeking home and/or waterbirths at their door just as community midwifery had been honed down and centralised hospital birth had become Health Service policy. One young midwife who had never even seen a home birth was assigned to us at some point - which did little to boost our confidence - but then we discovered that she had handed in her notice, and that was that. We were not to meet our midwives until the day before the birth, but we trusted that the right midwives would present themselves at the right time and did not feel neglected by the N.H.S.

To Abel's parents it must have seemed as if he had met a woman on the rebound from his marriage who was leading him a merry dance and rapidly brain-washing him into a weird and unfathomable way of life. The decision to plan a birth into water for their first (illegitimate) grandson could have been the final nail in the coffin, coming hot on the heels of his name change, but it was not, and I shall be eternally grateful. Not only had Don been named after his father's brother, who had died when he was a teenager, but the family surname of Gillett now had little hope of surviving. There is no doubt that his parents experienced a great deal of pain and a sense of rejection, but despite the bruises their prime concern was their son's happiness. Whatever strong judgements they held were kept securely under their hats in preference to the neutral message of 'Time will tell'.

My immediate family and friends were, thank goodness, supportive from the beginning. They trusted our decisions, moved with us through the different stages of learning and thoroughly enjoyed the unfolding saga. It would have been a big surprise to them if we had taken the conventional route of a hospital birth for the entry of our child.

The Healing Sanctuary at MetaCentre was our obvious choice of location. What better birthplace could we find than a room which had been used through the years for healing and learning activities? This beamed attic room with its view of the garden and Clent Hills beyond was, and still is, a sacred space.

The choice of a vessel in which to give birth was not so easy. Birthing tubs did not exist at that time and we racked our brains to think of a container of the right size, shape and depth. It had to be deep enough for me to move about in and for the baby to be completely immersed before rising to the surface but not so deep as to cause strain on the midwife's back - not to mention the strain on the floor joists! Visions of mother and baby flying through the water-filled air to the sound of creaking, gushing and manic screams were hard to avoid at this point, and finding the right pool was becoming a task of paramount importance. Eventually, we thought of the idea of a garden pond-liner and off we sped to check out the possiblility at the local garden centre. We asked a befuddled assistant which fishpond would be most conducive to giving birth, and with a nervous shuffle he disappeared to find a more senior worker whose response was to enquire whether we required a pond with or without fish. We made our own decision and hired a pear-shaped pond, 6ft by 3ft for £5.80 per week and prayed that it was up to the task.

It must have been a sight to be seen - our Morris Minor crawling up Adams Hill wearing a floppy fishpond like a hat which almost obscured the driver's view. No curious onlooker could have guessed its purpose. Abel made a wooden frame to support it and we draped a white bedspread around it to soften its appearance. Now in pride of place in the sanctuary, with candlelight and gentle music, the whole scene looked thoroughly inviting and the excitement was mounting. I quite enjoyed the jokes about me giving birth in a fishpond and I knew that the Press would have a field day when they heard about it. And they did hear about it because *I told them.*

The time had come to face my lifetime fear of the public gaze and I didn't really feel as if I had a choice about it. There was no question of me keeping quiet about our intentions to create a waterbirth. I wanted the whole world to know that we have a legal right to choose the way we give birth to our children and I hoped that before long we would also be able to report a beautiful story of a birth in water which would inspire others to explore this possibility. My parents were on holiday when the following press release was sent out, but I had no doubt that they would take all the interest in the goings on at Adam House in their stride without even a wobble.

PRESS RELEASE

FOR IMMEDIATE RELEASE

The Midlands' first planned waterbirth is due to take place on 9th November 1986 (or thereabouts) at a small Centre for self-transformation and holistic education, called MetaCentre, in the village of Clent.

The parents of this forthcoming 'waterbaby', Carmella and Abel B'Hahn, who live at the Centre, have researched this method of birth thoroughly and are convinced that it offers a multitude of advantages to both mother and child.

Waterbirth, pioneered by Igor Charkovsky in Russia and Michel Odent in France, has been seen to reduce the pain and length of labour dramatically due to the relaxing effect of the warm water on the mother's body. The gentle emergence of the infant into a second warm and womb-like space is said to prevent the normally inevitable shock and trauma of birth.

If all goes according to plan for the B'Hahns, Roshana or Benjamin, their first child, will be born directly into a birthing tub which is in fact a fishpond, hired from their local garden centre!

The couple plan to video the birth and to travel the country sharing their experience of the benefits of natural birth and waterbirth.

CHAPTER FOUR

Making the News

M'haletta

T he press release arrived in the first post of a variety of different media establishments on the morning of 27th October. In the Birmingham office of the *Daily News,* a Midlands free paper, it found its way to the news desk run by Claire, the news editor. She thought the publicity looked like an interesting possibility and asked Ann Adams, a senior *Daily News* reporter to look into it. Claire had already heard about the MetaCentre through David Scott, her Chief, who, after visiting a while previously looking for assistance for persistent migraines, had made some positive comments. Ann Adams contacted the senior photographer, Mike Fisher, made an appointment with us immediately, and arrived that afternoon at 3.30 looking for copy for the next morning's edition.

Ann and Mike, who were both about the same age as Abel and Carmella, were professionals from the outset, clear on what they wanted for their newspaper, incisive, whilst at the same time conveying openness, warmth and a willingness to listen. From those first moments of meeting, the exchanges touched personal chords in them both and they were caught up in the excited anticipation which, with their arrival, had begun to take a new momentum.

Ann explained what she was looking for - a strong story, unique, local, which in this instance had the added benefit of being slightly quirky because of the fishpond angle. She phoned the newsdesk and told them to reserve space, that there would be copy and photographs ready for the same evening and that there was definitely a story with a sequel brewing. The obvious location for the photographs was the sanctuary where the birthing pool was sitting comfortably, filled with water.

The stillness was there as it always is in that room, moving people to speak gently, to take more notice of themselves, as if they were the stones that could ripple the stillness of a lake. The carpet was white and the walls were swirls of cloud shapes which gave the impression of being in a more unworldly space than living rooms and bedrooms usually allow. There was a music centre and a bed, but it was the pool that dominated the scene, drawing them towards it like a magnet. The notion of a fishpond did not strike the same note of amusement when the birthing pool was seen in situ. The liner held the water gracefully, the sides where Abel had built a wooden frame had strength and the undulations of the moulded shape looked as if they were made to hold a reclining human body. They were surprised, aware I think then, that this was not a stunt but was something more subtle that had to be done, whatever the outcome.

Later, Mike was to tell us how much he had wanted to ask to be there to experience the waters moving with birth but had felt that he did not dare. He walked around the room testing the light and angles, choosing to have Carmella leaning over the side of the pool and rippling the waters with her hand, as it is difficult to catch a good image of still water which reflects like glass. There was only one object on the wall in the sanctuary, a plain wooden cross, which was directly behind the pool. It was Mike's choice to include the cross in the picture as a background symbol. The newspaper was particularly careful not to be associated with promoting cults, and so he thought that the cross image would dispel any misconceptions by people who might question this unusual event.

Ann took a serious approach to the concept of waterbirth and thought it would be of interest to the general public. She planned to follow the picture with a longer feature for the women's page. Abel and Carmella felt the meeting had been such a positive experience that they agreed to give the *Daily News* the option to print any pictures of the birth in exchange for developing and printing the film. There was never any question or mention of money involved. Ann made a careful note of the expected birth date, still a couple of weeks away, returned to enter the birth event into the newsdesk diary and we looked forward to seeing them again.

That night all went according to plan. The picture and article were accepted by the night editor and on the morning of Tuesday 28th, Carmella, beside the pool (with a smiling inset photo of Abel), appeared on the front page of Issue No 421 of the *Daily News* accompanied by the headlines:

HEAD FIRST IN A FISHPOND
Mum-to-be in pioneering waterbaby plan

The headline came as no surprise as, after all, Carmella had used the fish-pond angle herself to draw the attention of the Press and they were only doing the same to catch the eye of their readers, though some phrases in the descriptive text stretched the imagination:

> *...the 28 year old photographer and her fiancée Abel, are to have their waterbaby in goldfish bowl setting surrounded by cameramen, a film crew and other fascinated onlookers.*

It was impossible not to see the humour in the mental images which could be created at the thought of us all queuing up to sit around a goldfish bowl! Then followed the inevitable mixture of views from professionals, the information that a spokesman from the British Medical Association viewed the birth plan with 'considerable mistrust and the gravest concern'. It was conceded that waterbirth, though almost unheard of in Britain, was practised as a tried and tested birth method in America and France, so all in all, we felt that the batting had been opened on the subject of waterbirth and we hoped that we would have something positive and constructive to add to stimulate future public debate.

As Mike Fisher had intended, the cross was visible. Although we had no way of knowing whether it had caught the conscious attention of the readers, it had a particular significance for us. The cross in Christian symbology is primarily associated with the sacrifice of life through the death of the Christ, but for us it also held a direct connection to the Nativity story. The story of the cross had become one of our family legends to be handed down and recounted over and over, the mystical quality of its appearance always working its magic and leaving us wondering. This is the story of its discovery which had had such an impact upon Carmella when in Israel, told in her words:

*It was in 1980 that we began to use a top room in Adam House as a
sanctuary for healing. We called this room the Ramethon Healing
Sanctuary. We knew it was time for us to find a cross, a plain and simple
cross, nothing that held symbology of any organisation or group. I made
a decision to return to Israel that year, knowing it was my task to find
this cross and that I would find it on this journey in an unusual way. It
would be the only one of its kind and it would be called the Ramethon
Cross.*

*I went to Jerusalem and stayed for a week in a hospice on the Via
de la Rosa - said to be the road that Christ walked with his cross. Day
after day I scoured every corner of the city looking for our cross. It was
a hot, tiring, and unproductive week. The only crosses I could find were
mass produced, mainly gilt or ornate crucifixes. There was nothing with
the simplicity and simple vibration I was seeking. By the end of the week
I was exhausted and frustrated. Knowing that I had done all that I
could, I asked for higher guidance and immediately received a flash of
'knowing' that I had to get on a bus and go to Bethlehem.*

*I packed instantly and found a Bethlehem bus. It was a long,
rickety ride with chickens fluttering up and down the gangway and I had
the sensation that I was taking a trip into the past. On arrival, the
search began all over again in the same way, combing every street and
shop. There was nothing there for me. Feeling a sense of helplessness
and disappointment I felt moved to go into the Church of the Nativity
where the place of Jesus' birth is marked and there I asked to be led by
the hand to the spot where the cross was waiting.*

*I went outside and sat down in a cafe in the sweltering heat and
must have made a dejected picture because a man came across to my
table and asked "What's troubling you? Can I help?" I explained that I
had been looking for a special cross for over a week. He said "I know
everyone. You come with me and we will find the cross." His name was
Charlie and he had just been nominated for the office of Mayor of
Bethlehem. Clearly he was very well known and I trusted him
completely.*

*He paid for my drink and we left , walking through the town arm in
arm, as Jews and Arabs hailed him in different languages as we passed
by. There was something touchingly significant about walking through
Bethlehem being greeted by the two different factions so often in*

*opposition. We visited a few shops owned by his friends, but we could tell straight away that none of the crosses were for me. At last he said "Ah, I know!" He took me into a field past a sign which read : **WHERE SHEPHERDS WATCHED THEIR FLOCKS,** then down a dusty dirt track to a tiny hut. Inside was a small, wizened old man. He was a carpenter and all around him were heads of Mary, Joseph and Jesus that had been carved by his hand. Charlie explained briefly about our search. The man did not answer, he just stared into my eyes; then he turned and shuffled to the back of the hut. We followed. Hanging on the wall I saw 'our' cross - about a foot high, simple but extremely aesthetic, with the knots of the wood standing proud. He took it down and, through Charlie as interpreter, said -*

"This cross has been on my wall for over ten years, waiting. I have known it is to go to some special place but have never known where. It is for you. Take it."

A tingling sensation shot up my spine as if an electrical current had passed through me. I felt the whole of my body responding to it and at the same time my mind knew with certainty that the awaited connection had been made. He told us that the cross had been made with wood from the Mount of Olives. I was willing to pay all the money I had for such a treasure but the carpenter would take nothing. He needed no details as to its destination or the purpose for which it would be used and so I simply blew off the layer of dust and received it with a smile that must have lit up the shack.

How amusing it was to imagine three hundred and fifty thousand pictures of the Bethlehem Cross finding their way onto breakfast tables, into briefcases, riding on buses and trains, spreading their way into inconceivable corners of the Midlands and beyond. I loved the synchronicity of it all. The cross is also used universally as a symbol of archetypal man at full stretch, capable of infinite and harmonious expansion on the Earth and celestial plains. The expansion for us had indeed begun and was to continue at a rapid pace.

The *Daily News,* being the first to break the story, drew immediate interest from other branches of the media, all of them at this point local. As calls came in on the morning of Tuesday, 28th it was Carmella who took the lead, looking outwardly calm and in control as she buzzed around the house, one minute doing a radio interview on the telephone in the hall, the next nipping up three flights of stairs to ripple the waters in the pool as an authentic background sound for a rival station, and feeding local newspapers with additional information.

The 'pregnant mum' initially drew more attention than the 'pregnant dad'. I was consistently aware of Abel's strong presence as he waited, confident of his own verbal ability and photogenic image but careful not to project out too strongly whilst he discovered his role, allowing Carmella the space she needed to co-ordinate all these potentially hazardous contacts. With some trepidation she agreed to an interview with Central Television News, and I drew a deep breath at the thought of our private space opening to public scrutiny.

For different reasons the visual medium of television undoubtedly offered Carmella the greatest challenge. The equipment was daunting as it spilled out of the van. A giant spotlight dominated the lounge, turning an autumn afternoon into the dripping heat of a summer's day. Carmella has always had a reaction to extremes of heat and cold, excess of either bring immediate changes in temperature which are visible in her skin colour. This we had been told, when she was younger, was due to an excess of nerve endings in her fingers and feet. This real physical concern was compounded by her childhood memories of the inability to bring out words, let alone express her views in a situation in which there could well be some tricky and challenging questions. We had worked on these anxieties, which she saw as a limitation, in many different ways on our MetaCentre workshops and those light hearted exercises of 'The Grill' suddenly had an immensely significant purpose. Even though she had proven on many occasions that she had the ability to rise above the physical and emotional tripwires to speak her own truth, the realm of television was unexplored territory and I was extremely grateful to see Abel's natural composure in these somewhat unnatural circumstances.

The scenario began with the cameras picking up on Abel and Carmella walking across the grass in front of Adam House and entering the front door; then came the dialogue seated together in armchairs in front of the spotlight, followed by shots of them both by the pool. The radio and newspaper interviews had in part been a preparation. Carmella had been in a highly connected space all day and it held - just about! This television debut was the only occasion that her mouth was to look slightly contorted as she controlled the trembling of her lips. To our relief the concept of waterbirth was sensibly seeded by them both presenting as a team, and the camera crew left hopeful of making the early evening news.

The next task was to ensure that we had video recording equipment set up, and tape recorders by two different radios, tuned to different stations from which interviews were due to be broadcast at about the same time. We felt it essential to monitor exactly what we were generating and to look carefully at what was being presented. Both Carmella and I had worked with the media and were acutely aware of the infinite number of ways in which mis-representations can occur.

As it approached the six o'clock news-time we were absorbed in our respective tasks of watching, listening and preparing to record in different parts of the house, when we had two unexpected callers. It seemed to us to be a most strange time of day for two midwives to choose to call, but later we were to learn why this was so. With the expected birth only two weeks away Carmella had still not been allocated a midwife, and when the media brought the forthcoming birth to public notice, the Health Services were galvanised into action. Carmella and Abel's trust that the right midwife would appear in time was justified. Their timing at 6pm could not have been much more inconvenient but Maggie Herbert and Sheila Brookes were undoubtedly the right people. They made it clear that, normally, everyone having a baby would be offered the opportunity to get to know the midwife to some degree beforehand whether they were having a home or hospital delivery. Neither of them wanted to appear at the birth as strangers, particularly so in these somewhat unusual circumstances; so Carmella agreed to a quick examination and a return visit next day, then they left us to our own devices and we at last reached the point where we could reflect on the day's events and listen to the recordings.

We all watched the late Central News together and were, in the main, well pleased by its unbiased presentation. There was only one word which touched a nerve which came in the opening remark, 'Medical professionals are *outraged* ..". Words hold the power to create images by association and 'outrage' is a word that has persistently been used by the media in the context of public disapproval of criminal or other thoroughly unsociable activities. I found it hard to accept that we ourselves could be the cause of such reactions.

There was also a surprise that gave us immense pleasure. The camera had picked up our MetaCentre logo, a six-pointed yellow star within a circle, on the outside wall. As with the cross, the star symbol holds its own significant legends and levels of meaning. We had our own personal stories connected to our logo, and various unusual events had been associated with it; for instance, walkers passing by had called at the door to tell us they could see a beam of light shining from it, another had been drawn to a workshop by seeing the symbol in a dream. It was such a delight to see 'our star' flashing out in our living room in the knowledge that it was also in that moment reaching millions of others and it was also, of course, an entirely appropriate birth symbol. So all in all we felt the media had become our messenger of goodwill, sharing widely our serious intent to create a holistic birth using the element of water.

In the lateness of the evening we sensed that the public flurry was over and we would not be a news item again until the birth took place. Abel felt that he should take a journey to Bristol the following day on some urgent business that had been awaiting his attention, and Carmella and I agreed that a quiet day at home would not come amiss.

CHAPTER FIVE

(Entering the System

Carmella

The peaceful day of our desires failed to manifest. I recall sitting in bed that morning feeling somewhat lethargic and weary after the antics of the previous day - my body ached as it had done for many weeks and I felt a sense of readiness to release the weight I carried. Everything was in place except Abel who had left the house early for his last trip away before the birth and I was slightly uneasy about his disappearance. We were now in count-down time - only ten days until the due date.

Late morning, I went for a routine check up at the doctor's and whilst I was there had a small discharge of blood. Seeming to think it was of the utmost importance as I may start haemorrhaging, my doctor phoned the hospital immediately for an ambulance and asked me to arrange someone to pick up the car from the car park outside, which I dutifully did with a phone call home. I was taken completely off guard, felt absolutely nothing to be wrong with my body and was quite bemused to be bundled into an ambulance as an emergency case.

It was a farcical trip with most of the journey spent encircling the hospital car park in search of the elusive labour ward! First, we went to the wrong department where I was thoroughly reprimanded by a matron for not being in a wheelchair. I couldn't believe my ears but allowed myself to be helped into the compulsory wheelchair and pushed to the labour ward corridor where I waited... and waited, waving the letter from my doctor at every official-looking passer-by. I felt like an invisible woman at a railway station in rush hour, and even with the knowledge that if I was really haemorrhaging the delay could be crucial, I felt one step removed from reality and entertained by the absurdity of events.

At last my turn arrived and with it the beginning of the disintegration of my control. This was no longer amusing. I was told to replace all my clothes with the uniform of the system - a faded, knee-length blue smock which gaped open at the back, and to jump up onto the coverless bed. I felt myself being rendered helpless as I was hooked to a glucose drip on one side and a foetal monitor on the other and then investigated by a succession of five people for potential problems with my body or my baby. Hours later I was informed that all was normal apart from the fact that the small blood loss was discovered to be a 'show' - the first sign of the onset of labour. I was already three centimetres dilated, Abel was in Bristol and I was being strongly advised to stay put and to have my waters broken to speed up the process.

I was confident enough to state clearly that I wanted the labour to take its natural course, but the feeling of losing control due to the assumed authority of those around me was increasing. I was being treated like an invalid and began to feel like one when I was encouraged to use a bedpan in full view of several strangers. I felt trapped, crucifixion-like, on the bed and unnerved by the primal screams of a woman giving birth along the corridor.

It was late afternoon before I managed to get a message home via a midwife as I was not allowed to walk to the phone. She came in with a notepad asking me to list all the things I would need from home for my stay. I protested and reiterated what I had told all the other staff members - that it was my intention to go home if I was in good health and have my baby in the way I had planned. "That's just not the way things are done here dear" she said, but from her manner I sensed that she was aware of my intentions to give birth in water and I suspected that it was a hot topic of conversation amongst the staff. If she was aware, she made no mention of it and simply repeated what seemed to be the hospital line, advising me to stay within the safety of the hospital. I felt none too safe here as I dictated the list, feeling that my voice carried absolutely no weight but I found strength in the knowledge that my mother would be here soon and would give me the moral support I craved.

M'haletta didn't arrive for a long time and it was only later that I learned that the *Sun* newspaper had been calling home persistently for an interview and the midwife could not get through. I waited and prayed but at least I felt no labour pains. The call was made eventually at about 5pm just after Abel had arrived home from his successful day's business trip.

It was Abel who arrived first as he had moved at lightening speed, leaving M'haletta to pack my bag - just in case. He was obviously a little shocked to see me in this stark, white room amongst the wires and drips in a setting that contrasted sharply with the beauty of the sanctuary so lovingly prepared for our sacred event. He began by pacing up and down like an expectant father, not knowing quite what to do in this incredibly important situation. It was a relief to see his brain beginning to click into gear. Despite his strong desire to drive me home at once, he was intent on finding the decision that was best for everyone. We agreed to make an appraisal of the situation, taking into account every piece of information we could find and then to sit quietly and ask for intuitive guidance.

We already knew that we were legally entitled to discharge ourselves from the hospital and to call our community midwife. The baby's heart-beat was steady and strong, and according to the monitor the contractions were weak and diminishing. The blood was no cause for concern, we knew that everything could be ready for our ideal birth at home in less than two hours and indications were that the baby was not moving that speedily. The questions that niggled us were: Why did the last pieces of the jigsaw for our home birth (meeting the midwives, finishing the birth tub, and speaking with the media) fall into place yesterday if we were to have the baby in hospital? Yet by the same token, if nothing happens by chance, why were we in the hospital? Was there an unknown medical reason for us to be here?

The publicity situation heightened our awareness of the gravity and complexity of our position. The national newspapers were beginning to badger us for a story - the *Sun* had even been phoning the hospital looking for me - and we knew that this was a factor subsequent to the delivery that could cause embarrassment if we stayed in hospital and all was well, or equally so if we left and somehow jeopardised the baby's safety.

We concluded that the hospital experience would be invaluable to us in our future work with promoting natural childbirth and that it was offering us the opportunity of knowing that we were capable of giving up our personal desires if necessary. With this clear, we sat together in silence, meditated and asked for higher guidance whilst the rush hour continued past the door. I had an all-encompassing sense of well-being and a surety that my body and baby were in a perfect state of health and Abel received a strong indication that we should go home.

By this time, M'haletta had arrived and we were told that she would have to wait in the corridor as only one visitor was allowed at a time. On hearing this I found my power and my voice. We needed to be a threesome to discuss where we were at and to have her input from what we knew would be a very intuitive space, especially as Abel was now scared by the thought that as soon as we left the hospital premises he would be taking the baby's safety and my own into his own hands against medical advice. This piece of hospital policy was unacceptable and I demanded assertively that my mother be admitted which, after a brief wait, she was.

M'haletta told us that she was sure that both the baby and I were fine and would create a very positive birth experience wherever we chose to be. She was totally willing to enable a hospital birth or to set everything in motion at the Centre. There were few words used, spoken fast and clear and it was in this triangle that the firm decision to return home was made. After all, it would have been unwise to ask for higher guidance and then ignore it. And so M'haletta sped off in excitement towards home with the green light flashing, and I remember thinking 'Thank God I have action people around me'. My brain had been scrambled and I needed other people who I could trust to think with me and act for me.

Abel requested one further interview with a doctor to set his mind at rest that there was no information that we had not been given, and the doctor's response summed up for me the attitude of this system which had sucked away my power that day in its attempt to put me right. He said "It is safe practice to assume the worst until proven otherwise".

I signed the necessary discharge papers with a flourish and with an awareness that I had not even given them the responsibility from which I was now absolving them! I skipped down the corridor on my own two legs and had to suppress the urgent desire to shout out loud 'I'm free...FREE and I'm going home!'

On our way home we stopped for Abel to inform Tony Concannon, our acupuncturist friend who was due to attend the birth, that the birthday was approaching. As I sat in the car outside feeling the baby's movements towards birth an incredible firework lit up the sky in front of me sending a shower of stars over the roof. From that auspicious moment, I expected nothing less than perfection for this baby's entry into life.

CHAPTER SIX

𝔗he Coming of 𝔅enjaya

M'haletta

On returning from the hospital my feelings, on entering the house, were akin to coming home after a long, somewhat arduous journey. I appreciated greatly its enveloping warmth, the sense of safety and the effortlessness of being at one with my surroundings. After Carmella had left at 9.30 that morning, Charlotte and I had been the only two people left at home, and by 10.30 I had been alone. This was unusual. It was as if a cloak of stillness had fallen around the house and all I had to do was wear it. Nothing during the day had disturbed that state. The telephones rang from time to time, mostly newspapers following up on yesterday's story, wanting to generate a bit more copy, and then Marael Robertson called. Marael, a friend of long standing, a companion on my spiritual journey who had brought in the first wave of our channelled teaching said simply that she was in contact with the coming baby. She had felt an overwhelming sense of love enfolding her and had written down words which she felt came from the child, they said:

I am a seed, held within the warmed earth of spring.
I am about to shed the outer casement
And grow upward into the light, strong and beautiful.
I am enclosed within the womb of Infinite Love

Awaiting birth into the diamond light.
This love I feel is so different.
*It is as though I **am** the love yet it is **given.***
It is cosmic, yet of Self upon the Earth.
As above, so below... What awaits me?

At that time I had told no-one except Derek and Charlotte of Carmella's journey to hospital and had received no news from her or the hospital that she was thought to have begun labour. It is a wry thought that, whilst machine monitoring of well-being of the body is acceptable, contact of a more mystical nature would normally hold little, if any, relevance. This message was of relevance to me as it was my first indication, from a source that I trusted, that the birth journey had begun and all was well. It also heightened the awareness of the essentially loving capacity of this incoming being.

I did not have to go through any thought process as to whether to visit Carmella, telephone, or attempt a 'rescue'. In such situations I am acutely aware of moving within the greater flow, and took no action. It is my experience that in a heightened state of consciousness the mind moves beyond reason to a state of alert awareness, and there is an inner knowing which sets signals rather like traffic lights in motion that flash 'stop', 'at the ready' and 'go'. The inner signal was on red all day until Carmella asked me to take her clothes to the hospital and then it changed to amber. What I felt on leaving the hospital was the green light. The green light is not only a symbol of permission to move, but also a quality of energy that is projected in abundance by the nature kingdom.

The house was vibrant with activity. People had arrived already and my telephone call from the hospital had set tasks in motion. Derek had arrived home from work and I was so glad. Carmella had made it very clear that she would welcome his presence at the birth and had suggested he might take on the task of recording it on video but this had not worked out. We had not acquired a video camera, he had not acquired the necessary skills, and Carmella and Abel had simply let go of this part of the plan in favour of taking still photographs. Persh Sassoon was to be our number one photographer, and Derek had agreed to act as back-up. From the outset Derek had been open to Carmella and Abel planning a birth at home in any way they wished. When asked what he thought about it all he had answered "we do different things at the MetaCentre, and this is only one of them." Derek is a Virgo by birth sign, most comfortable with familiar patterns, and it had taken him many years to become comfortable about doing things differently. He had not sought out information or become involved in any practical way and had remained on the periphery, keeping any reservations he might have to himself, but come the day he discovered that, as this had been the prime topic of conversation for months, he had absorbed a great deal. Now it was time to move onto the stage. He had been moved by Carmella's invitation and had felt certain he would be present at the birth, and if there was anything at all that he could do to bring about a positive outcome there was no doubt of his willingness and whole-hearted support.

Wendy McDougall, my son Marc's girlfriend, had also arrived home. Wendy had been living at Adam House for some while as she worked locally. At twenty-nine she was an experienced social worker, working with emotionally disturbed young people. Wendy had no children and had had no opportunity of any experience of childbirth but had often reflected on the effect that she believed pregnancy and birth had on children's development in later years. She had watched videos with us, had read the literature and was both personally and professionally interested in this birth event. Marc was working away in London and she was the person who kept him linked into developments by telephone. All the family, wherever they were, were on their toes by now.

Carmella had agreed with Wendy that she would let her know on the day how she felt about her coming into the sanctuary when the birth was imminent. The excited anticipation of this possibility showed all the more because Wendy was usually such a private, self-contained person. Wendy was a constant energy, used to the house, calmly following any instruction or suggestion, moving with Derek in the physical activity of emptying the tub of cold water and re-filling with hot. Her presence was smooth, a steady, unobtrusive under-current that flowed with us.

David Powell, also single, aged twenty-seven, was almost Wendy's opposite. David had also been living with us for two years following a traumatic personal time, finding space to reconstruct his life. David worked as an electrician. Deeply immersed in philosophical studies, his head teemed with an endless flow of unanswerable questions. He had been interested in all the technical aspects of erecting the pool, such as how the plumbing worked, but also was sensitively concerned as to how Carmella would handle being on view in such an intimate way. He had been suggesting all sorts of ways in which she could cover herself up, such as buying what he described as 'diaphanous robes'. His presence at the birth had also been loosely discussed and he thought it an opportunity too good to be missed, as he had no experience of birth in any way. At many courses and workshops in the sanctuary David had shared all manner of unusual experiences with us; it seemed, therefore, somewhat strange to me that David had arrived home from work and left again immediately for an evening appointment and I wondered whether he was having second thoughts about being present.

My second task, after ensuring that all was in hand in respect of the pool, was to make contact with the midwives, choosing first to telephone Maggie Herbert at home where she was just sitting down to tea. Maggie had already been alerted via her manager of Carmella's hospital admission and had followed that information up with a telephone call to the hospital in the afternoon. She had been told that Carmella seemed to have started labour and was probably going to stay there, so she was somewhat surprised to learn of the change in plan but I felt that there was excitement in her positive and immediate response, knowing that she was going to be involved after all. It was agreed between us that Maggie would now act as the liaison person to make all the appropriate contacts - with Sheila, with the other midwife, with Carmella's doctor, and with her own management who had told her firmly that they must be informed if the midwives were called out because 'its a bit different and we must be on our toes'. There was an air of competence and friendliness about her which came through then and later in her person as she walked through the door. We never had any doubts that these two midwives would flow into this evolving pattern of birth and, what is more, would enjoy it!

By the time more telephone calls were made, which included calling Sandra, my eldest daughter who was living in Devon with her family, Patricia had arrived. Patricia was a teacher of children with special learning difficulties. She had been one of our most regular participants on MetaCentre workshops whilst sorting out her personal and spiritual path and had that evening expected to be attending a small group studying the process of raising consciousness. We had called it 'In Tune with the Presence' which, in the changed circumstances, seemed apt for our evening's agenda. I had been unable to contact Patricia by telephone and so she arrived to find herself in the midst of the birth preparations. Ever resourceful, she simply switched into the scene, checked out with me what needed to be done, and then went into over-drive. One of the main themes on our workshops had been the concept of service, and we had all worked together to let go of the need for any recognition or reward, serving unobtrusively and with a spirit of enjoyment. Patricia had been an enthusiastic server and I had no hesitation in agreeing that she should do whatever she thought was needed. Thinking ahead she foresaw that later many people would need feeding, and so she rummaged in the food store and soon a table began to fill and the smell of baked potatoes wafted from the oven.

Charlotte was hovering with her boyfriend, Peter, a 6ft 2in carpenter who frequently communicated with a delightful turn of humour, and as the excitement built in the air, Peter proved to be the one who was best able to express it. They were on call to be our 'outriders' for anything or anyone needing transport. It was a great relief to be released from the thought of these necessary physical details. I was doing other things, less tangible perhaps but equally necessary as I saw it. Then lookouts saw the car arrive. Carmella and Abel were here and everyone surged towards the front door.

Carmella

The first sight of Adam House brought tears to my eyes. It looked like a big, friendly beacon with its windows casting light all down the hill and smiley, waving people spilling out onto the doorstep. As I stepped across the threshold I knew that **I was entering a system where I could reclaim my power, a place where I would be supported and encouraged to connect with my highest source of inspiration.** The party atmosphere was live with excitement and anticipation and I was the centre, the one who would be bringing the birthday gift. There was no other agenda or distraction and everyone seemed to know their task.

The lounge was my first base. There I was totally relaxed and thoroughly enjoying myself in the company of Wendy who was in charge of timing the contractions which had now begun to build. There was a lot of action in the house, but not of the rush-hour type. It was cohesive team action. Abel and my father were upstairs preparing the birthing tub with the right temperature water, Patricia was cooking, my sister Charlotte and her boyfriend Peter were in and out of the house on an important mission to find the right film for the birth photographs, and M'haletta seemed to be holding an overview, making all the important phone calls and generally ensuring that the harmony in the house was held. I had total trust in everyone and my only task was to act as a channel for the entry of my baby.

The team at this time was still expanding. The midwives we had met the day before were here now and we made friendly contact before I sent them off with all our waterbirth information to study - a little late in the day, but better late than never! A friend of mine, Persh, who had guided me through several rebirth sessions in preparation for this day, had been fetched on one of Charlotte and Peter's whirlwind trips. She was here in two roles - as birth supporter, having had a great deal of positive experience with birth, and as a photographer to catch the birth on film if possible. Her ex-partner, Tony, with whom she had had three children, also arrived and I was aware of the potential for sadness here, yet at the same time I was confident that they would both rise to the occasion whatever their personal feelings.

Tony, a tiny, slim leprechaun of an Irishman, was my acupuncturist and I felt safe with him and his needles as my alternative form of pain relief if it proved necessary. I did not want to take any drugs as I knew that they would pass through to the baby's system and had read recently that there is irrefutable evidence of a link between drug taking in later years and drugs used at birth. I had chosen this ancient oriental form of medicine' because it is a holistic practice, working with the body's vital energies on physical, mental, emotional and spiritual levels. Tony had a specific interest in acupuncture and childbirth and was skilled enough to read the six pulses in each of my wrists and give me information about different aspects of my condition. My pulse reading when he arrived showed that all levels were in good condition and as long as I stayed in touch with my own vital essential energy there would be no need for help from the needles. He threw out a prediction that this birth would happen about 6am and then disappeared to build a rapport with the midwives.

At 8pm I went upstairs to the bathroom and watched my image change in the mirror as I breathed through one of the strongest contractions yet. I was thinking 'Here I am, a pregnant woman in labour with my first child, who I will never hold in my womb again. This is so momentous, this move into motherhood, and about **720,000 of us do it every year in Britain** alone.' Then a flash of memory came to me of a recent dream. It was a simple dream in which I was being made aware that the real work of labour would begin at 8pm at Adam House. An hour or so after this, socialising lost its attraction and I retreated to the sanctuary where the inner circle was formed.

There was a sense of a change-over at this point. Now the action, the essential work, was being achieved in the inner circle whilst the outer circle settled into a state of waiting and cradling support. Abel, the midwives and Persh were with me now, and we were the core. Hours upon hours passed of gentle chatting between the increasing challenge of riding the contractions. I used the bed, the chair, and Abel to kneel or hang over in my attempt to find the most comfortable positions. It was an instinctual process and nothing stood in my way to prevent me hearing my body's messages. Persh, confident and relaxed throughout, added words of guidance every now and again, and took a nap for a while in the early hours. The midwives were unobtrusively present checking the baby's heart-beat regularly and making copious notes, and Abel wore many hats. He was my prime supporter, breathing with me at the height of contractions, also keeper of the pool temperature which he maintained at (38^0c) by a ritual of boiling up a kettle of water periodically He was the director of music - changing the tapes, and he was the messenger man, moving from the inner to the outer space relaying details of my progress. He described himself as feeling suspended on a platform of energy, full of joy and calm-ness. Of his messenger role he said "I have a distinct memory of stepping outside the sanctuary, which had a specific atmosphere, into the rest of the house and being enveloped by an expansion of an atmosphere of peace and cradled support which was almost tangible." I was glad he was my man, and proud of his strength and sensitivity.

I learnt from him that all was silent downstairs apart from the music of the Taizé chants wafting out of the music room where M'haletta, Derek and Wendy sat in a meditative state. I guessed that M'haletta was choosing consciously to stay out of my immediate vicinity at that time because she had taken on the role of spiritual midwife[1] which necessitated her staying in a centred, calm space, attuning to the highest perspective and facilitating group consciousness. It is likely that as a mother she may well have weakened into an emotional space had she been facing me in pain for so many hours and would therefore have been unable to hold that higher state. Also, facilitating group consciousness and 'setting the note' required being available to respond to all within the walls of Adam House. She was the unspoken **conductor of the birth support orchestra with the responsibility of keep-ing everyone in key. Just one person out of tune and that one is heard above the rest.** The other part of her task - to receive spiritually the new-born, could be undertaken downstairs by communicating in thought with the baby as s/he moved within me towards birth. I knew that M'haletta would be in the

[1]The concept of the Spiritual Midwife is covered thoroughly in *Holistic Birth and the Spiritual Midwife* - see page 240.

perfect position for the entry.

Everyone else, it seemed, had gone to rest before the call. They knew they would be called to the birth as I had sent out the word that I wanted everyone in the house to be present. It was not a *personal* want, as I have always been self-conscious about even showing my knees in public. I simply knew that it was required, on some level, that the supporters came in to act as witnesses as one whole group. No-one was to be left out, and the embarrassment that I felt initially at the thought of being on show in such an intimate way evaporated as I moved into the all-enveloping last few hours of labour.

The temptation to enter the pool was ever-present, but I wanted to save the effect of the warm water on my body until I was urgent need for its support. At 2am I relented, and that first sensation of being in water was heavenly. No longer was I an ungainly elephant but more like a dolphin, able to slip and slide into whatever position my body cried out for. The pain was steadily increasing and nothing could have prepared me for this unimaginable onslaught. As time went by and still the pain increased, I said to myself **'I can't do this any more...HELP!'** Quick as a flash came the response to the call. I heard the words in my head **'It is not I who does the work but the Father in me'** and I relaxed and invoked every sacred being I could think of to join me. I then felt a surge of energy, a force beyond my own merging into me, holding the little me suspended in safety as my body continued its momentous task. It felt as if my head was in heaven and my body was anchored firmly to the Earth. It did not occur to me to take drugs in this setting - it would have felt sacrilegious.

Abel was transfixed by me from this time onwards, using direct eye contact to focus with me through my heaven and hell. Later he said:

"I was in awe of the way Carmella's body took over. She knew exactly what to do and when to push without any instruction and was in a totally different state of consciousness than any I've seen before. I felt humbled by the natural phenomenon taking place before my eyes."

It was 5.30am when my body decided it was time to push, and I sent out the call, via Abel, for the witnesses. It took about ten minutes flat for everyone to be present in a semi-circle around me. When all these extra people entered the room, far from feeling on show in a fishpond, I felt an intensification of love energy which increased my sense of being in a safe, cocoon-like space where nothing negative could survive. This was not a show but a sacred sharing and they all knew it. At one point David was missing and I became hyper-aware of his absence - there was a missing link and I could not retract into my inner space again until I saw him come crawling through the door, completing the feeling of wholeness. M'haletta closed the door behind him and took up her position at my feet.

After forty minutes of pushing, a midwife suggested that it might be another half an hour before the birth, which was enough to bring out the wild woman in me. No way could my body experience splitting in two for that long, and so I gave an almighty push accompanied by an almighty shout, and there, between my legs, was our baby's head. With the second push a slippery little form with a mop of black hair shot into the water to an exclamation from a midwife of **"I've never seen anything like it"**.

Four hands dived into the water to catch this new-born child. The cord, which was wrapped around the body three times, was slipped off - and there he was, my son, Benjamin Jaya, lying on my chest with his legs continuing their swimming action. His magnetic, dark, Tibetan-shaped eyes captured my own and time stood still as soul touched upon soul. Slowly I became aware that we were not alone, he had to meet his father, and no doubt everyone was awaiting their connection. I felt stunned, elated and totally shattered, but I still had enough awareness to notice the light of a new day beginning to shimmer through the curtains. It was 6.15am.

M'haletta

There had been a wrench in the area of my solar plexus when I connected visibly to the scene in the sanctuary, registering all that was necessary. I grasped Tony's hand for anchorage, and within seconds, had regained the space I knew I had to hold, letting go of any physical concerns, emotional connections or mental exercises.

During the night I had sensed two definite shifts in energy. I had been sitting alone at about 11pm when the first shift registered. It is noticeable to me, rather in the way that anyone, attuned to a car engine, can identify the moment of a gear change, although there is no audible sound. This awareness was accompanied by the impression of a domed canopy forming above the house. The rhythm, the vibration inside, then settled at its new pitch. A few weeks previously we had held a workshop called

'Heralding the New Life' and the musical theme had been the Taizé chants. At this workshop Carmella had spoken words which she identified as coming from the consciousness of her unborn child, and I sensed the importance of picking up on this familiar sound to use as my connection to the in-coming life. It was about three hours later, when the music of the chants built to a crescendo, that the second change occurred. The vibrations not only intensified, but I sensed **a swelling sensation as if the energy in the house had expanded and lifted,** rather like a hot air balloon rising.

Later, some of those present were to describe to me how they experienced the energy on entering the sanctuary, for me the main sensation was of my connectedness with everything and yet nothing, a perfect state of non-individual relationship.

My physical body was directly in line with Carmella lying outstretched, the Ramethon cross tucked in the corner above her head. My inner awareness simply guided me to 'remain in line', to be in line with the emerging life form, in line with the crown chakra of the child.

Everyone knew their part and performed it well, as if it had been rehearsed a thousand times. Even as Abel and the midwives reached out to receive the body of the child we also caught him in our web of consciousness. Our minds and our eyes were our hands. Softly, over and over in the stillness of my inner self I called his name, which I knew was the first word he must hear as a sound projecting from the heart. Perhaps that is why silence is so vital, so that the child can hear the love pulsating on the stream of thought that words so often are inadequate to express. It was not the time for any ceremony or Rite of Passage. Benjaya was safely with us, making his entry in what appeared to be his own predetermined way and, in this instance, the water had been the perfect medium for bridging the gap between different states of existence.

For some long time before the birth, a memory had been tapping on my mind of an event which had taken place when Carmella (then called Virginia) was six years old. When sorting out some old papers, I had come across the original account of that event, written in 1964 as a 'True Story' for a women's magazine, though it was never published. Perhaps it was waiting for this event... twenty two years later, to share it.

Virginia is six years old. She seldom speaks, though I know that she can, because she speaks to me when no-one else is around, and she laughs too. She has huge eyes, but they are often heavy with some unspoken sadness that I cannot reach, as if she carries some hidden sorrow.

She has been at school now for a year, and as far as I know talks to no-one, not even answering a polite 'yes' when the teacher calls the register. I do not understand... and neither I think does she. Sometimes she tries to say something and her voice is a croak, sounds are strangled, tears fall again and again, frustration, embarrassment, despair. She seems to have the expectation that we should all be able to read her mind and respond to her needs without words - but we cannot.

It is September. She has moved into another class where the vicar's wife is teaching. There is no difference, though now it has become clear that she is clever. She hears everything and lessons are perfectly produced on the page.

The Christmas Nativity play is being cast and the vicar's wife, with inspired wisdom, selects Virginia to play the Virgin Mary. She brings home the script and studies it silently. It is to be performed to all the parents and so there is an understudy primed. If ever a choice had been made to hold an audience captive, then this is it. The parents all know her and have shown a puzzled compassion in their concern for her 'disability'.

She enters confidently on Joseph's arm, her waist-long hair flowing as she moves purposefully forward, radiantly alive. And she speaks:

"I have travelled a long and weary road"

Every word rings with crystal clarity. She is Mary. Not only is there no hesitation in her part, but it is obvious that she knows everyone else's as well. There is silent amazement. No-one breaks the spell of her sound.

A miracle? It seemed so in that moment. She was not over all the hurdles but she had made a beginning. Virginia had risen above her self-consciousness by *becoming* Mary. She had played the part allotted to her faultlessly before a discerning group, and I pondered on the synchronicity of it all. Had this earlier pageant been a rehearsal of things yet to come at another turn of the spiral? Who knows? Yet that same electrifying force had been with us in the sanctuary, as I had experienced it those many years past, bonding the 'audience' who were there fully and compassionately with her. How, then, could I have failed to know in some inner space that Virginia/Carmella could rise again in a new version of the old story and hold that central focus of the mother whilst knowing all the parts? And this time her family had not failed her. We had read her mind sufficiently to meet her needs without words. She had asked this of us as a child and we had not known how. It had indeed been a long and often wearisome road to this point for us all.

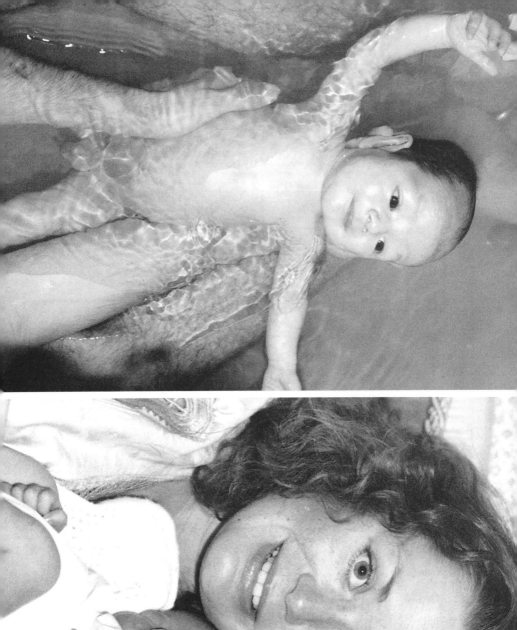

CHAPTER SEVEN

The Snowball

M'haletta

Benjamin Jaya

**First Born
of
Carmella and Abel B'Hahn
at dawn on 30th October, 1986
into water
in the sanctuary of
Adam House
Adams Hill
Clent**

O ver the morning and afternoon of Thursday, 30th October, the birth announcement went out, first to family and friends. One by one the birth 'witnesses', as we had begun to call them, had left to go about their working day. A euphoric atmosphere remained in the house and there was simply a need to rest within it for a while. Bringing in the media again seemed rather an effort and we were in no hurry, but having made our promises to inform the

Daily News and Central Television, at 5pm Abel made the announcement to them by telephone. The speed of their responses was astounding. The Central Television camera crew beat the *Daily News* by a cable-length, and Benjaya was making his television debut, under the spotlight with Abel and Carmella in their bedroom, when Ann and Mike arrived. I played host whilst they waited their turn. Neither of them were expecting to make a front page news story.

Nothing untoward had happened which could grab readers with chilling headlines, and we had all agreed not even to mention the hospital detour of the previous day as there was an obvious risk of being drawn into dialogue which could have been presented in a negative light. This we particularly wanted to avoid as we recognised that the previous day's events had also been a part of the plan and had offered more insights which had the result of heightening our appreciation of the alternative plan which had run so smoothly.

The television crew were sensitive to the situation, asking only about the birth experience which, of course, was reported as being overwhelmingly positive, and the camera zoomed in for the first time on Benjaya's live image. Then Ann and Mike had their bedside interview, took their pictures and, as promised, were handed the roll of black and white film to take away for processing. No-one had any great expectations that any of the pictures would prove useable in a newspaper, particularly as Carmella had been naked throughout and the lighting had been dim and rather shadowy. They were in no hurry, having reserved space on page three for a happy family after-the-birth picture, so we drank tea and laughed, trying from time to time to find words to express the quality and magic of the night's experience, whilst knowing that it was untranslatable into 'newspaper' language. Then they left us to wait for our next television news slot and we remained totally unaware of what was happening at the *Daily News* office that night. Ann tells it this way:

Ann Adams

This birth had become really important to me and I was stunned when Abel phoned at 5 o'clock telling me the baby had been born. I wanted to do something straight away and couldn't get there quickly enough; even so, Central beat us to it. But at least we had the birth film. Mike dealt with the film while I went back to my desk and did the write-up. The next thing was that I noticed a commotion around the newsdesk and saw Mike showing the pictures. The Picture Editor, Mike and Claire, were looking at them and they were absolutely... They said:

"Come and look at this, you're not going to believe this picture, it's one in a million!"

I couldn't believe it either when I saw it. I thought 'That is incredible! It's the sort of picture you only see once in a lifetime.' There are so many pictures passing through on a newspaper that you just give them a passing glance, but that picture - everyone just stared at it. It really did create a stir.

I just knew it should go on the front page and lead into the story inside. And that is what the Deputy Editor decided. It was a brave decision. I don't think many newspapers have the guts to put something so completely different right across the front page of 350,000 copies. We did it, and when it appeared every single national daily was after us and **all hell broke loose!**

M'haletta

Later, when I went to spend a day at the *Daily News* office, I interviewed other people involved, one of whom was Mark Higget, the Deputy Editor, who filled in more of the story from his standpoint:

Mark Higget

It is my responsibility, along with the Night Editor, to put together the front page of the paper. By 5 o'clock on the 30th we had decided on the content. We knew that Mike Fisher might come back with a picture; but we had decided to go with what we already had in front of us.

But when we realised what Mike had brought in... At 8 o'clock at night the whole front page had to be redesigned. We had about an hour!

We had known this birth was going to happen and I was anticipating a picture - but this surpassed *anything* I could have imagined. Technically, it had everything. I could not remember a picture of its kind with so much impact. If it had appeared in a National, on a slightly slower news day, I think you would have seen it used as a poster - the whole of the front page would have been devoted to it.

The only word that I could find to describe it at the time was *'Biblical'*. Clearly, the Nativity came into it - what a pity that Christmas was still six weeks away! I don't know if there was a *practical* advantage to Abel being topless, but that did add to the effect! - he *could* have been wearing a Led Zepplin T-shirt!

The headline - **THE JOY AND MIRACLE OF BIRTH** - was down to my Night Editor, who had judged it sensitively. Had the picture been a little different, the heading, too, would have been different. The fishpond angle would have killed the picture stone dead - though the fishpond *headline* did serve a purpose, for it drew attention to the story in the first place...

But there really was no contest - it simply *had* to dominate the front page. Only on great occasions - such as the royal engagement and the royal wedding; or the Challenger Shuttle disaster; or the raising of the Zebrugge Ferry, had I used a picture as big or bigger. So you can see the company you were keeping!

At a personal level it touched a chord, for it was about twelve months after my little girl was born. Katy was not born in water, and it was a long, hard day, which is still fresh in my memory. I was not allowed to hold her - she was whisked away, without thought or ceremony, to be cleaned up. This picture brought that memory, all that emotion, back to the surface. It is obvious that your picture was taken minutes after the birth, and I thought it would touch a chord with fathers, certainly those who had been present at a birth, or who might have wanted to be, but were denied the experience.

It was my good fortune to be in London the following day for a conference of editors, deputies and managing directors. I managed to get a copy of the paper in time to take down; also an original print so that we could compare reproduction quality. *It really stopped the show! There was nothing to compare.*

Most other presentations were frittered down to about a minute.

M'haletta

On Friday 31st, copy No. 424 of the *Daily News* followed its usual distribution pattern. At Clent we are a few miles outside its circulation boundary (Birmingham area) and, well before the phone rang, with Mike Fisher at the other end telling us we had made front page news, it had already begun to make an impact on *Daily News* readers. Tony Devany was one such reader whose eloquent description of his experience of the picture's archetypal essence is shared in our opening pages.

It was Abel who drove out to find some copies. Seeing it for the first time was weird as we realised that the seemingly inexpressible essence of the birth had been encapsulated in this one image which held everything we would have wished to say. On page three was another spread of a smiling Carmella cradling a sleeping Benjaya captioned in inch-high lettering:

WONDER BABY - BORN IN A POND

So the incomprehensible jottings in my journal were working themselves out. Carmella *shall bear a child and s/he shall be called 'wondrous one'*. That on the first full day of his life the child was presented as 'wonder baby' was then significant for me in that it meant the rest of the message - *the child comes to work from the moment of birth* - could also be relevant. Certainly the picture, captured a few minutes after his birth, was taking a momentum and path of its own without any activity on our part.

Then the commercial world burst in upon us. Obviously the national papers peruse the locals to promote stories of local interest more widely. The *Daily News* was being inundated with calls from nationals wanting a copy of the picture. There is strict protocol to be followed between newspapers and no-one could re-print without purchasing the picture from whoever held the rights. Though the *Daily News* had been given the option of printing anything without charge, Carmella and Abel were still its owners. Pressure mounted fast. The *Daily News* was fielding all enquiries through Mike Fisher who was at home having a rest day which was to prove one of the busiest of his career! He liaised for us, not only with the stream of nationals, but also at the same time was chasing photographic distribution agencies to discover who was best placed to handle the situation and who, also, had access to the international press. He passed all information on to Abel by telephone as it came in, playing the role of our middle-man and negotiator.

The day was a testing time for us all. It was necessary to ensure that we remained in an absolutely centred space, making decisions from the highest motives and not allowing ourselves to be swayed by financial gain or false limelight. There were many areas of risk, not the least the exhaustion which was creeping over Abel. Carmella was at least physically resting and yet Abel did not seem to have stopped one activity or another and was now taking the weight of the mental bombardment. In consultation with Carmella the decision was finally made. They were not prepared to sell the photograph to the highest bidder, which would have realised one large sum. They wanted to retain overall control but considered themselves as its custodians, its guardians in a way, enabling the picture to find its widest distribution. For this it was necessary to use an agency. Rex Features in London were engaged and Mike Fisher undertook to arrange for the picture to reach them immediately. All those wanting copies of the picture then went directly through the agency, who had a list of press rates which would be properly administered, the agency and the 'owners' sharing the income. It was therefore in their best commercial interests to promote the picture widely, a task which would have been impossible for us.

On receipt of the photograph, Rex Features wanted accurate and more comprehensive text to accompany it. For instance, buyers might want to be able to select text from various angles - from the human interest to more detailed information on waterbirth. So after some debate it was agreed that I should interview Abel and Carmella, asking all the questions that we collectively thought the media might have wanted to ask. I sat up through the quietness of the night and by first light we had a text. Carmella joined me to act as editor, sitting in a sea of flowers in her bedroom with Benjaya in the crook of her arm, and we both felt that the first great wave of the work his arrival had instigated was over.

The result of all this activity was a crop of reproductions of the birth picture in most of the national dailies the following day, and the text was relatively accurate. There was no negativity what-so-ever. The papers all let the picture speak for itself and the *'outraged'* voices, had there ever been any, were silent. The picture tabloids came into their own, printing relatively large pictures, whereas papers such as the *Independent* used a smaller image with more informative text. Later, the *Daily News* told us that in all the crop of letters they received there was not a single complaint or criticism which they found astonishing. Usually there is *someone* who feels a sense of disquiet on the sensitive subjects of birth and nudity!

Going out for a while after these events became an adventure, and time consuming, particularly for Carmella and Abel. It was fascinating to observe how, when an individual has laid themselves open to the public, it seems to give permission for people, previously strangers, to ask questions at a very personal level or simply to seek out more information, even on subjects they may never have thought about previously. In this way we learnt a great deal first-hand about the general reactions of 'the public', the over-riding response being a spectrum from curiosity to fascination. It also drew from people stories of their own birth experiences, many of which were deeply moving and quite sad. The general opinion was undoubtedly that change is urgently needed that will bring us back to regarding the coming of life as a natural, sacred and enjoyable event, wherever the birth takes place.

During the days and months that followed, the snowball rolled on and on across Europe into far corners of the world, America, Japan, Australia, South America, until we lost track. The *Weekly World News* at 55 cents a copy is not a paper with which we were familiar, but they certainly took our prize for the most inventive and inaccurate headlines, when on 16th December, they boldly proclaimed:

BABY BORN IN AN AQUARIUM

Couple tries underwater childbirth in their living room

CHAPTER EIGHT

The Kaleidoscope

M'haletta

he next event of major significance for me came in an unexpected invitation to go to Italy to participate in a New Year celebration with a small, intimate group of people of whom I knew only one. A year previously, while on a workshop in Scotland, I met Nicoletta Cherubini, a professora of Italian who taught at Sienna University. It was one of those rare, inexplicable meetings in which we had sensed connections between us that transcended a passing friendship and we began to correspond. She was intent upon working for peace and unification in the world and was experimenting by bringing together her closest friends, to discover ways of working which could be applied on a wider scale. During these first four days of 1987 I was both observer and participant as I recognised the ingredients of a holistic process weaving its magic and taking us into expanded dimensions of thought and creativity, even though we had no common language.

In this state of feeling in perfect rapport with life and the people around me I opened a book and my attention fell on a particular paragraph which was this:-

This is the immediate challenge to the people of the Earth: to create a fabric of experience and esoteric knowledge which, by its nature and completeness, propels them into the next dimension of learning.

Agartha; A Journey to the Stars. (Meredith Lady Young)

Without doubt the nature and completeness of Benjaya's birth placed it for me within this description. Now I was with others who were also consciously seeking to create of the same fabric and to reach the learning that stemmed from such experiences. Had we learnt as much as we could from the birth event? Had we been propelled as far as we could go? The answer had to be 'No, we had not'. **We often think we live life in a common reality which we share with others around us but our inner worlds are diverse, filled with activity of which no-one else is aware, colouring our experience of events.** Each witness would undoubtedly have their personal perspective offering them the lessons and learning that they needed. If they would reveal the more subtle levels of their experiences then we could hope to learn more.

So on my arrival home I contacted all the witnesses. The richness of their experiences lay within the diversity not only of their occupations, but also of their personalities and past. Two probation officers, two teachers, a social worker, a photographer, an acupuncturist, an electrician, a carpenter, two midwives... some familiar with our environment and holistic principles, others not at all. Each birth witness held fragments of that kaleidoscopic pattern that had made up a whole. Gathering in those fragments was my task, extracting the learning from it was later one for sharing with Carmella. We were well used to evaluating our life events, small and great, and the process to us was a natural one.

All who had been present accepted the invitation, with the exception of Sheila Brookes, one of the midwives, who felt it inappropriate as she was still employed by the local Heath Service. The others came, one by one, revealing whatever rose from the heart of that event for them. It was by then three months on from the birth and the timing was perfect. A natural internal editing had taken place and the welter of detail which so often crowds the conscious mind had been refined to that which had made an impact leaving images and feelings that had remained as lasting impressions. Could it have been the action of walking purposefully again up those stairs, to the top of the house, that began to reactivate memory? We simply stepped back together effortlessly into the energy of that night as each dipped into their own recollection of their personal history. As I relived the birth scene through their eyes and minds I became aware that deeper reservoirs had been nourished than could be expressed in the language available to us in words. All used the term 'energy' in their attempts to convey the subtle shifts in atmosphere and vibration that were sensed that night. Their words illustrate some of the seeds of learning which they offered to us, together with the permission to share them in whatever way we chose.

Patricia's Story

I had believed I was arriving for an evening study/meditation group and when I was told Carmella was in hospital my first reaction was relief. I just couldn't cope with all the thoughts of the dangers involved, you see, of the practicalities of taking a pool upstairs and filling it without putting dangerous weight on the floor and all the concerns about having a first baby. With all the anxieties I held I certainly felt it wouldn't be right for me to be present at the birth, but that didn't stop me wanting to give a hand to get things moving because I can be really efficient when my Grandmother instinct takes over. I was so keen to get the pool empty I started throwing water out of the window! I cannot get away from the sense that people went into slow motion and yet in retrospect I think I was moving and thinking extra fast. I wasn't intending to stay. Then Carmella arrived. I could see the birth wasn't imminent and my pace slowed down.

When I stood still long enough and became aware of the total group cohesion, any sense of potential problems just flowed away. This is very important to me, this awareness that, individually, I struggle with anxiety, but in a group such as this it just seems to be erased, transmuted. I was still there when the message came downstairs that all those present in the house were welcome to be present at the birth and I knew then that I was meant to be a part of it.

I have never been present at any birth other than giving birth once myself and my own experience had been absolutely terrifying. I had begun labour when visiting friends and had to kangaroo the twenty-two miles back home in an old car. I couldn't convince my husband that labour had really started. I was petrified. Most things you can turn back from at the last minute but birth is different, there's no turning back! When I reached hospital everything went from bad to worse. The gas and air mask didn't work properly; my doctor, who had foreseen complications, couldn't be found. In the birth class they had spelt out that we might need to be cut along the vagina and the tension was there, had been implanted in my mind you see. They lost count of the number of stitches I had... oh yes, it is quite obvious now that I had been projecting anxieties from my own personal experience onto birth in general all these years .

I dozed on the couch, waking just before Abel came to call us. There wasn't any interaction that I recall, just a slow, quiet ascent. I felt a kind of respect. We weren't going up as voyeurs, we were going to be part of something special and you don't chat amongst yourselves in those circumstances. It's as if your mind is walking ahead of you, making contact with what is to come. Maybe that is why we sat around in a silent way. We wanted to be with her rather than watch her, which is different.

When I went into the sanctuary there was an immediate impact, an indescribable reaction in my solar plexus, yet the scene looked so natural. I could see the bath was actually going to stay up and the floor was not caving in. What was it I had been so concerned about? I'd lost the thread of all those niggling little thoughts and worrying details and just sat on the floor with my back to the door.

When it was time for the birth I experienced a mounting excitement... and then there he was - a new human being slipping into life so gracefully through the water, so different, so beautiful. But it was not just the water, it was being there in that safe, familiar, embracing energy in the sanctuary, the muted lighting, the relaxed environment, the loving support, so solid that it was almost tangible, and the stillness. A sense of awesomeness hung in the air.

There was rightness of how I came to be there despite myself, if, for no other reason, I was there to clear my own particular set of negative thought patterns relating to birth, but there is another important connotation for me which is harder to explain. You see, I had come straight from a hospital in Western-Super-Mare, from my dying father to a new birth, and those energies are so similar. Dad died shortly afterwards and I hold these two scenes together in my mind. I know they are related in some way although I don't know exactly how. The first building that I walked into after stepping out of the hospital was the MetaCentre and I felt sure Dad was stepping out of life into some other safe, familiar and beautiful space.

Now I have it, the feeling that hit me when I walked in! What I got was a tremendous sense of the pattern of history. T.S. Elliot writes of 'timeless moments'. I get this sense of time past, time present, time future... a pattern, I can feel it again now. It's wondrous! There's a massive birth thread that goes back through all time, and as I walked through the sanctuary door I was swept into this pattern like an ever flowing river. **Death is the same, it's the same great thread.**

$\mathcal{P}eter's$ $\mathcal{S}tory$

There was magic in the air that night, that's what I felt - magic, excitement, suspense. The closest thing I can compare it with is the waiting before opening presents on Christmas morning when I was a kid. I just couldn't wait!

You wouldn't believe the chaos it was out there when the action started. I zoomed about with Charlotte four times in three different cars, one had hardly any petrol in, another ran out. We were flying around for films, a heater, people. I didn't know who was who or anything. Every time we got back we had a bulletin on what was happening. I didn't want to miss a thing, but when Charlotte mentioned going right into the room my first thought was 'I can't! I don't know what I might *see!*' The idea was a total shock at first and then it just grabbed me, that I could *be there*. I was *going* to be there. I was dumbstruck for a minute then the excitement really got to me, I kept laughing and joking saying "help, I'm peaking again!" I was getting carried away and didn't know what to do with myself. I was sitting on the edge of my seat already!

It was just like going to bed on Christmas Eve. New life was coming into the house and for me it was the first time ever, being a part of something like this. When Abe woke me up I was scared. Charlotte was moving so fast that I think I made it in one leap trying to keep up. When I walked in all I wanted to do was to merge into the wallpaper, be very quiet so that I wouldn't be noticed or cause any hassle whatsoever. I didn't feel like I was intruding though. I admit I did have a thought of 'should I really be in here?' then I sat down quick on the edge of the bed and thought 'well, I'm in, so try getting me out of here, Bob!' I was wondering what was going to happen but I *wanted* to see then. I remember doing a quick visual of things, then I just sat there enthralled and never took my eyes off that bath once. I was like in a trance just staring at that bath.

I felt I had to be totally quiet during the birth. I almost held my breath trying to keep dead quiet. I remember a midwife saying that the head had appeared and then he was out, flying like a torpedo and this little child floated up to the surface. It was just amazing.

I felt certain that as he was coming out, that was the time when he seemed to be starting up, ticking over, when the energy was pouring into him - the start of the human being. That's when both the body and soul are combined as one, when they start acting as one, when the senses are picking up. It's like a car that has petrol in, but when the starter motor is turned on it starts to move.

He must have been about an hour old when I held him, when I could get my hands on him and really feel what he was, a ball of energy, well, that's how I see it. Everything had been ready and right in the early morning in a house so out of the way, with the world just waking up, another life arrived. That's what I think about a lot now, about life arriving all the time in lots of different ways.

My family said "What, birth in a fishpond!" but when they had me explaining it from the inside they accepted it. They were astounded that I'd been there, that I'd *seen* it. No more than me! It was a privilege to see a life coming in, it's not an everyday thing for most people is it? Seeing a baby born in the water just caps it off in my opinion. After seeing that now I've got a better idea of what it will be like having my second!

Charlotte's Story

I certainly wanted Carmella to have her baby at home. Hospitals are so impersonal, being surrounded by strangers who just don't know, who cannot possibly know, what sort of person you are. Surely anyone giving birth would want family around to give that feeling of security, support and confidence, wouldn't they? Um... I suppose it does depend on the home and people in it. I certainly would anyway and Carmella *definitely* did. As long as she was at home she could have the baby any way she liked, in water was fine with me!

I nearly went berserk when she was whipped off to hospital. I knew it couldn't be right and we had to get her back home, but when she didn't come all day I couldn't understand. I didn't want to wait, I wanted to go to the hospital and fetch her and kept being told "wait, she has told us to wait, she'll let us know when she's ready". I was ready. I'd been ready all day. If it had been my decision I wouldn't have followed her instructions. That was awful leaving her there. *She was in the wrong place!* I can hardly remember anything about the day except for the relief when she was home and then I just knew everything was fine and it was just a question of time.

In one way it was good to get into the action outside but there was such a sense of urgency in me then to get things done and get home fast. They were like two different worlds, one out there and one inside. Out there I was really getting irritated with people. I wanted to kick out at somebody, something. When I get annoyed I don't usually feel so edgy, so physical with it. As soon as I stepped back into the house I stopped being urgent, everything slowed down and was very calm, in me I mean, as well as in the house. It was, yes, like a bit of panic when I was away. I wound up as soon as I set foot outside. The trip to fetch Tony and Persh must have taken about an hour, which seemed like forever. I was nearly going mad with all the delays. I don't know how I stood it!

At last when we'd got it all together we could have a good laugh. Pete was hilarious! Carmella had already told me I could be there if it was all working out okay, but when she said it was okay for Pete to be there I knew that I needed him to be there for *me!*

I tried to sleep but was on edge every time someone walked up the stairs. When Abe knocked I was out of the door and in the sanctuary before he'd turned around, I think. We settled in the corner but because of the size of the room you couldn't help but feel you were *in* there, a part of the action, but a *still* part of it, if you see what I mean. I had to sit on my hands to stop myself grabbing at anyone who moved. The words 'Don't move anybody, - **just don't move'** were drumming in my head. It was funny really, after all the urgency to get things moving this was just the opposite. It *was* together and I just knew it didn't have to be disturbed.

I was glad it wasn't me in that pond. I wanted it to be over quickly for her... and for me. I remember the perspiration on her face and although she didn't make noises of pain, I knew that there *was* pain and she was sort of moving with it, through it somehow. I didn't want to make contact with anyone else in the room except Carmella although I did have a quick glance around and saw everyone had their eyes fixed forward, glued to Carmella. No-one showed any signs of emotion or tension but I could feel it in the atmosphere. It was electric.

Then he was here and I was with him, but I knew he wasn't just a baby. I don't think in terms of body and soul, the two are not separated in my mind.

M'haletta

Charlotte's story had a personal relevance for me which no-one else would have been likely to recognise. Her behaviour had been very much out of character and I was surprised to hear the strength of her inner agitation and urgency to ensure Carmella was 'in the right place'. She is well used to going with the flow of events and I wondered whether there could possibly be a correlation between this behaviour and her own birth. Her anti-hospital stance was not born of any personal experience, having never been a patient in one!

Charlotte was the last person to be born at Adam House in October 1967. Being my fourth child I had felt confident and relaxed, having had no previous birth problems and I felt that I knew the process well enough. But all did not run in the expected pattern. The contractions started, and in due time the midwife arrived, the contractions stopped and the midwife could no longer find a heartbeat. She looked at Derek who sat silently on the bed and shook her head. It was a full-term pregnancy and it was being soundlessly implied between them that the life had gone. I recall lying motionless and silent as I wanted to be able to identify the merest flicker of movement in me. It did not come and all I heard was the midwife calling the ambulance to have me taken to hospital to have the 'dead' baby removed.

The memory of Charlotte's birth which remains is essentially of that period of delay, the mental agony of the waiting, the stillness and silence when I too did not want to move or be moved. But they came for me and, as I stepped out of bed, the action began... but not at the hospital, I remained at home in the 'right' place. It was soon over, the cord had been wrapped around her face and neck and she arrived bruised and battered, held back by the entanglement. Her heart never had stopped beating even if we could not hear it.

This posed questions for me as to **what degree our own births have seeded experiences which, when triggered, can be transferred to other situations.** Charlotte's unusual degree of physical agitation at delay; the certainty that 'home' was the right place; her inner need for stillness and silence were all possible indicators.

David's Story

I'd had an evening appointment and when I returned home everything was ready, orderly, calm and I felt quite superfluous. So I had supper, snatched a little sleep and woke spontaneously at 5 o'clock next morning. I still felt a bit apprehensive about the whole thing, about how many people it was going to be possible to get into the room, a host of details like that. When Abel gave me the invitation I made my way upstairs and then made camp outside the sanctuary door. Others came up and went in past me and when M'haletta opened the door and beckoned me in I gulped and crawled in on my hands and knees feeling very awkward about the situation.

I looked around and tried to take in the state of each of the people in the room and I was touched by it all - how Carmella was so relaxed as if she'd had ten babies in these circumstances and Abel's caring attitude, contrasting with thoughts in my mind of fathers who the closest they get to the maternity ward is the lounge bar. There was a certain amount of distress in me for what I imagined Carmella might be feeling - my projection! I wondered what it must be like, what pain a woman had to go through and the actual physical distortion of the anatomy and how that would feel and I just couldn't think of any sensation that would equate with that in my experience. I think I can relate to the feminine aspect of myself but I can't relate to the feminine aspect of giving birth.

Carmella's nakedness definitely had an effect on me. I'd suggested to Carmella that she might be bothered about such things, but *she* didn't seem bothered at all. That was a big shock to me, that someone who could be so self-conscious was not being self-conscious. I was fascinated by Carmella's state. She didn't seem to be experiencing any neurosis, was totally open, clear and wide awake and yet at the same time *was* in a higher state of consciousness, forgetting about her own comfort. It felt to me as if she was doing an important job and just wouldn't allow any distraction of a lower nature to creep in, although I'm sure there wasn't even a conscious pattern of thought going on.

As soon as everything began to move my attention switched from studying Carmella to all kinds of thoughts about the baby, or rather about the incoming being who was going to be a baby. I was wondering whether it was a celebration for that being, or not. Before this moment I'd had a fairly conditioned approach to birth, a rather flat 'Oh congratulations, someone's had a baby'. Now I'd begun to think about the actual mechanism of how a being comes into birth and how that being will learn to live and acclimatise. What problems would it bring or create for itself to deal with? Would it be happy, healthy, well loved? It's like we're one side of the curtain and I was trying to imagine what it might be like on the other side before the curtains open.

When Carmella began to push and sort of groaned, it went through me, I couldn't get it out of my head, how it must feel. Then I was taken completely by surprise. I had a television image of birth being slow, first a head and then a shoulder and the baby being sort of twisted out, but suddenly this baby was there in the water, midwives dipping in with their hands, and he rising up onto Carmella's abdomen. It was awesome. I was so overwhelmed then by my own internal reaction I didn't notice anything else.

I was surprised at the authority, the calm, which Abel brought to the whole thing. Sometimes he even gave out little commands to the midwives as if he'd done a hundred such births. Then I looked around again and realised I was probably one of the ones who had done the most worrying. I had been concerned about so many things, but once in there I had been able to sit and soak up the atmosphere. The heat was incredible, the humidity. Everyone was really working - externally holding that focus on the centre and internally.

I've been conditioned, in the way most western people have, to see birth as a precarious thing and to fear it, which perhaps accounts for my original concerns. Until recently, I realise birth would have been quite a taboo subject and it would have been the province of women. I was privileged to be present. If I am ever in the position of becoming a father I would want to be in it with the kind of commitment I'd seen demonstrated. I saw a special process happening of three people, Abel, Carmella and Benjy all working to bring themselves together as a family.

When I got to work I felt so positive that I told everybody I met that day about it, even the customers whether they wanted to hear or not! Things like this put back the reality into life. I had a very strong sense of reality out of the whole thing and it's still with me. We can be so distanced from life's natural realities in the twentieth century high-tech life-style. All in all I went through a sort of catharsis. I've wondered about the whole process of birth a lot, especially the mystery of it.

Wendy's Story

When I came home late afternoon I knew that I wanted to be involved straight away, to be physically active. This went on until early evening when I found myself hovering, going around everywhere to see if help was needed but there came a point when everything that could be done physically was done. I had sat in the sanctuary for a while with Carmella and the midwives, timing the contractions and when I came down had moved around joining in groups in different rooms. In the later hours, as I sat with M'haletta and Derek, the three of us just being together, listening to the Taizé chants playing, I felt I was doing something that is inexpressible, keeping a vigil perhaps. I didn't go to bed at all, just sat in a chair dozing off a bit in the early hours. I was dreaming about the baby and when I woke up I thought 'it's going to be a boy' but I didn't say anything.

When I heard that Carmella was happy for me to be there at the birth I *wanted* to be there. I *had* to be there. It was 'the group' going in, not individuals. I felt that we were just one group although some didn't know others. That didn't matter at all because we were all focused on the one thing, something greater, more important than ourselves.

When Abel called "It's time" I didn't rush. Inside the sanctuary it struck me how soft and clean it all was without being sterile and bare. Before, I was imagining the possibility of blood and mess everywhere. It wasn't like that at all. I was very aware of going in there positively because I smoke, but all that day I would not go outside and have a cigarette because I didn't want to bring anything negative into the house, never mind the sanctuary.

I felt strange initially, outside the situation. I took the space on the bed next to Peter and as soon as I sat down seemed to just merge in. I glanced round briefly and could see everyone was focused on Carmella, then I felt I had the rhythm of it and I don't think I took my focus from her again. We were not staring at her, more gently holding her with our eyes. Abel had said to be aware of our breathing and to keep a rhythmic flow and not to hold the breath in. That seemed important so that's what I did, focused on my breathing.

Carmella was in a high state of consciousness, just about the opposite of unconsciousness. When I walked in she said something to me about sitting down and I was surprised she was so aware. It seemed that as everyone went in she recognised their presence in some way and then let it go. Nothing broke the flow of things until the moment the baby was born;

then I felt a tremendous, overwhelming upsurge inside me. He seemed to just 'whoosh' in and I felt it *inside me*. It didn't seem important to know if the baby was a boy or a girl. I really felt very emotional at that point.

The midwives looked very balanced one on either side of the pool but they didn't stand out as being two different people, professionals in uniforms, they just flowed into the whole of it. I remember the midwife wanting to clear the baby's air tubes and Abel didn't want that, so for a moment or two I felt concerned. I wanted everything to flow on in a natural way because everything had been so perfect. I didn't want it to be spoilt. Then Benjy coughed and cleared the airways himself and I was really glad.

One scene strongly imprinted on my mind was when Abel had his arm around Benjy and Carmella, the point at which the photograph was taken. I think that moment must have been when we were all strongly focused for that photograph to come out the way it did with the light energy in it. I feel I'm in that photograph. We were all in it.

I'm just so sorry that Marc missed it. Some weeks before I didn't think that he would have wanted to be involved, but when he phoned on the day Carmella was in labour I felt he *was* here. He was so excited and he expressed concern for Carmella and asked me to tell her that he would be with her. I know that's the sort of thing people often say, but I did have an incredible feeling of his presence. How these things work is a mystery to me, but I think Marc *was here* and involved in some way. His energy was in that photograph with mine, with all of us, I felt it connect with us and nothing can change that.

When I wrote to my mother and told her about Benjaya's birth I remember writing that it was **'beauty in its purest form'**.

Derek's Story

My first real involvement began at 6.30pm at a very practical level. The task of co-ordinating the emptying and re-filling of the pool was more complicated than it seemed. I felt a certain amount of non-coherence in the absence of any time-scale to work to. What sort of temperature was needed? Would it get cold before she arrived? Would she get straight in? There were so many variables and I just had to keep making reasonable guesses, but all of that was underpinned by a sense of immense relief that their plans were not going to be thwarted, as I'd begun to think they might be.

There was a space between the practicalities and the birth. It seemed a long time. The information and directions from the group in the sanctuary to the group below seemed to me to bind us all together as one complete group, although we were all spread out.

When the call came from Abel I felt high anticipation. At the same time I was experiencing a bit of discomfort about seeing my daughter naked in a bath of hot water. It was an experience I'd not had for twenty odd years. When I went into the sanctuary I found that having the camera and the responsibility that went with it gave me a role to play, a focus that kept my mind from extraneous thoughts. I began thinking about the task straight away, asking myself when would be the right time to take the shots, what angle should I work from, and so on. Also, I had to take into account the atmosphere. A group-consciousness had been raised, and if I stood up, knelt down or moved about, what effect would that have on the group and the atmosphere? I was most conscious of this all the time, aware that there was only limited space in which to work. I had Persh to consider, the midwives' movement obscuring my vision, but more than anything else I was concerned not to spoil that atmosphere or disturb the energy in any way.

It was obviously the same for everyone else. No-one was making sudden movements, loud noises or unnecessary communication. There is a certain look about a group of people in a state of heightened awareness which indicates that they sense at some level that they are all connected, so there is no need to be going through the social rituals and games to feel safe.

The atmosphere was perfect to give birth in; peaceful, tranquil without being soporific. There was a sense of activity within the stillness. Then I lost all track of time. Nothing happened for me as a series of events and I cannot remember any more details. Everything has fused together, which is captured and held for me by the photograph. I look at it and see a biblical scene from the *Old Testament* and I think 'If Herod had been present at such a birth, would he have put all the first-born sons to the sword? Would he?' And I wonder about people in the world today. If only they could witness or experience birth in this pure form, would it change their actions and attitudes, their whole relationship to life? I think it might. In a subtle way it is the story of Moses and the mother who cared enough to cast a child adrift, trusting in the safety of the waters in order to save its life.

Tony's Story

Essentially, I will support whatever works during childbirth for the couple. I work a lot with couples to get them attuned to what they actually want. From about two weeks before a birth I tend to get a bit like an expectant father myself, on edge waiting for the phone to ring. Sometimes, in pregnancies, I get concerned for various reasons, but with this birth I had the sense of it being stable, that there was a harmony around and all was working according to plan.

I attend lots of homes, and one of the things I find very important, which is one of the first things I pick up on, is the atmosphere. I find it easy to determine the condition of the mother by the atmosphere in the house, even if the mother is not present at that point. Coming into MetaCentre there was a sense of being at ease. It was a safe, stable, harmonious and settled space to step into. I like, when I'm working, to know where things are, where people are, what's going on, so that whatever happens I can integrate that quickly into what I do. We immediately sorted out where I would sleep and anything I might need. I met the midwives, took Carmella's pulse and determined the state of play.

Oriental medicines work with the body's vital energies - physical, mental, emotional and spiritual. In childbirth, acupuncturists bring all that into play, considering not only the mother's energy but also the energy that is coming through her from the child. This they do by monitoring the pulses which correspond to the twelve major organs and functions in the body, six on each wrist. In childbirth there are specific energy relationships between pulses which can identify whether a woman is pregnant, whether labour is imminent, whether there are breech complications, and how accelerated the energy is towards the actual birth. Carmella's reading showed all was stable. Although the contractions were coming fairly quickly and there was no reason to suspect a long labour, I predicted the time of birth as 6am. As it turned out I was thirteen minutes out! I think I must have picked that out of the heavens.

Inserting needles for analgesic purposes in no way interferes with the natural birth process, but I felt it unnecessary to do anything at that point. I talked at length to the midwives about acupuncture, and they shared birth experiences with me. There was a tremendous rapport between us. Then I went down to eat and to spend time with Abel. So much emphasis is placed on the female at times around birth that the man can tend to get forgotten or cut off from the experience. I am very conscious of supporting men at birth, not only to be actively involved, but also to use the experience to connect to their partner's energy. Abel had obviously already gathered a momentum which enabled him to be supportive, and I was also aware of how attuned he was to everything else that was happening. With an agreement that I would be woken closer to the birthing time or if needed, I went to bed and slept soundly.

My initial impression of entering the sanctuary was a powerful image, definite and clear. It was at one and the same time harmonious, calm and integrated, but a strong dynamic integration, and it struck me how synergistic this energy was. It was so easy to become a part of it.

Seeing Charlotte and Peter, I slipped into remembering my own youth, wondering how I would have handled something like this then. In a way all births are humbling. Life is fuller and greater than we can ever imagine it to be, and that expressed itself through your face, M'haletta - the fullness of feeling that was held in the radiance of your expression because all was going well. I looked around at others, too, and was so aware of Persh and the experiences we had shared together in terms of our children. I was full of recollections of the warmth and joy we've shared and of the sadness too of our recent separation, wondering how 'together' we ever are with someone else. We share everything that there is and yet there is always that elusive part of ourselves that is alone.

Suddenly in birth there is a moment which is the peak, then it's over. I thought Benjy swam very well... then as he lay there with Carmella and Abel, this was for me - a very holy time, a complete inner and outer expression of what birth is about, the wholeness of the bonding of mother, father and child. It can be true of all births if we let ourselves connect with it.

When I mention this birth in lectures, as I have done since, the number of people is always a matter of concern. I thought it worked perfectly. You can have any number you want at a birth providing they agree to be there out of a willingness to be a fully integrated part of the natural momentum, whatever is happening. As long as everyone is connected consciously or unconsciously, to that momentum, then it doesn't matter how many people are there.

I didn't use the needles before the birth as the water had been so relaxing, but when Carmella came out she did have some strong post-labour contractions which seemed to ease after I had treated her.

It was then that Abel wept. This was very healing for me; so many memories to be dealt with left over from the births of our children... the helplessness and powerlessness I have felt when faced with my partner's pain. Abel was crying for me too. Perhaps this also supports the idea of having more people at a birth, because there are so many facets of a birth, so many experiences that we all internalise from our own births, or birth experiences, that need to be healed; so much that is valuable, essential and specific to us all who attend births, not just the parents. Also, to be able to talk freely in terms of energy might lead us into a whole new realm of thought, and into creative ways of playing our roles when we have learnt what is happening beyond our immediate, tangible, reality.

Persh's Story

I'd spent three weeks in Spain with Carmella that summer and when we had talked about me taking on the photography at the birth and I'd been really excited about it then, though it all seemed rather unreal and remote. October came, and Charlotte and Peter were at the door, and I hadn't even bought a film for the camera! I'd moved house, parted from Tony less than a week before, and simply didn't have myself totally together. I didn't even recognise Charlotte at first, then when I did I wondered why she was visiting me! My reaction was 'Oh no! I haven't organised anything. I'm not ready' I had to deal with leaving my three children in bed for the night and my whole focus was on getting my own household under control so I would have nothing to distract me once I'd left. It wasn't easy!

We collected Tony on the way and we talked a while when we arrived before I went up to the sanctuary. It felt right that I was there with Abel and Carmella, and that's where I stayed throughout the night. There was little conversation, we built rapport by opening to each other on other levels although somebody would occasionally speak quietly. There was more eye contact than words between Abel and Carmella, and there was certainly no social chit-chat of the sort that fills space when silence is uncomfortable. The energy was gently focused on Carmella, we were all there for her, there was no other agenda, and the midwives were terrific.

Carmella was in the pool for several hours and the busy little ritual of boiling up the kettle to top up the water was great. I even dozed off for an hour in the early hours. The photography was my official function and I felt it was both a responsibility and a challenge in the dim light.

About half an hour before the birth I was aware that something had shifted. The energy had changed. I was bright, alert and very present. My attention was sharpened, it was like a change of gear, a speeding up. Abel consulted the midwives and they agreed it was time to call in the others. I was a little aghast when they trouped in, but the energy was lovely as everyone settled down. It felt like when you blow bubbles and a whole lot of bubbles come and join onto one - everything gives a little bit as they join together, and then they sort of settle.

The birth scene for me was through the camera's eye. I took six or seven shots while Benjy was under the water, unsure of how much would come out. I was vaguely aware of the cord being cut and continued with shots with tears in my eyes. Only once before had I taken photographs with a hand-held camera at an eighth of a second, then both my elbows were resting steadily on a church pew in natural light. How I managed, with the tears and the tremor in my body at the wonderful thing going on in front of me, I'll never know. I had thought at first it might be cramped, but then it didn't seem to matter what the physical conditions were. The energy of the person working with them seemed more important. And Carmella was fantastic the way she handled the labour with such terrific inner strength, staying in tune with herself and what was happening.

When I saw the photograph on the front page of the *Daily News,* I felt I had been helped. I expected the pictures to be blurry and rather dark. I still cannot understand how the lighting in the sanctuary could have produced that effect. The lines were sharp, there was no shake at all. It doesn't add up at one level. The definition is incredible. That is what I've read solar light energy looks like. Look at her hair, the lines on her face, Benjy's hair... and that's in a newspaper! See the hairs on Abel's arms? If you talk to someone who teaches photography they're likely to tell you it's not possible. This may be saying something about light energy, that when we are in a totally connected higher state of consciousness, in a space, an environment which is also clear, we can key into different qualities of light. I just don't know.

I think birth is a very spiritual event and people are pulled into that energy whether they give it a label or not. It was the birth of a whole being we witnessed - no part of him was being denied. I could feel a personality resonating and *he* chose how he came in as well. Abel was in charge, holding the overview in one sense, but that baby was also in charge.

Maggie's Story

I was doing relief work in the G.P.'s surgery when I first heard that a twenty-eight year old girl wanted to have her first baby at home. I'm a supervisor of midwives, trained in home deliveries, and when I learnt that the midwife who covered her doctor's practice had never seen a home delivery, I asked my supervisor "Would you like me to do anything about this?" I was told "No, it's not your practice. Stay out of it." Time went on and I heard that this girl, Carmella, wanted a waterbirth, and I knew her doctor's midwife had resigned, so I asked straight out "Would you like me to do this birth?" The response was the same, so I had to let it go; although I'd heard there was some resistance around to doing 'the water business'. I didn't feel that way at all, although I knew nothing about it.

Then one morning, when I was in the hospital, the manager approached me and said "Get out to Clent this afternoon to see Carmella B'Hahn. Take her a pack, she's got no equipment, and the press are coming this afternoon". I was going to be on holiday when the baby was due so I arranged to take a colleague, Sheila Brookes, who I'd known for twenty years. First I had a busy afternoon clinic to take care of, so that was how we came to make our first contact at such an inconvenient time. I don't know whether Carmella felt neglected by the National Health Service, but I certainly would have in her position.

The next day I heard that Carmella was in hospital and was expected to stay there. I had a mother-and-father of a headache when I got home from work that day and felt dreadful, which was most unusual. I had cooked a meal but couldn't eat much and was sitting at the table when the phone rang - Carmella's mum telling me the new plan. Then the headache miraculously disappeared. I phoned Sheila first, then I did the duty phone calls, as, by now, management had decided that this was all a bit different and they wanted to be kept informed of what was happening - 'We must be on our toes'. My husband is one of those flying doctors with the accident squad and I knew I could call on him as well as Carmella's doctor in an emergency. For some time afterwards he was very involved in Carmella's story.

It was really good to arrive and get involved. Everybody was cheerful and sociable and it felt a bit like a party at first. Carmella gave us some material on waterbirth and we went upstairs to sit reading for a while. People I have spoken to since have said "Weren't you frightened? I'd have been terrified!" But why? It was a perfectly normal process and Carmella was super. I can't remember feeling anxious on any score, except perhaps for a bit of concern that there were so many people likely to be at the birth, which is unusual; but if that was how Carmella wanted it to be and she was happy, that was fine.

I remember sitting on the stairs talking with you, M'haletta, and commenting how calm you were. People get so agitated and impatient at births, but it was obvious that you have had a very different sort of training and your way of life is so different that this wouldn't be the same for you at all.

My one big regret is that I didn't have the opportunity to get to know Carmella better, though I'm really glad we seemed to get on so well together because birth is such a vulnerable and emotional time and personalities can be so difficult. I was impressed with the pain relief of the warm water. I feel we are becoming too reliant on the use of drugs and machinery these days. We are too conditioned to speeding up the delivery and doping the mother so that she doesn't participate very well. Carmella was participating fully and knew what she wanted and did what she wanted, but then she had obviously studied childbirth and she understood what her body was doing. So many people don't bother to find out, they think it's just going to happen to them, so why should they need to know anything?

When the time came for the people to come in I thought it might be a bit difficult for me, but it wasn't. They came in carefully and quietly. Even the cameras were not a nuisance. The most difficult thing of all for me was keeping quiet myself! We are always, as midwives, feeling we need to encourage the mother, constantly making little comments like 'come on, this is good, you're doing fine'. Most girls want to chat to keep their minds occupied, distracted from the contractions. Carmella wanted it quiet in order to focus and I discovered how difficult it was *not* to do the reassurance bit. Abel had asked us not to be doing 'oohs and aahs' and calling out 'It's a boy - or girl - and isn't he lovely, and so on'. It's difficult because most people do that. There are set patterns of communication in certain circumstances and it's hard to change them at a moment's notice; to do things differently. And all of you *were* different, as if you had some inner frame of reference that was of more importance.

We kept focused on Carmella and our own tasks. This baby entered so fast, one minute I could see an inch of head and the next he was out!

The cord was well wrapped round him and this was where we did need the two pairs of hands. He was so buoyant! They had wanted a gentle transition through the water, and bringing him to the surface just happened naturally; no-one gave any signal. I don't think I'd really believed until that moment that he wouldn't breathe until he was out of the water. Although I know in theory that breathing is stimulated by contact with the air, it's another thing proving it! This is one of the things I've had to explain to a lot of people since. It was Sheila who called out "I've never seen anything like it!" It was just an expression of amazement. I know how she felt, I felt the same - it was the way that he shot out like a water creature. Now I understand much better why people are wanting to use water more as a medium for birth.

I couldn't help but be aware of the comparison to working in a hospital environment. There is so much going on that it is impossible for one person to devote all their time to one mother. You cannot hope to build the sort of intimate group atmosphere that we had. I know they have tried putting on pretty wallpaper, but there is more to it than the trimmings. This birth setting had been so well thought out and it worked well for us too. It wasn't strangely way-out by any means. The only real strangeness was the water. People have individual choices and attitudes toward things, and I think we should adapt to how other people like things to be for them, and to learn from that. Too often we try to impose our own standards on people. That is what the system seems to be all about. It is a system that says 'there is a right way of doing things which is *our* way', particularly in nursing and medicine. We do impose ourselves, I know we do. That is part of what I enjoy about working in people's homes, where we are guests. As soon as a person walks in through the door of a hospital or surgery they metamorphose from being a person to being a patient, and it's not good.

There was a spiritual quality about this whole scene which came through in the way that everyone was relating to each other, from the tone of the music and so on. I felt very calm and connected to your behaviour, in fact from the minute we arrived I think Sheila and I stepped into your way, your stream. I never once felt like an intruder from the very minute we closed the outside door behind us. A lot of people would have been inhibited about something as intimate as childbirth, but you were not. Many girls would not want their parents to be present, certainly not their father, and very few fathers would want to be there. You have a very different attitude towards each other to a lot of families; you obviously have some very special relationships.

M'haletta

When the tapes of the interviews were transcribed we had a dossier of invaluable reflections. The house was so full of activity that Carmella and I waited until we had the opportunity to go away and find a clear space together for two days at Abel's parents' home. It was a luxury that we used to the full as we spread out the pages, classified and collated the common threads, and absorbed the enlightening personal details which expanded our thinking into unexplored territory.

The birth event had resulted in the simultaneous raising of consciousness for a group of diverse people to the point where new learning had taken place, old wounds had been healed, attitudes born of unsound beliefs had changed, invisible energy-fields had been acknowledged, and each individual had felt the value of their own presence, even in inactivity. It was as if we had managed, through our interviews, to capture a life event as **a living hologram,** a kaleidoscopic view of interplaying patterns and synchronistic experience, rather than the less whole, or partial picture viewed from our own limited perspectives.

Recognising the immense value of our learning, and keen to share our insights we then set about weaving a mixture of personal experience with our holistic theories, producing booklets[4] and designing workshops for midwives, birth supporters, and pregnant people.

There had, of course, been another person present at the birth who had not been offered the space to speak - Benjaya himself. And I could not help wondering what he might have communicated if he had had the chance. Some long time afterwards, on a day when I felt my mind to be in rapport with his, I mentally asked him to speak to me of his birth, and this is what the pen wrote:

My birth into the body of a boy was a gladsome thing. First came the life-line, a webbed thread of spinning sound infused with life. Then came the life as womb-child, taking flesh, building bone and brain; and then, ah then, that sacred moment when the womb-child left his womb, his home, his world, his watery abode, to take to the air.
Had you thought of birth this way, as a taking to the air?

---

[4]See page 240

From the darkness I came forth into the light of my new world with spinning motions as the brain connected to the eyes, and mind was reborn.

Had you thought of birth this way, as the anchorage of mind?

*Torrents swirled as sound and light rushed toward me and entered through my cloak of skin. Every cell was motion suffused with sound. And within that sound was heard the call of my mother, a call unceasing, joyous with wonderment, not from the lips, but from the heart. I **heard** that sound.*

Had you thought of the sound of joy breaking as a crested wave on the shores of a new consciousness?

Awareness of the body's existence as flesh touches flesh, then the hand and the eye of the father is upon me and I experience an electrification as the life current runs between us in our first Earth's embrace.

Do you know of this, the currents of the hand and eye which make their silent mark?

On then I flowed toward the belly of the mother and an explosion of warmth as the fires of flesh are lit.

Did you sense the heat as the flame of life leapt high?

The waters were my swirling cloak, for I, as few can yet proclaim, came dressed in snow. For what is water but the melted stars? So, too, I wore the cloak of love... yet every child can thus appear, only to be uncloaked by a shivering world.

And so the dream of life began...

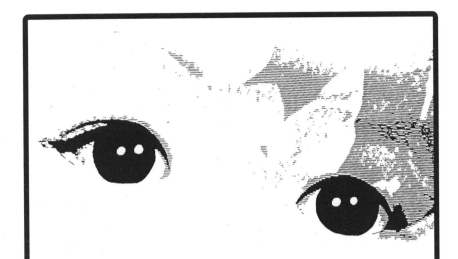

Sustaining

the

Life

Courtesy of Wolverhampton Express and Star

CHAPTER NINE

𝒫arenting 𝒫rinciples

Carmella

𝒯 the euphoric feeling of 'mission accomplished' after Benjaya's birth was short-lived and the realisation that the parenting mission had only just been launched finally sank into our consciousness. Abel and I felt naive and incompetent in the face of the massive task before us and we recognised, in the first few days of his life, that **Benjaya would bring us lessons and opportunities far greater than any spiritual teacher could possibly offer.** To say he offered us challenge seems like a gross understatement. We were shaken to our roots by his existence.

The claim that all waterbabies have a calm and gentle disposition was soon knocked on the head in our household. What we had birthed so beautifully was a squirming ball of fire - a strikingly handsome, acutely aware, vocal and wilful powerhouse with insomniac tendencies.

We needed all the help we could get and, thank goodness, we were given it on all levels. Before he was born Benjaya himself had given me advance warning of the way he wished to be parented. In the later part of my pregnancy we held a celebratory workshop at MetaCentre called 'Heralding the New Life', and it was here, in the sanctuary, during a high point of the weekend, that my son spoke through me. Suddenly I felt choked with an emotion which was certainly not my own, and I knew that if I opened my mouth our child-to-be would speak. I was conscious of my heart beating as I took the plunge and allowed the words to come spilling out. The essential message was contained in his first three sentences: the rest has slipped away with time.

You may not think that we have fear here, but I am afraid. Birth to me, and to those with me, is like a death, death to who I really am. Please keep me conscious of who I am when I come.

There was not a dry eye in the room and tears were running down my cheeks. I could feel his pain at the thought of separation from his Godforce, so alive in him at that moment; and his fear of knowing that in taking human form **his true identity could be soon overlaid with conditioning and illusion. Death or birth... birth or death?** It was at this time that I became confused as to **which is which.**

And so, before Benjaya's arrival, Abel and I were committed to keeping him God-conscious. Thankfully, we were given many more parenting principles on which we generally agreed, and despite falling far short of them time after time, at least our sights were set upon the same goals.

When I was six months pregnant I had made an impulsive decision to join friends on a three-week holiday in a cottage a-top a blistering hot mountain in southern Spain. I soon discovered that I was too unsteady on my legs to brave the 45° slopes down the mountain often and I began to feel trapped and emotional - and homesick for flat roads and rain. As a last resort I turned to higher guidance for help as to how I could spend those long hot days profitably. I should have asked sooner, because as usual I was given the needed guidance. It comes as a kind of word-flow in my head which by-passes conscious thought, and when I begin, by writing in my journal the first few words I hear, the rest just keeps on coming at such a rapid rate that I have trouble keeping up. The first words were these:

Know that there are those who watch over you night and day; who feel with you, sleep with you and hear your prayers of thought. However, know this: we cannot intervene until conscious request for help is given, for how can we fill a full chalice?

You now don the cloak of motherhood, but it is not merely the child that you serve. We would have you work side by side with the microcosm and macrocosm of motherhood. You will find that a love and devotion towards the child within your womb will allow your heart to reach out to the vulnerability in all peoples. And if you can successfully parent a child in body, then you can parent the child in all men and women who have not had the fertile soil in which to be successfully nurtured.

In practical terms in response to your question we would answer thus. Follow these suggestions and you will take home a harvest of fruits to those who love you and those who know not of you. A house will be provided where you can sit in stillness. Prepare the body with healthy foods and the mind with healthy thoughts and sit each day to receive teachings of simple truth upon Education for Life, plain truths which will become commonplace in times to come...

The following day I was offered the use of a beautiful, cool house with a balcony offering a vista to the eyes and soul in exchange for watering the plants. I accepted enthusiastically and sat in meditation each day to receive the promised guidance, which has proved essential to my mothering.

Education For Life-The Principles

1. BANISH ALL THOUGHTS WHICH SEPARATE ADULT FROM CHILD and put one above the other. Recognise the pure, simple, unadulterated wisdom of a child, and be open to learning as much as you can teach.

2. TEACH ALWAYS BY EXAMPLE Words without corresponding action are empty shells and children will mirror your deeds. If you have not personally reached the goals you wish to impart, then share stories from the lives of those who have, and speak honestly about your own lessons in working towards that goal. Children need to learn about stepping-stones to the horizon.

3. PRACTICE THE ART OF LISTENING The prime cause of 'bad' behaviour is feeling unacknowledged, unheard, or ignored. Change your perspective to that of the child. If the child is old enough, ask questions about how s/he feels and communicate that you can hear what is going on. Agreement is not always necessary to dispel tensions.

4. FEED YOUR CHILDREN WITH LOVE We are all living reflections of our diet - our diet of food, thought, television and entertainment, books, atmospheres and all that enters into our minds and bodies. The more pure the diet and free from pollutants, the more healthy we will be.

5. DO NOT BARGAIN WITH FOOD Food is for creating a healthy physical body, and if used to bribe or punish, the message is given 'food is for pleasuring the senses'.

6. LIFE IS THE GREATEST TEACHER Constant involvement in life, and creating experience for all the senses in equal proportion, is the highest form of education. Head-knowledge alone is useless. Stimulate imagination, thought, touch, taste, hearing, smell, sight and intuition. If other places or lands cannot be visited then create imaginary scenes, dress up, learn words of other languages, and learn from the created reality.

7. WHATEVER YOU NOURISH GROWS Teach the child that s/he

has the power to change the day - positive thoughts make fun days and negative thoughts make troublesome times.

8. BE AWARE OF BALANCE IN ALL THINGS There is a time for silence and a time for sound; a time for attention and a time for self-amusement; a time for eating and a time to rest the body from food. Freedom can be as detrimental as discipline when it is given in too great a measure.

9. LAUGHTER HEALS If you want to fly high with your child, then take yourself lightly and see the funny side of life.

10. AS WITHOUT: SO WITHIN All things have right relationship with other things, which brings harmony. The external world can be used as a mirror to reflect a child's inner state.

11. ALLOW A CHILD'S CONSCIENCE TO SPEAK Each of us has a natural sense of dis-ease if we do something contrary to our inner truth (like Pinoccio's Jimminy Cricket). Encourage this 'knowing' rather than 'blaming'. Blaming sparks a battle with the child's defence systems.

12. AVOID SCOLDING AND PUNISHING CHILDREN What right have adults to scold or punish a child unless they themselves are willing to be scolded and punished by others? It is our responsibility to show children clearly the result of the action, and to use misconduct and mistakes as an opportunity for learning, encouraging forgiveness and trust, rather than creating fear.

13. TEACH JOY IN SERVICE by loving your work. Work is an integral part of life and should not be separated and categorised as duty, whether for financial reward or as a distasteful necessity. Show your children that work helps to enrich the whole of life, and if yours does not, then change it, or change your attitude towards it.

14. ENCOURAGE QUIET TIMES EACH DAY. Many children in today's manic world do not know how to sit still or to be receptive. Create a relaxing environment in the home - play gentle music, tell an inspiring story, take a candlelit bath together or teach simple meditation to bring out the child's feminine qualities.

15. THE MORE YOU GIVE THE MORE YOU WILL RECEIVE

To encourage sharing in children, adults must be seen to be giving generously and receiving graciously. Ask yourself 'how attached am I to my possessions?'

16. AVOID OVER PROTECTION If a child is constantly protected,

how may s/he ever find inner strength? Learn to discern when it is appropriate to help and when to allow strengthening through struggle.

17. NEVER IMPLY STUPIDITY Self-worth and self-image begin in

the cradle - and probably before - by the absorption of tonal and behavioural messages. Avoid labelling a child as shy, wilful, backward, as labels do stick. Always encourage the child's positive attributes. Weakness in character is an opportunity to love more - it is easy to love perfection.

18. INTEGRITY OF CHARACTER IS BUILT BY PERFECT HONESTY which is evidenced by the matching of thought, word, emotion

and deed. If a child's words do not match the action or emotion, then by-pass the words and speak to the emotion or apparent cause of the upset. Often there is hidden need crying out for attention, shielded by words.

19. TEACH RESPECT FOR THE BODY The physical body is a

magnificent vehicle capable of amazing feats if well treated. Tell stories of physical accomplishments and inspire the desire to cherish the body with love, good food and exercise.

20. TEACH RESPECT FOR THE EARTH'S BODY Ensure that the

child understands that the Earth is a living being which needs love and respect; that if her body dies then our own will also die because she feeds and clothes us like a big mother.

21. LIFE IS FULL OF NATURAL CYCLES - ups and downs; waxing

and waning; birth and death; light to dark; summer to winter. Teaching children about nature's ways brings them closer to knowing themselves - the most useful gift they will ever receive.

CHAPTER TEN

Working Wonders

Carmella

M'haletta's prediction that our child would work from the moment of his birth was not the whole truth. It should have continued: ...and this work will primarily consist of making his parents work. If anyone is responsible for the direction of our lives since our meeting, Benjaya is. We tried to prevent his conception, but in he came, later kicking me into the decision to plan a waterbirth, against all odds, which catapulted us into a new career.

The magical photograph which carried the news of his birth around the world invoked a constant stream of interest from the general public, and we were inundated with requests for information and practical help regarding waterbirth. Keen to respond, we borrowed a caravan from my brother Marc, which soon became a beehive of activity and was christened the Birth Resource Caravan. It was from this little haven in MetaCentre's garden that we answered countless letters and phone calls and studied any literature we could find on natural birth practices and waterbirth worldwide. There was much to learn.

Abel and I attempted to juggle our work with co-parenting our son, but it seemed that because I had breasts - his prime source of food and comfort - I needed to be involved to a much greater extent.

When Benjaya was four months old I wrote in my diary:

I am head over heels in love with my Tibetan-eyed boy and still I revel in his magnificence, despite the sacrifice and sleepless nights. It is sad that Abel does not share my own fulfilment. He is vague and kind of helpless about his role and has difficulty in relating to this tiny vulnerable creature, although he pulls his weight in all respects. His thoughts on first sight of his son are still relevant today. He described them as going something like this: 'How can I relate to something so small? He's like a different species from another planet. What on earth do I do with him? I'm supposed to feel things... I'm a father now, but I don't know what I feel.'

After the birth, when I had been cleaned up and made ready for bed, I had put Benjaya to the breast. At first he didn't know what to do, and then it was as if he had suddenly remembered as he latched onto the nipple and started sucking. Abel, at this moment, exhausted physically and emotionally, burst into tears and so I had a baby sucking on one breast and him sobbing into the other. The dynamics of our trio reminded me of this graphic scenario for a very long time. I felt at the apex of a triangle with two boys wanting my energy. My strong, dependable man felt left out and resentful and I, completely consumed with mother-love for my son, failed to understand his inability to love his son unconditionally and I failed to give him the nurturing he needed as I felt that my energy would not, and should not have to, stretch that far. (So much for 'parenting the child in all men and women ...'!)

In April 1987, when Benjaya was six months old, Abel and I were still together enough to make a public commitment to each other in a highly unconventional, self-created marriage ceremony. It was a magnificent day of sunshine and celebration at a hired stately home in beautiful grounds, with its own yachting lake. Benjaya had his own blessing ceremony in the afternoon and all was captured on video for posterity. Our first vow was to **assist each other to achieve our highest potential** and that is **the foundation stone of our relationship.** During the ceremony we offered each other bitter and sweet liquids to drink from two chalices in recognition that life is never happy-ever-after and that we would be required to support each other through bitter and sweet times. Precisely how sweet or how bitter, we were not to know.

Financial donations were welcomed instead of wedding gifts, and with the proceeds, plus the moneys earned by the birth photograph, we took off with our son in a back-pack, for a six-week honeymoon research tour of Californian Birth Centres. It was a thoroughly enjoyable, occasionally gruelling, trip which was definitely not a honeymoon, and we returned with a firm belief that Birthing Centres could be viable in Britain, and an enthusiasm to be involved in the creation of one at a later date. For the time being we needed to continue our education and to recognise that 'small is beautiful'.

In October 1987, with the help of an Enterprise Allowance award, we turned professional and gave birth jointly to our business BirthWorks. I designed a logo of Benjaya's face rising from a lotus flower and later discovered from my symbol book that the lotus means birth and death; spiritual unfolding; Divine birth issuing forth from muddy waters, its stem like an umbilical cord. Our services grew slowly to include: birthing tubs for hire and sale; production and sale of waterbirth and holistic birth educational material; lectures; attending births; birth preparation classes; counselling; and Holistic Birth Training Courses for midwives and pregnant couples.

Although we quickly became known as the waterbirth people, our vision was much wider than simply encouraging the use of water in labour. We wanted to play a part in eliminating the massive fear-consciousness surrounding birth and to heighten general awareness of the sacred nature of birth. It was also our aim to assist people in using the pregnancy and birthing process as a catalyst for personal empowerment and positive transformation. Sometimes we felt as if we were making headway rapidly, but often people thought we were living in cloud-cuckoo-land.

BirthWorks had a long, hard, but worthwhile labour, and the complications were many and varied. There was the strain on family relationships as we set up business at MetaCentre; balancing the business needs with Benjaya's needs. We had to contend with fearful and sceptical medical professionals and microbiologists; stringent health and safety regulations; lack of space and finance - and more! I have often thought that we must have been insane to have attempted to run a business in the same house as our son. His needs alone were full-time, and I battled time and time again to release my zombie-like state to become normal enough to function coherently after another adventuresome night of baby games in the lounge.

Despite continued attempts to leave MetaCentre in those early days, we failed to find anywhere else to live. We had taken over two bedrooms and a downstairs room which acted as our office, dining room, pantry and storeroom. Abel took over the damp, cold cellar, which flooded from time to time, as his workshop area which was where he built the prototype of his birthing tubs amongst a high proportion of the local frog population.

We lived on the breadline. Everything we earned we reinvested in the business. BirthWorks' survival was threatened on many occasions, and it was the unceasing support of our parents, both moral and financial, which encouraged us to go on.

Benjaya, the raison d'être of the business, accompanied us everywhere. I imagine few children could have had such an inauguration into the process of birth at such an early age. I remember one scene during a lecture which Abel and I were giving to a group of midwives in a northern hospital - Benjaya, aged eleven months, sat on the floor at the front, cross-legged like a miniature Buddha intently 'reading' a copy of *Water Babies*. He retained a fascination with birth and would never tire of hearing the story of his own birth. The facts of life were ingrained in him by the time he was three years old, as a natural progression of his constant questioning on the subject, which we felt obliged to answer honestly.

When Benjaya was two years old we managed to move house and find a space of our own, leaving MetaCentre occupants to wallow in the feeling of expansion and to redecorate the house from top to bottom. We joined a community of four families who lived together in a big pink mansion and surrounding cottages in Long Ashton, Bristol. Hill House was an exciting haven for the eleven children who lived there, and we were exceedingly happy to have been accepted as members of this particular community. After a babyhood full of adults Benjaya could now grow into boyhood with lots of other children and acres of safe space in which to romp and roam and express his abundant energy. Abel and I felt no need to produce a sibling for his sake, and were content with our trio.

Our boy was increasing in rascal charm, physical and mental agility, and willpower. He made up countless jokes, and together we had much hilarity. One day, after he had done something he knew he shouldn't have, he said "God maked me do it because he maked us all, didn't he?" He knew what he wanted and put every ounce of his energy behind achieving it whatever we felt was best, resulting in many a battle - particularly with his strong-willed father. He was also a loving and wise child and revelled in our night-time, candlelit rhythm of song-time, when we sang inspirational songs and simple chants together, followed by prayer-time, when we gave thanks for everything in our day.

It was during this quiet time that he asked penetrating questions about the nature of life, discussing intelligently the concept of the 'big me' and the 'little me' and insisting on reading repeatedly a book which included the concept of reincarnation. He spent many an evening puzzling over who would be his choice as a mother to return to after he had died, and finally decided that it would be me. Then he was thrown into confusion as he realised that big people usually die before little people so I would not be here after he died, but still he asked me "when I die will you be sad, and will I meet your old cat?" He was only just able to talk when he first mentioned reincarnation. We were reading a book about the seaside when he pointed to a picture of a jelly fish and said casually "I was stung by one of those in another life." Then he turned the page.

Benjaya's closest playmate, William, just days younger than himself, had recently lost his mother to the sea. In an extraordinary finale she had swum out into a rainbow on her birthday, had had a heart attack and drowned leaving her husband Rob, a Rudolf Steiner teacher, to parent their five children. I thought that perhaps this had triggered Benj's intense interest in death and what happens afterwards. It certainly caused me to contemplate how it would be for me if Abel or Benjaya died. Unthinkable' was always the answer.

It was at Hill House that our second business, named after Benjaya, was conceived. Jaya's Company is a manufacturing business, also dedicated to spreading the healing power of water in the form of flotation tanks, portable spa tubs and baptistries - all designed and built by Abel using all that he has learnt from his design of birthing tubs. Jaya is an Indian name meaning 'victory' and is often used as a salutation - victory to God!

Sadly, the community was forced to close down in May 1991 as we were unable to find new members with enough funds to cover the shares of the outgoing family. It was a great wrench for us all to separate - some had been there for nine years - and we all mourned the death of what we had built together. How would we ever find a place with such potential again?

Abel and I chose to put down roots in South Devon for two reasons: 1. We wanted Benjaya to attend a Steiner School which offered a holistic approach to education. 2. We wanted to live in a community which would support our way of life: like minded people around us; alternative medicine available; organic food in the shops. The Totnes/Dartington area answered these needs. In Britain, it is probably the area most densely populated with alternative thinkers and practitioners.

We enrolled Benjaya into the Steiner school for September 1991 and lived for the whole summer in a caravan and tent on a caravan site six miles from Totnes and a mile from the village of South Brent, where we had dared to rent a large workshop on a rural trading estate. It must have been one of the wettest summers for many a year, but I enjoyed spending most of my time with Benj close to nature, exploring Devon whilst Abel worked long hours to keep the business going in our new, though more remote location. On one of our nature walks, Benjaya was looking puzzled and I asked why - "There are so many dandelions," he said "but who made the first one?" He was becoming more nature-spirit-like by the day. The outdoors was his element and on his speedy legs he explored every nook and cranny of that campsite, talking congenially to campers as he went. He and I were both magnetically drawn to water and spent long hours by rushing rivers and beachcombing for treasures by the sea.

The Steiner kindergarten, a wooden building nestling in the grounds of a big manor House (the big school) was a magic kingdom full of gnomes and nature tables, coloured veils and wooden toys. I wished that I had had this cocoon of support and aesthetic surroundings as a school child and was very happy to give my son this opportunity. He fitted in well and was already used to the gentle Steiner way, having attended the Bristol Steiner school for two terms before we left.

At the end of October we moved into a little semi-detached house in South Brent belonging to new friends of ours. It was Benjaya's fifth birthday on moving day and Abel surprised him with a gift he had made secretly in the workshop - a beautiful wooden bed on stilts with his name carved on the front. It had a ladder to go up and a slide to come down - a child's dream bed. He had friends at school and was content with his life - apart from an urgent desire to travel to Sherwood Forest "to take from the rich and give to the poor".

Benjaya's teacher, Gordon Woolard, in a Rudolf Steiner kindergarten child study, described our five year old son in this way:

Benjaya, with his large, open, dark eyes, brings wonder and faithfulness to the world. He expresses a fund of life-forces in all that he does, says and thinks and stands and sits with notable uprightness.

He loves to run and drive himself hard, after which his heartbeat is remarkably powerful. He rides on a bundle of life-forces, lithe, supple, sleek and ready to move. When running, jumping, balancing, twisting or climbing he does not have to pay much conscious attention to what his body is doing. He is one of those children who has that wisdom written into their body. There is joy in his movement. In this respect he excels beyond the others and is apart from them. Perhaps that contributes to his being something of a loner amongst the rest.

Upon this harmonious bodily foundation he can be restless and hasty in soul. Sometimes he is moody, changing quickly from one extreme to the other and not lightly but passionately. One moment he will smile widely and the next cry floods of tears. Nothing is done by halves, it is always to the full. One can be sure, however, that if he cries there is something real to cry about and if he smiles then it is because something is worthy of it. In this respect he has an uncomplicated soul, in touch with the world, sincere. He does not over-nurture private feelings of resentment towards others and is notably free of malice.

In this way, something objective, universal lives in his soul. While he can freely deal with injustices to himself from others, he carries a constant underlying respect for them. They, like everything around him, seem to interest him but not bind him. Perhaps the word compassion would convey this inner strength accomplished in him.

Beyond this talent of his, though, is his sheer warmth of being, brimming full into his will to work and play and be. His presence is strong but doesn't push others over inwardly. Bridging the distance of his way of non-attachment is the look in his eyes: direct, honest, seeming to say 'here are you and I'.

I was immensely proud of my son and still loved him fit to burst. I felt that I had succeeded in keeping him conscious of his true identity and prayed it would continue - that he would retain his close relationship to God. Abel, after five long years of resenting Benjaya's uninvited presence finally recognised that he truly wanted his son in his life and was greatly enriched by his presence. He sat with him one night in the candlelight and gave thanks for all that he had given him. I was immensely relieved -

a milestone had been reached.

Left: Benjaya playing in a birthing tub
The Tibetan on a San Francisco sidewalk
The 'Trickster' with friend Meriel
& Albie bear

Above: In the Kingdom of the Gnomes

Below: In his element - the nature kingdom

CHAPTER ELEVEN

𝔇reaming the 𝔉uture

Carmella

Could I cope with the idea of being parted for a week from Benjaya? A winter holiday on the Canary Isle of Lanzarotte was the surprise Christmas/birthday gift from Abel's parents in 1992...*and* they offered to look after Benjaya for the whole week (February 5th - 12th). What couple who had never had a holiday together alone would look that gift-horse in the mouth? I was over the moon about the holiday but worried about Benjaya as he had spent little time alone with his grandparents before. I expected him to be resistant and uneasy, but he was neither and said to me just before we left "I don't know why you worry about me Mum, I'll be perfectly all right without you". It was my lesson to let go of my precious boy, and these words were to be a great comfort to me.

The week in Lanzarotte was a very powerful one. I felt deeply attuned first to death and then to birth. Here are some excerpts from my diary:

February 7th

I have felt strange here. A depressing place for me, filled with an eerie lack of life. Dead volcanic lava and ash everywhere, half finished buildings and no builders ever in sight. This island has exploded from

*the inside out and the fire still simmers close to the surface. It is said
that Lanzarotte was part of Atlantis and I feel as if the Earth balked at
the negativity of humankind. It will take many years to erase the aura of
death from this place, it is so short of life-forms and the beautiful
timeshare towns emerging everywhere are to me like make-up
attempting to disguise a scar.*

*Nevertheless, the sun is shining and the pool outside our apartment
beckons, even if it is icy cold. I miss my boy, but I'm grateful for the
precious space with Abel.*

February 12th

*Help, I'm confused. What's all this about? It's 5.30am and I have been
dreaming half the night about preparing myself for pregnancy. But it
wasn't like a dream, I thought I was conscious at the time, but then I
woke up, so I must have been in some other state of consciousness. It
was not a symbolic dream, but a direct experience.*

*It was just me having a deep communication with another being. I
was sharing all my resistance to having another child:*

> *"I don't want to start again now...at last I'm free to write and work...Abel
> couldn't cope...he wouldn't want another one... NO, we are clear and
> decided".*

*One by one my arguments surfaced, and one by one this being, oh so
gently and lovingly, persuaded me that I could look at this another way;
that it would be an extremely exciting option to have another child.*

*I'm scared! I went to bed as one person who felt that my family
was complete and woke up as another who now wants to conceive
immediately. I've been manipulated in the night. I don't feel safe. Where
are all my protective beliefs that I carried when I went to bed? What is
real? How am I going to tell Abel all this? Perhaps he has been worked
on too.*

Abel looked normal when he awoke and we sat on the terrace eating hot
croissants in the rising sun. In a trembling voice I told him about the night's
encounter, expecting him to be emphatically against the idea of extending
our family.

"Well," he said "I'm more open to the idea this morning than I've ever been before."

I spilt my coffee!

We agreed that we would let the idea percolate a while to see if time would alter the extraordinary turn-about in our thinking. We knew that if we made the decision to go ahead we wanted a conscious conception with both of us carefully preparing ourselves to welcome in a new child. We believe that the quality of the sperm and the egg which come together at conception are a direct reflection of the state of being - mind, body and spirit - of the parents at that time, and we, both Aquarians, wanted perfection in any potential conception.

It was an exciting end to a weird holiday and, on return, Benjaya was also in an excited mood. He had thoroughly enjoyed his time connecting with his grandparents and presented me with the fruits of his last day's work - a beautiful bunch of **everlasting** paper flowers. I checked out what he thought about the idea of having a brother or sister and he was crystal clear: "A brother who I can share my toys with and look down on from my high bunk".

The question 'will we or won't we conceive?' dangled in the air day after day and was the hot topic of communication with our friends. The dream-being had won me over and I never really wavered in my desires after that fateful night, although I gave myself a week before stating my 'YES' loud and clear. It was Abel who was teetering on the brink and needed more time.

I felt that he was almost there by February 25th, but by now I was beginning to suspect that it might be too late for him to be in control of the situation. My period was late and wisps of nausea came over me from time to time. But it couldn't be - could it? How could this happen to us twice given how rigorously we insist on contraception? I went for a pregnancy test that day at the local Health Centre and nervously awaited the telling phone call at home, alone.

"Hello, Mrs B'Hahn? I'm very happy to tell you that you'll be expanding your family soon."

"Thank you," I said, and started to shake. My feelings were in conflict. I was awed that another being had managed to start growing a body within me in its own sweet time and relieved to a degree that the decision had been taken out of our hands. I trusted that all was well and good on the higher levels, but I was exceedingly nervous about Abel's reaction. I didn't want to go through another difficult process with him feeling out of control, but consoled myself by thinking that he was so close to saying yes that surely he would be able to let go easily. I was terribly wrong.

Later that day, Tuesday, I wrote the following in my diary:

For a short time I was happy to be carrying our second child. I was filled with joy at the thought of becoming four sooner than expected, but how can I hold that joy when Abel is stunned, in traumatic shock, and unable to be anything but depressed? I have seriously underestimated what it means for him to say 'yes' to his second child and to avoid a repeat of the suffering that Benj has endured because he was not consciously invited in. I am attempting to understand and to be compassionate but I simply cannot comprehend why this man, who is usually so quick to see the light, is unable to just let go and welcome this child now.

Abel simply wants to scream 'NO' right now, but it's too late unless I am willing to have the baby aborted, which I know would destroy our relationship. I know that I would experience an abortion now as killing our baby for the sake of his ego, because he has a major problem in surrendering. This is a living nightmare and I am worried about the effect the energy is having on the tiny growing foetus.

Abel will not even come near me at the moment because of what I represent and I feel utterly rejected by him. I pray and trust that he will find a way through this soon without major scars.

Benjaya was my saving grace and his response to the news of a sibling on the way was startling in its intensity. He was filled with wide-eyed delight and wonder. He kissed me, loved me, and sang songs to the baby in my womb. We were in cahoots, he and I, protecting and loving that baby for all we were worth.

In an atmosphere of gloom we set off on a whirlwind trip to the Midlands that same Tuesday for Abel to have a business meeting the next day. We stayed overnight in Stroud with close friends, Sharon and Girish, and their waterbaby son Nikhil, which proved to be difficult as Abel and I were expected to sleep in the same bed! As far as I was concerned he wanted to murder our baby and I wanted to obliterate him and his emotional trauma from my life until he had come to his senses. We didn't sleep much!

The next morning, whilst Abel was at his meeting in Birmingham, Benj and I went to visit my sister, Sandra, and two of his cousins - Josh (aged 11) and Amy (aged 8). Sommer, their elder sister, was in India at the time with M'haletta. Benj was urgent to share our news, which was received with great excitement. I watched the children playing ball and shouting with laughter, and I cradled my womb wishing this child a joyous life. Where would we be without the lightness of children? Today they had lifted my spirit.

On Thursday, back at home, I prepared for the coming weekend's course at Dove's Nest, a Spiritual Education Centre in Sussex based on the teachings of Omraam Mikhael Aivanhov. I was billed as the first speaker on Conscious Conception and Ideal Birth and could not escape the ironic twist that there I was, pregnant for the second time without conscious choice and off to share with others how to conceive consciously. Nevertheless, I was confident that I had a great deal to share on the subject and could use my present situation as a learning experience for others. It would have been good to consciously conceive but **maybe this was our ideal conception, i.e. one which offers the most learning for all concerned rather than one in which we were in control.**

Friday morning the sun shone brightly and I took Benjaya to the market in Totnes. We thoroughly enjoyed ourselves and, seeing all the daffodils in vibrant bloom, he sighed

"Mummy, I'm so glad it's spring."

I felt moved to buy him anything he wanted, within reason, and he settled on a wiggly paper snake and a crystal for his collection. Later, after my first visit from the midwife, we took a bath together and sang to each other and the baby:

We are one, you are inside me
Every step I take you're there
Every breath I breathe you're there
We are one.

On Friday afternoon Abel drove me to the train with Benjaya happily singing to himself in his car-seat. They stood on the platform hand-in-hand waving to me as I sped away - my sweet happy son and my traumatised husband. It is an image that will be imprinted on my mind forever.

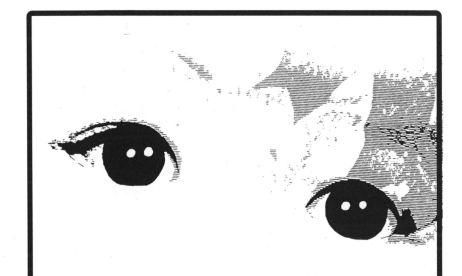

A

Goodly

Exit

CHAPTER TWELVE

A Full-Scale Emergency

Mike Major

I'm Mike Major of the Cornwall Constabulary, stationed at South Brent, where I have been for the last twenty years. I'm a police officer with twenty-nine years service and I'm one of the three local Community Constables for the South Brent Area.

We were alerted on Friday, 28th February, 1992 at 16.22 hours by the Ambulance Control who had received a call from Miss Walls who worked in an office at one of the units on Brent Mill Industrial Estate, reporting that a young boy had fallen in the river behind the units. I was just down the road when we 'had the shout' as we call it, so I was the first police officer to attend the scene at 16.23, quickly followed by the ambulance and then by further police units. It's helpful for everybody concerned when you've got a local officer on the scene who knows the area and the people.

My initial job at the scene was to verify the facts as we had received them and this was done by speaking to Miss Walls, the two children who had alerted her to the fact that a boy had fallen into the river, and to the boy's father, Abel B'Hahn. I established that he had been looking for his five year old son, Ben, and was unable to find him. By 16.33 we had verified all our information. The facts all dovetailed together, we had a missing boy and a report of a boy in the river, so this was then a full-scale emergency.

A police helicopter and other available police units were requested to come and assist in the search, and a supervisory officer, in this case the Inspector at Totnes, was called to attend the scene immediately. By 16.39 we were in the process of alerting our police diving unit at Plymstock. By that time we also had two members of the public who had stripped off and were already swimming in the river. They were searching in the hollows where some parts of the bank are washed away underneath by the river.

A search of the river from the banks was immediately commenced on both sides above and below where it was believed Ben had fallen in. Police officers were assisted by members of the public. At the same time we were checking out the home address in case Ben had in some way reached back home. We have to look at all the possibilities in situations like this. We also had police units checking the whole of the village in case Ben had fallen in, got himself out and wandered off. All of this was in operation within a matter of minutes. We had also put in a call to the fire brigade for them to attend with emergency lighting, should it be required. The ambulance carried lighting and portable generators, and flood lights were offered from the workshops so we were thinking forwards to the possibility of a search continuing into the hours of darkness. We were offered the use of a small boat from one of the workshops and that was put into the river with a couple of men in it to search the deep pools. We also requested the attendance of the water bailiffs because of their knowledge of the river. They attended and liaised with the inspector. By this time we also had a superintendent at the scene.

By 17.00 hours we were advised that contact had been made with the diving team who were out on a training exercise. Thay had now collected equipment and were on the way. From then on it was a question of continual searching of the river, moving downstream from where Ben had fallen in. We checked up to half a mile on both sides of the bank.

At 17.45 we found one of Ben's wellington boots in the river a few yards downstream. The reason why it took so long to find it was because this is the River Avon which crosses Dartmoor, flowing out through Shipley Bridge and meeting the sea at Bigbury-on-Sea. On the moors it picks up peat deposits which make the river a brownish colour and in places it is difficult to see through as the peat particles hang in the water.

Shortly after that we found a second boot trapped under the river bank just below where Ben had fallen in. This then firmly established that an unfortunate accident had happened and obviously, with the length of time that had passed, we were now greatly concerned that we were not to going to find Ben alive.

On finding the wellington boots, which were quite distinctive, being green with frog faces, we had to get them positively identified and Abel confirmed they were the boots Ben had been wearing. Up until then I think everybody was hoping against hope that we'd got it wrong. There's always a chance when children fall into cold water, the body temperature drops and the brain remains alive for quite some time. If they are found, there is a good chance, but as time goes on this factor diminishes. It was a good hour or more since Ben had disappeared. To me that was it, then. I knew for certain we were going to be looking for Ben in the river. It affects everybody. Up until then we could stay on an 'up', hoping, but the point had come when firm realisation dawned that it was not going to be a happy ending to the story.

We kept the main search to police officers so that we could have some control over the way it was being done. The police officers were working in pairs so one could stay and another come back to base if they found anything. We had fifteen police officers plus the helicopter. It's surprising what the helicopter can see. It carries a thermal imager on board for detecting bodies, but cold water presents problems because the temperature of a body would soon drop. It did a long search of the river. A young child with baggy clothes on can float for some considerable distance with the current.

We also had two water bailiffs on the scene by then and they were advising us, after looking at the state of the river, that they felt Ben might be a little further downstream as the waters were running fast. Our initial hope was that he might still be in the deep area where he had fallen in, but the swimmers couldn't see quite to the bottom. The water bailiffs suggested he was most likely to be down at the mill pool which was about 100 yards downstream where the river makes a right-hand turn behind the timber mill. There the river eddies and slows to form a deep circling pool...

By now the light was beginning to fall. We had some emergency lighting set up and were waiting for the diving team to arrive. We took people out of the river because we didn't want to stir up sediment and obstruct the divers. A lot of people were scrambling about on the rocks. In the failing light we all strung out, keeping our eyes closely on the river.

At this point I decided to take a young officer with me and go downstream with the water bailiffs to the mill pool. One water bailiff had brought his chest waders, like a big oversized pair of wellington boots with a brace and bib that he can get into and stand in the water. He had a line and a grappling hook and we had a couple of powerful lamps. We went off quietly, leaving everybody else out of the way because it was our strong feeling that we were going to find Ben in the mill pool.

At the mill pool one of the water bailiffs kitted up and waded in while we scanned the water and directed from the bank. Within a few minutes I spotted something faint and light-coloured moving about below the surface. It appeared to be an arm or hand waving about with the flow of the water. The water bailiff was able to reach him, tie a line, and at 18.45 hours, Ben was recovered from the river.

It's difficult to explain feelings at the time. You are disappointed that you've not been successful and begin to ask questions of yourself - whether you could have done something else, done it quicker and so on. But I don't think there was anything more we could have done that would have had a different outcome. It was the first time the young officer with me had ever been involved in anything like this and he had to walk away as we lifted Ben out of the water.

What tends to happen with bodies that go into the water is that they sink briefly, come up, sink again for a little while and then surface again. By the time we found Ben, his body was finding its own level in the water. It had probably been circling around in the pool for a while. At some stage he would have come to rest on the river bed, either in that pool or possibly further downstream. The river is deep where he went in. He was wearing a woolly jumper and baggy playing trousers that would have held a lot of air. Even if he had inhaled a lot of water the air in his clothes might have kept him afloat. He would have floated quickly down the river out of sight.

Local children have always played in the area where he went in, which is known as 'the beach'. The bank is steep and you have to climb down eight or nine feet, clambering over tree roots. By what I understand, the oldest boy had climbed down and Ben followed next. He was going down backwards when he put his foot onto a root which gave way and he fell backwards into the river at a point which is between six and eight feet deep.

We alerted the ambulance and they came down to us quietly and did all their emergency procedures to establish whether there were any signs of life. There were none. It was then necessary to bring Abel to the ambulance to carry out a formal identification, as this is a requirement of the law. Once that was completed I had to go with the ambulance to convey Ben's body to the hospital at Plymouth and hand it over for examination by the pathologist the following day. Because of the circumstances in which Ben died, the law requires that there is a coroner's inquest. He will then make a decision as to the cause of death.

Later that night I met Ben's mother, Carmella, and I took her and Abel to the hospital. We came back home and I took down all the statement details the same night. In circumstances like this you've got to be very logical and practical to get the job done, but I also think it's essential to establish a good rapport with people and I like to think we did that.

Usually I try not to dwell on such sad events and they fade from my mind quite quickly, but I shall remember this for a long time to come because of the way Ben's parents coped with it, which was so different to what I usually see. In circumstances like this you find people often get aggressive and angry, and they weren't. They saw a natural process happening here. Ben had come into the world in water and he'd left this world by water, and I could see they would be able to come to terms with it. Some people never do.

CHAPTER THIRTEEN

Don't Just Stand There - Do Something!

Abel B'Hahn

When I took Carmella to the train that Friday afternoon it was as if there was a glass barrier between us. Three days earlier I had learned that she was unexpectedly pregnant again and I was not remotely ready to accept what I thought had not been my conscious choice. I felt terrible about this situation and was wrestling a demon inside, but I did feel particularly good with Benj that day.

Carmella was to be away for three days and I had planned carefully how I would look after him. I'd prepared paper and crayons and set out a game on my work-table at the unit. On the way back from the station we picked up a hitch-hiker and Benj was asking all kinds of questions. It felt wonderful to be able to answer and share with him why I was making the choices I was making. It felt like a real father/son exchange and I realised that at last the time I had longed for had come. He was old enough for me to enjoy relating to him through his inquisitive mind.

It was a gloriously sunny afternoon when we arrived at the workshop and he wanted to make a wooden sword, which he always liked to do. I planed the wood, he banged in the nails and went outside to ride his bike, waving his new sword above his head. That was my last interaction with my son - giving him what he wanted, feeling good about looking after him, and expressing my love for him.

He was outside for a long time and so I went out to check on him and saw him playing with two other children at the front of the workshop. I brought his bike inside and carried on working. A while later I went to check on him again and couldn't see him, so I walked around the back to the river thinking that he might be playing along the bank. I walked along the riverside and stopped to speak to someone briefly on business, telling him that I was looking for Benj. When I returned to my part of the estate, Frank, who repairs motorbikes in the opposite unit, started walking towards me and I called out "Have you seen Benj?" His response was "Oh, shit!" and he told me that a little girl had come round to tell them that a boy had fallen in the river.

It took only seconds for me to compute that it must have been Benj who had fallen in. I'd only been walking there a few minutes ago, an intuitive move I'm sure, but not intuitive enough. I walked down the river again for some distance searching for signs, but there was no sign of anyone. I was thinking 'Where has he gone? What should I do? He must be very cold and distressed, perhaps trying to climb out or maybe even hanging on in the water somewhere.' Then I thought that he could be down at the bottom, but if he was and I'd jumped in at the wrong place and not found him straight away it would have been too late and I'd have been of no use to anyone. I was thinking 'I've got to work out where he would be rather than recklessly jumping in and thrashing around'. But there was another voice inside me screaming '**DON'T JUST STAND THERE - DO SOMETHING!**'

Other people arrived then and started doing things, clambering down and hunting, and although I felt relieved that there was some action, I could only think 'I'm his father and I'm just pacing around trying to hold myself together and to think'. I was almost crying. I knew that somehow I would have to contact Carmella who was on a train to London. He would need her after an experience like this. I was trying to work out how to find both her and him, all mixed up together. Things were happening so fast. The police had arrived and the place was crawling with people. I could even hear a helicopter overhead. Customers, local people, the police were doing everything that I could have done, and so I went to try to contact Carmella.

I dialled Directory Enquiries for the number of Paddington Station, was given a number and hung on for five minutes, only to be told that it was the credit card booking line. I dialled another number they gave me, and by the time they answered the phone I couldn't speak. I knew that the man was thinking 'we've got another joker playing around' and I only just managed to get something out before he put the phone down. I explained that Carmella was on the train to Paddington and that her son had had a serious accident and he said he would page her at the station and get her to phone me. Then I realised that I was tied to the office and could not go and look for Benj.

I was assuming that he was alive. The idea of Benjaya dying was preposterous. I imagined that he was somewhere down river, hurt, cold and calling out for us. There was a long time thinking these sorts of thoughts and feeling suffused with helplessness and worry.

Carmella did phone at 5.20pm and I told her to turn around and come home on the next train because Benj had fallen in the river and was on his way to hospital. This wasn't true, of course, but for the first time in our relationship I simply could not tell her the truth. It was a bad line and I didn't know if she had even heard me properly. As I was talking to her the vicar walked in ...and out again. I don't know if he knew I was the father or not.

There were two policemen assigned to stay with me and they were great, talking a bit about their children and asking questions about Benj, but mainly I just paced around the workshop unable to escape the horrendous reality. I fetched my ropes for the police to haul a boat across the river and found my ladders when asked, but went back to my pacing like a tiger in a zoo. Whenever I said "It will be too late" the policemen said "Oh no, we've heard of children being under for half an hour or so". In the beginning I was thinking 'Okay, yes, he could be underwater, and we could catch him in time and resuscitate him... come on, COME ON,' but as time wore on I knew in my heart that he was dead. The son I had so recently welcomed fully into my life was drowned in the river.

I phoned my mother, but when she answered I couldn't make a sound. Then, instead of giving any warning I just blurted it out leaving her in a state of awful shock. I tried to phone the friends I wanted, Julian and Arabella, but they were away. Then Frank, the motor cycle man, came in and told me that Benj had been found. I hadn't been told officially yet, and when I responded he realised he'd spoken out of turn and was embarrassed. That was when the policeman came to me and said:

"Can I have a word with you Mr B'Hahn?"

Mike Major arrived and escorted me into the ambulance where the body of my son was laid out on a stretcher. His beautiful, big brown eyes were half closed and clouded and I collapsed onto his chest making a hell of a racket. Mike Major pulled me off and I didn't appreciate that. I wanted to have longer to express the emotions that had been building to fever pitch in me for the last three hours. It felt appropriate to cry and howl as much as I needed and I thought that perhaps the people around me simply couldn't cope with the rawness of my emotion. I'd seen the electrodes on his chest and knew they had tried to resuscitate him, so if they knew he was definitely dead, what was the hurry?

Benjaya was driven away to the hospital and the police drove me home to our empty house with Benj's small shoes in their place by the door. Here, with reflections of his aliveness all around me, the waiting began again - this time for Carmella. Two policemen and June, whom I hardly knew, from the next-door workshop were left with me and I felt the need to be considerate and pleasant. I made them tea and toast to fill the interminable space and then the vicar arrived and introduced himself and I made him tea as well. At one moment I closed my eyes and tried to raise my consciousness a bit but realised that wasn't going to work with them sitting there, so I said: "Look, I'm just going upstairs to meditate for a bit" and took fifteen minutes to myself.

It was impossible then to escape the painful memory of the glass barrier between Carmella and me when I left her at the station. I began worrying about what could be going on in her mind about me. Would she blame me? She wanted a family of four; I wanted her to consider an abortion. She left me in charge of Benjaya and now he was dead and would never have a brother. Then it occurred to me that she might not even know he was dead because I hadn't told her. Who would tell her, how and when? I needed urgently to find out how she was and that was the abiding feeling that filled those waiting hours.

CHAPTER FOURTEEN

ʜis ʟegacy was ʟove

Carmella

ebruary 28th, 6pm (Diary extract)

Is this a nightmare or a dream? I arrived at Paddington Station after a three hour journey to a loud-speaker announcement about me: "Will Mrs B'Hahn please go to the information office". My first thought was that Abel was making a very romantic gesture and trying to reach me with a message of apology about his behaviour before I reached my course destination but as I waited in the queue at the information desk I began to worry about the possibility of an emergency. It took about fifteen minutes for my hope of romance to be shattered.

The man at the desk told me gruffly to phone my husband at work - nothing more and so I waited in another line by a public phone, knowing that it would be difficult to hear with all the loud-speakers, hustle and bustle. The phone I'd been waiting for didn't work and the queue dispersed to other phones. Eventually, with my heart in my mouth, I heard the ringing tone. Abel answered and with a tight, controlled, emotionless voice which sent shivers up my spine he said:

"Sorry to drag you off the platform but there's been an accident, you must come home on the next train."

*Pips...**loud-speakers**...money falling through*

"It's Benjaya - he's fallen in the river. We don't know if he's all right. He's been taken to hospital."

Noise...noise...*I can't hear...* *"Where shall I go?"*

"If you can't find me, get South Brent police." Pip..pip..pip...

PANIC. *I had been feeling queasy already but now I felt terribly sick and my eyes simply couldn't read the signs. 'I have to get home NOW' was hammering inside my head, but HOW? I started to breathe more deeply and tried to focus on the information board. The only words that stood out were NEWTON ABBOT 5.45pm. 'That's near enough' I thought and in a daze found myself a seat on the train.*

I'm on the train now and it's so, so slow. What's happened to time? Why won't this train go faster? I can't stand it. My precious boy could be dying and I've got to sit on a snail of a train not knowing anything. Which hospital could he have gone to? Where shall I get off? Will anyone be there to meet me - friends maybe if Abel's at the hospital? I doubt it because they would expect me to be on a Totnes train.

I need to love. Just love and release into God's hands. I mustn't blame Abel. Forgive and surround my boy in love. Don't think about what might be, just experience the now.

I AM LOVE. I LOVE BENJAYA AND RELEASE HIM TO WHATEVER IS BEST FOR HIM. I LOVE ABEL. I LOVE OUR NEW GROWING BABY.

The horrific thought that Benjaya might have brain damage and be a 'vegetable' keeps pushing its way into my head and my stomach churns in revolt, bringing a bitter bile into my mouth. How could I live through that? I have to reprogramme my thoughts in order to stay sane: 'Benjaya, wherever you are I am sending you love for your healing process, be that to live or to die peacefully. May the will of God be done.'

The loud-speaker has just announced "No saver tickets on this train". Oh my God, my ticket is a saver ticket and I anticipate a scene - the train is full. The conductor won't believe me, my story sounds pretty far fetched. He will have to believe me because no-one on earth is going to eject me from my seat...

The conductor has been now and punched my ticket without even looking - all £52.60 worth. The first hurdle is over.

Saturday morning, 5am

*Woke at 4am into the nightmare of silence and no boy to sing me awake
then come for a morning snuggle. Abel is now howling with grief in
Benj's room. My beautiful boy died yesterday whilst I was on the train to
Paddington.*

*I need to backtrack to catch up on yesterday's events. It will be
excruciatingly painful to write but I have a compulsion to catch the
process on paper. Maybe it will be of use to me or others in times to
come.*

*The three-and-a-half hour train ride back was sheer hell despite
my efforts to reach for the highest space I could. I was so queasy that I
couldn't eat and felt weak as a kitten. It must have been obvious that I
was in a bad state but normality went on all around me. No-one
ventured into my pain-racked space - except with their eyes before
quickly averting them again. Two people even sat next to me with their
faces in their papers as I sobbed. What a sad, separatist world it is -
how many of us dare to care? I wanted to shout 'my boy could be brain
damaged, dying or dead' and raise a response but I feared cracking up.*

*Again a loud hailer assailed me: "This is your conductor speaking.
If there is a Mrs Beehan on board the train please make yourself known
as I pass through". I made myself known and he told me there was a
message for me to get off at Newton Abbot where I would be met. I was
relieved, expecting a friend to drive me straight to the hospital.*

*Eternity lived through, the train pulled in to my station, but there
was no friend waiting. The platform was flanked with police - one at
every other door and I knew, as did everyone in my carriage, that they
had come for me. It all seemed impossibly unreal. The policeman at my
door said, as I stepped out "You're Carmella aren't you?" and I nodded.
Other police converged towards me and took my bags, my arms and my
life force energy as they ushered me into a cold British Rail office.*

*Just like in the films someone told me I'd better sit down and then a
young, blond policewoman spoke kindly into my daze:*

*"There's no easy way to say this Mrs B'Hahn but we found your
son's body in the river this evening. We thought you'd want to know
as soon as possible. He's now at the hospital in Plymouth. Your
husband's at home. We'll take you there."*

A male officer was on his knees at my side, holding my hand and forcing back his tears. "I have children, I know what you must be going through" he choked.

At top speed we whizzed down roads unfamiliar to me. My feelings were remarkably similar to those in the second stage of labour - I felt **separated from my body, watching the drama from a higher perspective and yet completely shattered, with an unbearable, stunning pain.** *The same thought of 'I cannot live through this level of pain...but I am' passed through my head.*

Home at last, I faced the man I had left just hours ago with my happy boy in hand. My main concern was that he might be feeling self-recrimination but I could tell from a glance that if he did it was not serious. He looked strong yet totally vulnerable. We hugged and shed some tears. **What could words express at a time like this?** *All our other difficulties had already faded into insignificance, for both of us I think.*

Suddenly I was aware of all the spectators and of the phone ringing incessantly. Abel answered all incoming calls and dealt valiantly with the shock and pain of his family and friends (word had spread locally via our next door neighbours). I felt the need to give recognition to the police, the vicar and June who seemed stuck to the settee and so devastated that she needed me to comfort her. I told her to go home and cherish her children. We were both strong then, Abel and I, telling people:

"He came into water and has left in water. We know he's all right, it's us left behind who are not. He served us well for his five years of life."

We heard later that the vicar felt rather superfluous then and it was sensitive of him to refrain from pressing his own beliefs on us.

It seems a strange thing to say but I was already gaining great comfort from the fact that it was water, nature, that took our son's life. The symbol for us Aquarians is the water carrier: water is the element with which we have worked together as a trio for five years and **I cannot help but see a divine plan encompassing the emotional trauma of the loss, elevating my spirit as I grieve.**

At 10pm after waiting...waiting...waiting for the go ahead, we were driven by Mike Major to Derriford Hospital to see Benj. I was absolutely clear that this was my highest priority, no matter what the time or the inconvenience involved. Abel was apprehensive but also wanted urgently to see him. It was he who had seen him as he came out of the river and I shall always be thankful that I was spared the trauma of that experience.

On the half-hour journey in the police car I was steeling myself for
the horror of seeing my boy's lifeless form and requesting help to find
my courage, knowing that this was probably going to be the most
difficult task of my life.

With an intake of breath, squeezing each other's hands for support,
Abel and I stepped into the small, plain room in the basement where
Benjaya's body had been 'laid to rest'. There was the oh-so-familiar and
handsome form which had brought me so much pleasure, unfamiliarly
motionless, decked in a white satin gown and a purple cover with a
cross on it. He was like a marble replica of my son, **so life-like yet
without his essence.**

Abel sat by his head and cried, his face crumpled with the
torturous pain of it all, whilst I anointed his forehead with Sai Baba's
vibhuti.[1] As I did so I remembered with a flash that, out of the blue at
lunch-time that day Benjaya had put some of the same ash on his forehead and told the midwife "This is sacred ash from India. It will keep
me safe today." Whatever did he mean?

I have realised that seeing the body is an essential part of the
grieving process for me. **It was a peaceful sight** and I felt a sense of
stillness and love in the room. For this reason I felt it was imperative to
capture this image on film in case my mother and Sommer do not
manage to get home from India before the funeral - God forbid! (Why on
earth is my mother so far away at a time like this? Perhaps so that I can
find my own inner strength in a much deeper way).

I arranged to visit again at 3.30pm the next day with my camera
and with anyone else who might want to join me. Then we were sped
back home and the detailed questioning began for the statement. I
discovered that there will have to be an inquest to establish the cause of
death and we were warned "Tomorrow his death will be headlines in the
media". Just like his birth. Couldn't die without the whole country
knowing could you, my boy?

It was 11.30pm when the front door closed and for the first time we
were left alone in our empty house. So, so empty. What to do? How to
be? We didn't know how to function. I began by putting two pairs of

---

[1]Sai Baba is an avatar living in India. He has performed miracles since childhood, teaches
that there is only one religion - the religion of love - and has a worldwide following of
millions. Sacred ash, known as 'Vibhuti', is manifest from his hands and appears on
photos of him. It is used for healing or blessing.

small, worn-out trainers in the bin and started to clear up the house thinking 'I must have order'. We cried, we talked about Benj and cried some more. Abel had not put down Benjaya's coat since we arrived in, and was clutching it to his heart as if it still held his life-force - which it probably does.

I took Benj's crystal collection, his gnomes, the snake we bought this morning, Captain Hook from his treasured pirate Lego and other special things and arranged them all together in a little tableau in the lounge with a picture of him and a lighted candle. I guess this could be called a shrine, a focus on him and his life. A candle, Abel decided, would stay burning here until his cremation.

I remembered then that this last week he had started to give away some of his favourite things to his friends and that I had stopped him giving away one of the gnomes that I had hand carved myself. He also was adamant that he was not going on a planned group swimming trip on Sunday, which confused me as he loved to swim. I also remembered with a bit of a shock that, with Abel's help he had made a pirate flag a few days ago with a skull and crossbones on it and had been playing games about pirates killing each other in the water before they reached the treasure. Did he have conscious knowledge of his fate, I wonder?

Abel and I tidied his bedroom together. It was uncharacteristically in chaos as the bookshelf had collapsed that morning and tumbled books covered the floor. The pain of picking up his discarded dressing gown and holding it frozen, not knowing where to put the dressing gown of a dead person, was excruciating.

Alone now, I tucked up his soft animals for the night and climbed up onto his birthday bed. I lit the candle we had lit together the night before and gave thanks for his life with us. I told him that I was looking after all his precious things and suddenly remembered that about a week ago he had asked me "When I die will you be sad and will I meet your old cat?" I had answered then that I hoped he was not going to die before me but that if he did I would be very sad. As for the cat, I said that he would have to wait and find out. And so now I told him not to worry about us, that we were very sad to lose him but that it was okay with us that he had to move on. "And have you met my old cat?" I asked him," or Jesus, or anyone you know?" As I did not catch a response, I warned him that it is very difficult to hear answers in this cruder world and that I wouldn't be able to respond to him like I always have. Then I heard loud and clear "I love you Mum...and Daddy", and when I picked

*up his favourite bear, Albie, to take him to my bed I thought I heard him
say "leave him with the others".*

*Then in the early hours, exhausted to our bones, Abel and I fell
into a fitful three hour slumber.*

Saturday, February 29th

*This morning was one enormous pain-wave punctuated for a few
seconds by the bizarre sound of a little burst of Abel's laughter at
5.15am as he watched a comedy film in a vain attempt at escapism.
I was in the bath at the time, praying for support, anything to ease the
pain and to help me brave the task of the phone calls that we had to
make to break the news of this horror into the lives of people we love.*

*At 7am I dropped the first bombshell into my sister Sandra's home.
As the policewoman said, there is no easy way of doing it and so I just
told the truth "I have some very distressing news. Benj has fallen in the
river and drowned". She heard me immediately and I heard her pain
well up and trickle down her cheeks. What can one say in answer to
such shocking news? She said she'd phone back later and went to tell
her children.*

*Adam House was the next in line and how I wished that my mother
was with my father, instead of thousands of miles away being contacted
by INTERPOL. My father answered.*

*"Hello Dad, I know that you're going to a wedding and that this should
be a happy day but I have to tell you something that will make you sad
- Benjaya is no longer with us."*

"What? Say that again"

"Benjaya has fallen in the river. He's died Dad, gone home"

"Oh my God!"

*He told me he would do anything I wanted. I just had to name it, and I
told him that perhaps it would be best if he waited for M'haletta to come
home before coming down to visit. He agreed to break the news to
Charlotte, who was not contactable by phone, and to make sure that*

Marc was told. After that he had an appointment as best man at his oldest friend's wedding - God help him.

Sandra phoned back to say that all of my siblings were coming immediately. I know it is vitally important for their process to come and connect, to share their grief and experience first hand how we are coping.

I phoned my friend Kitty, who is here now. She came bearing remedies for us from her homeopath partner, Gordon, and an immense amount of compassion. She is a dream, blending in, cooking for everyone, crying, loving and throwing out bits of wisdom borne of her own experience of losing her brother and her father.

Neighbours, close friends and the vicar have all flowed in and out in varying states of devastation. Abel has been on phone duty all morning answering calls from friends, organisations offering help, the Christian Community, the police, the Sai Baba group and others I forget. He also made many calls to friends to break the news before the media reports reached them, crying on and off at their responses which have been as varied as instant howling to "You're kidding".

I spoke to three newspaper reporters this morning and was quite coherent and keen to give them my perspective. One other reporter was out of line and intrusive and was forcibly removed from the doorstep.

Lunch-time saw the arrival of my family (Marc, Charlotte, Sandra and two of her three children) into our tiny cocoon of a front room and together with Kitty and another friend, Arabella, we sat in a circle and shared from our hearts. It was so real, so painful and so right and I felt strong and vulnerable at the same time, sharing both the trauma and the gifts that our boy has given us. A few jokes were even cracked and the laughter fell well into our space of togetherness.

The next phase began with a knock on the door and the entry of Abel's family - his brother Rick, sister Lisa and his parents Thea and Norman. His other sister is too far away to come. We answered their detailed questions, cried some more and ate a little.

My queasiness at the sight of food keeps reminding me of the tiny babe growing within me - such a treasured being now that s/he is our only link to parenthood that remains. How uncanny that the due date should be Benjaya's birthday. I cannot help but wonder if he will return into this body but I doubt it as that would be an impossibly quick turn around.

*Everyone felt it necessary to go and see Benjaya's body on our
3.30pm trip to the hospital and so in convoy we went, with Rick driving
Abel's car and Abel sitting in the back next to Benj's empty car-seat and
books. The pain is triggered so easily and I cried most of the way.*

*We numbered eleven and in twos and threes we saw him - raw
emotions hanging out and hearts reaching out all over the place. I took
my pictures and noticed again the peace and obvious lack of lifesource
in the body that has held such vibrancy.*

*My family left then, having played their part well. Abel's returned
home with us and are staying nearby overnight. I came up to bed to rest,
feeling drained and utterly exhausted but how can I rest when I cannot
escape the pain? I fell time and time again into racking bouts of sobs,
comforted by Lisa. Here is a woman with whom I have little in common;
we live in different worlds, but now she is marvellous, totally open in
her compassion, questioning and caring. Today it seems she believes in
life after death having felt the peace in the Chapel of Rest and knowing
that he is in a different place. How wonderful that we can talk about
these things.*

*The Gilletts left us for a while to book into a hotel for the night and
the void loomed again. Both Abel and I were **inwardly screaming for
them to return soon as we cannot bear the silence**. We survived until
their return with dinner, which I couldn't eat. Lisa has taken on the role
of watching over me and making sure I eat at least a morsel.*

*Dr. Hill popped in to give me some advice. He said that the trauma
will not affect the baby physically and neither will eating tiny amounts.
He gave me some sleeping pills to help me survive the nights ahead,
telling me that for a short duration they would not cause harm to the
baby.*

*Alone again now, diary complete, we must brave bed again. I have
taken half a sleeping tablet and warned Abel not to say anything to
trigger more trauma. I must remain calm enough to sleep.*

Sunday, March 1st

*Miracle of miracles we both slept until 6.20am, temporarily healing our
exhaustion but not my queasiness. Abel's family returned at 8.30am by
which time Abel was desperate for their presence. He can't bear the
space, the raw loss which screams from the silence, mainly through*

Benjaya's bedroom door. His little light to tell him it is time to get up was shining this morning and the absence of his happy singing voice cut us like a knife.

As the morning wore on I began to feel my spirits lift. St Petroc's church in the village were including a 'Requiem for Ben' in the morning service for the sake of the villagers who feel this local 'tragedy' so strongly. Abel and I did not feel ready to face so many people so we sent Thea, Abel's mother, to represent us and to read a letter to the congregation. According to the press, 300 people turned up which touched us deeply.

Dear South Brent Community,

We feel the community care and spirit deeply and want to thank all of you for your loving thoughts at this time. We especially thank Michael and Amy and all those who were involved in the search for our son.

Benjaya was born in a water pool and it seems fitting that he left through water. We want to share with you the image of his birth [large copy of the birth picture] and ask you to recognise that within this death experience there is also, for him, a birth. He spoke often of death with no trace of fear and for him it was a natural part of life's process.

He loved to sing and his favourite song was 'Love is Something if you Give it Away' which we hope will be played to you now along with the song 'We are One' which he sang to the baby in my womb only hours before he died.

His legacy was love so let's do more of it!

Abel and Carmella B'Hahn

Abel's family left by lunch time and another surge of energy came in - reporters to take copies of Benjaya's photograph, friends Tim, Rod and Alice, and phone calls at the rate of about five per hour. This task of speaking to others about death and grief is extremely healing and I am boosted by knowing that once most people have spoken to us they feel their spirits rise. It is obvious that to connect as closely as possible, preferably **to be here and experience the centre of the cyclone rather than imagining the horror from the fringe, is a healing balm.**

Abel courageously braved the world this afternoon, keeping his commitment to play table tennis with Julian and leaving me in charge.

*Amazingly I have been feeling more and more peaceful and powerful as
the day has worn on. My time with my friends was wonderful and in our
group meditation I saw a vision of Benj as a vibrant sun sending me
deep joy. It occurred to me towards the end of the day that I may be
feeling so high because it is the third day after his death, the day I
associate with the rising of the soul. Perhaps Benj has been released
from his initial protected healing space into the light. What a joy it is to
be with people who want to look for the divine design in this death as
well as the human tragedy. This is my healing balm.*

*Rod, Alice and Tim went off to the hospital to see Benj whilst Abel
(who had tentatively enjoyed his trip out) and I had a visit from a
delightfully respectable and highly obliging undertaker who gave me the
giggles. He was as sombre as I was not. He was dressed from head to
toe in black and insisted on sitting (or rather perching) on a hard
upright chair. We agreed to accept his company's service as far as
looking after Benjaya's body was concerned and were deeply relieved
that their policy is to waive all charges in the case of tragic deaths of
young children. We had not considered the financial implications of
death. We also became very clear that we do not want a half-hour slot
(or even two) at the local crematorium for his funeral. We will find or
create a beautiful space which encourages us to express ourselves fully
and freely - a send off of which our spirit-boy will be proud.*

*After more ins and outs of friends, Kitty, our 'death midwife',
arrived to stay overnight to help fill that dreaded void. After an
inspiring day I'm getting a sore throat and cold and am cross, **the first
time I've felt anger since before the death and I wonder if somehow I
need an outlet for this emotion.***

Monday, March 2nd

*I had no sleep with my blocked-up nose but life goes on. My Dad rang
this morning from the probation office where he works. He admitted that
he had been sobbing all morning and has christened himself the 'Indian
Wailer'. All the staff know because they have read it in the papers -
which we have not seen. It has been on national television news too.*

*This morning the sense of expansion has increased and I have felt
encloaked in love and in touch with a higher realm. There have been no
tears. Love, flowers in abundance, cards and well wishers have*

continued to pour into our house. It is like a shrine here, a holy place where reverence seems appropriate. Reverence for what? **A new-born baby's presence has this effect.**

A close friend, Lizzie, popped in and I told her how like labour and birth this time is - the awful pain in order to give birth to something pure and healthy and far greater than the pain. She said "It's quite clear to me that you've chosen to suffer this apalling pain because of your future work. Now you can help people going through both ways". Yes, you're right, Lizzie. I've always wanted to work with death. She has recently given birth to a son called Benjamin, which is somewhat poignant now. Peggy, my next-door neighbour had been given the task of finding a venue for Benjaya's Celebration/Funeral and wonder-of-wonders the village hall is free all day next Saturday, the very day we want it - a perfect venue in the centre of our community. Soon we will start planning the event but we are not quite ready yet.

After a nibble of lunch I took the plunge and walked out of our front door aiming for the workshop. I have never felt like a turtle before, wanting to retract my head into my coat at the first sign of danger. Only five yards outside the door, I walked by a group of children arguing about which house Ben lived in and I retreated further into my collar. Is this the hot topic of conversation around the village? Will I be recognisable to everyone? I had to cross the bridge and forced myself to look at the pool in the river where Benj's body was found. It wasn't too bad - quite a lovely river in fact.

With growing confidence, having reached the workshop, I went out at the back to face the place where he fell. My main feeling was of gratitude that I had not had to suffer the hideous human drama that occurred here as that would have deeply affected my attitude to working here. I dealt calmly with all the business affairs, put messages on the answerphones saying that due to a personal tragedy we would respond in a few weeks time.

On the way back home my feelings of confidence were somewhat shattered by noticing the hoardings outside the petrol station: 'South Brent Mourns River Drowning Boy'. I knew that it was my son they were talking about but it wouldn't compute fully. The conspicuous feeling sent me straight back into the memory of going out after he was born, when I thought the whole world must recognise me from the media reports. **Death, birth, death, birth - they refuse to be opposites for me.**

There has still been no word from my mother and this is playing on my mind a lot. Surely INTERPOL have managed to find her by now; the message went out on Saturday morning. What is the delay? I expected her to have phoned by now. I must find out if we have any way of contacting her by phone. I am anxious to know how it is for her to receive such dramatic news so far away. And how is Sommer, her travelling companion? Are they supporting each other? I know I have to let go and trust, like I tried to on the train.

It's now 9.40pm and I am shattered, constantly sneezing and in desperate need of sleep. I must have an early start tomorrow.

Tuesday, March 3rd

Slept all night without incident. Anna Ash from the Steiner school phoned early to say that the school have enthusiastically accepted my request to beautify the village hall next week. That's the first major task delegated. This event will have to be a group effort; we'll ask everyone to bring food, cushions for the children and a candle each.

This morning I had to drive to Plymouth to meet my friend, Deb, who had undertaken to help me find a suitable outfit for Saturday. It was eerie being out in the world as I discovered that my senses were super-aware of potential danger to myself and the baby I carry. The responsibility for taking extreme care weighed heavily upon me and I felt that just one false move causing us harm and Abel could be destroyed. 'How can the world simply tick on as if everything's fine when my boy is dead? And **how many of us are there looking normal but suffering immense trauma at this very second?'** *are the thoughts I cannot escape.*

Still in one piece, I arrived, parked at a very wobbly angle and took my film of Benj in the coffin to the 1hr processing lab., warning them that the contents might be disturbing. I then put money in the bank, feeling very proud of my abilities as if I were recovering from a serious mental illness - which I guess I am. So far I have been completely incapable of making a cup of tea or doing anything remotely domestic. The shock has stopped me in my tracks in some areas and left me more lucid in others.

Deb, bless her heart, had already scoured the shops and earmarked a dress that she thought was ideal. I bought it immediately with relief, collected the photos and almost ran to the car. Were people really staring at me or was I paranoid? I guess they could have been because we have been front-page news, including pictures, in most of the local papers, let alone the television reports.

Increased lucidity occurs when I am dealing with the media. It is compulsive for me, this task of sharing our story, a golden opportunity to say -

Yes it hurts like hell but there is another way of looking at death...

On return home, a magazine reporter was waiting for me and during the interview I felt a higher energy take over, firing me and filling me with awe and gratitude for this death experience. What the reporter will choose to say to the conservative readers I don't know but I feel as if I have been programmed to talk about the transitions of birth and death in a new way. Perhaps that is even the main reason I came into life.

The mail that arrived today was choking in its depth and beauty. Abel and I have soaked most of the cards with tears. One old couple who read about us in the papers wrote: 'We've had a nice tree planted in Ben's memory; flowers soon die but a tree will go on forever'.

Abel is bearing up well just being himself in the moment crying, howling, laughing and talking a lot about his experience of grief. He has cried more this week than in the rest of his life put together.

Two friends, Polly and Jenny, parents of Benjaya's friends, came to visit us this afternoon bearing gifts from the children. Apparently Tom, aged five, was very cross when he heard about Benjaya's 'accident' and said "Well why wasn't he wearing non-slip shoes?"

I dealt with more reporters, delegated to lovely friend Leonard the job of finding accommodation for Saturday's guests and the making of posters to invite all of the villagers, then I sat down to dinner and sobbed into my green pea soup. When the giving out stops I give way. I couldn't even manage to butter my toast. Thank God Lizzie has set up a meals-on-wheels rota and every day a different friend arrives bearing our daily nourishment.

Wednesday, March 4th

My outfit for Saturday was ready this morning but Benjaya's was not. We did not want him to remain decked in a robe with a cross on it and so the task of finding his last earthly outfit fell to me. With Lisa's support and a stabbing pain in my heart I chose his favourite, bright yellow 'snowman' jumper, 'Greetings from India' T-shirt (given to him by my mother), red trousers and socks, his best new knickers and his batboy play cape because he would have chosen that. Lisa and Abel will take them to his new room at Ivybridge Chapel of Rest for the undertakers to dress him this afternoon.

I am intrigued and mystified as to why the wedding theme keeps popping up. Alone they mean nothing, but six wedding connections?

1) Dad was best man at a wedding on Saturday
2) Abel's family were kept awake by a wedding on Saturday night
3) Friends' wedding photos were amongst the photos of Benj in his coffin
4) Luke, Sandra's baby who died, was conceived at the time of our wedding
5) I need to wear my white, silk wedding trousers to match my new dress for the 'funeral'
6) Sandra and I keep calling the 'funeral' event 'the wedding' by mistake

My throat is still horribly sore and I have a heavy cold but somehow it feels part of the process. I feel so accepting of this death experience that it is a relief to know that I sound distressed and will therefore not be labelled as abnormal...yet.

My sister, Sandra, arrived late morning. She came down to Exeter yesterday to attend the funeral of her husband's aunt and so is bombarded with grief from all angles. We went to the workshop together to deal with messages and make necessary phone calls. There was one message of condolence on the answerphone from a woman in Birmingham whom we had never met but who had followed our story in the papers since Benjaya's birth, and another from Abel's wood supplier who was swearing and railing against God. Death certainly does take people in interesting ways.

Johnny, our next-door neighbour, then took us to the village hall to take in the layout of the place, which made a few of the senior citizens' heads turn from their bingo cards. I noticed on the way home that the posters inviting the villagers to Benj's Celebration/Funeral are up in two shop windows.

With Sandra gone until Friday, and Lisa and Abel out seeing Benj again, the house was empty and I took the opportunity to oh... so...

*carefully... vacuum the lounge floor. I was so **aware of disturbing the high vibrations by the noise** that I lit a josstick afterwards and put out really strong thoughts to steady the energy again and the cocoon seems unharmed. I am the self-appointed guardian of the energy and if anyone turns on the television, lights a cigarette or brings in negative energy, woe betide them! I put up all the latest cards and pictures and Interflora flowers in borrowed vases, answered the phone a few times and did lots of arranging for Saturday. I was thoroughly enjoying being at peace, feeling close to Benjaya and the baby but physically going downhill with an awful pain down the side of my face.*

By evening the phone calls and the constant task of working through other people's grief with them began to wear thin. I've been awake since 4am and hearing the depth and desperation of yet another person's process was almost too much to handle. It is time for bed not counselling and the phone will just have to remain unanswered now.

Thursday, March 5th

Today I am well slept for a change. Abel went off to have an acupuncture session this morning whilst I gave an extensive interview to a freelance reporter. Again it was a healing experience, leaving me feeling even stronger within myself. I do hope that all these articles are written sensitively and are worth the energy I have so freely given.

Next I went to Ashburton for a crystal healing session with friend Caroline Wyndham. As I lay there with the crystals pouring heat and energy into my body, I seemed to merge into the body of Benjaya and felt as if I was him playing with going in and out of his body in the coffin. I knew that he would not leave me but would continue to work closely with me and Abel on our path.

Abel has been again to Ivybridge to see Benjaya with his friend Leonard. They both said he looks so beautiful and Abel said that he looked as if he would just start breathing again and he leaned down to listen in case he had. I have decided to go again tomorrow as there will be few chances left to connect with his physical form.

Friday, March 6th

Benjaya's school held a memorial service this morning and Abel and I

*were the well and truly honoured guests. At 8.45am the whole school -
pupils, teachers and some parents were gathered outside the school
building, awaiting our presence. We stood at the back whilst Trevor, one
of the teachers, stood on the steps before us by a little 'altar' table
decked in flowers and spoke with tenderness of death. He said that **each
of us is here at home on the Earth right now but that we are also on a
journey and will return to another home,** as Benjaya has. He likened
Benjaya's short life to that of a snowdrop which pushes its way up first
to herald the spring, a flower short lived but received with much
gratitude by us.*

*We were then invited up to the front to light a long burning candle
which, wind permitting, has been burning all day. I imagine that the
wave of warmth and almost overwhelming humility I felt on standing
before this crowd was to do with the love that was pouring from them in
that moment. I stood there with my arm through Abel's and my long deep
purple coat flowing in the wind and after drinking in the silence felt
moved to speak.*

*"It has been a very sad and difficult time these last few days and I
want to thank you all for your love, your cards and your candles. But
it has not all been darkness. On Sunday I felt the awful pain lift for a
while and was filled with a sense of joy and expansion. Benjaya is
light and we can all connect with his light. I want to say to you
please don't ever take each other for granted because we've no idea
how long we will be together on the Earth."*

*The children, as if in answer, then began singing Dona Nobis Pacem, a
Latin chant, in three-part harmony. It is one of my favourites and I
joined in loudly. The sky was darkening, the birds were singing and
cockerels were crowing. As I stood there on the steps with all those
children's open faces looking up at me as we sang together, I was struck
again by the sensation of **playing my role in an astoundingly life-like
drama.***

*Benjaya's last teacher, Mariea, then led me and Abel and her
kindergarten class, with their little trowels, to the orchard for a plum
tree planting ceremony. Will, who had planned to go to Sherwood forest
with Benj, said "I'll pick a plum when they're grown and make sure it
gets to heaven" and a little girl asked me: "Are you really upset that
Benjaya has gone to heaven?" "Yes," I said, "but happy for him too".*

I am filled with a sense of awe, which is also shared by Abel, that our son's death has touched so many people and continues to do so daily.

*When we returned home it was only 10.15am and the day was just beginning. Sandra arrived and together we went off to see Benj. It is the first time I have seen him in his own clothes and he does look asleep. I was deeply moved, feeling the stabbing pain of loss but also able to change in the moment and be light and jokey to match Sandra's mood. I stood on chairs and nearly knocked the coffin over as I took photos and we both knew that some people might consider us to be highly irreverent in our childish giggles. I sense that **perhaps laughter is a vital release valve for energy that either pours through us somehow or is pushed down, festers and causes disease.***

I still get exhausted extremely fast and after our jolly escapade out, which included a walk by the river and animated discussions about the big day tomorrow and the future of the little one within me, I almost collapsed on return home. All I wanted was for Kitty, who was back again cooking for us, to stroke and caress my head whilst I rested. She was marvellous and I entered a state of deep peace where I wanted to remain forever.

Abel went out to his Steiner Hall design group and I was left to potter around and prepare for tomorrow, gathering photographs of Benjaya and a collection of his special things for a table display so that people who had not met him would be able to connect more easily to his essence.

The phone rang, causing me to jump out of my focused task. I knew it was my mother and leapt to answer it. After quickly ascertaining that I was indeed as strong in spirit as she had imagined, she began an excited story about her travels, beginning by saying:

"It's all right, I have been with him and he has been with me..."

I listened with a sense of relief and wonder to a brief synopsis of her magical mystery tour. No doubt I will hear the detailed version soon.

CHAPTER FIFTEEN

A Traveller's Tale

M'haletta

During the closing months of 1991 I had become increasingly aware that someone within our close family circle was preparing for the journey we call physical death, yet consciously I did not know who that person would be or in what circumstances it would occur. Whilst I didn't dwell on it, sometimes when talking with friends I would hear myself saying that we were expecting to be working more closely with holistic death at some time in the future, to balance our holistic birth courses, adding that whilst I had had some varied and unusual experiences of death, I felt it would come closer to teach us more of its whole and holy nature.

Life pulsates within this family of four children, two sons-in-law, four grandchildren, my husband and myself. Who would our 'teacher' be? Afterwards I could see **many signs and symbols had been there in the months preceding Benjaya's death** if only I could have 'read' them.[1] As it was, I thought no more of the possibility of Benjaya's death than that of any other member of the family. **Nothing that I or anyone else might**

---

[1]In Initiatic Science to 'read' means to be able to decipher the subtle and hidden side of objects and creatures and to interpret the symbols and signs placed everywhere by Cosmic Intelligence which consistently offer information in a multiplicity of ways.

have thought or done would have changed the eventual outcome. Of that I am certain. Our teacher was to be Benjaya, our youngest family member.

The last workshop that I ran, shortly before leaving for India, was at a local college. It was on the subject of psychotherapy and the group had chosen the theme of 'balancing the polarities'. We played this out visually, using the poles of birth and death by creating two separate positive images from a variety of objects and creative materials, each filling a square table. To depict 'birth' the students chose to arrange Benjaya's birth photograph on a nest of feathers, surrounded by crystals and other objects of significance to them. 'Death' was represented by a poster of the Taj Mahal, that white majestic monument to love and death. In front of the Taj is a pool, which balanced the pool in the birth scenario, but on the death side only, they chose to add a wide blue ribbon to represent a flowing river, surrounding it with greenery until the death image seemed to hold a vibrant life of its own. When they were content with their collages I asked them to take the tables and place them together so that there was no separation, no chasm, no divide between the images of birth and death. Then I spoke of the closing of the chasm in the mind in our relationship between the two. Time caught us unawares and I told the group that our next move would have been to amalgamate the two scenes to discover the picture that then formed. As it was we did this exercise in our minds. The image for me was of Benjaya, Abel and Carmella lying in the Taj Mahal in that extraordinary light it holds, and seeing it as a great birthing chamber. I felt that I could do no more to bring the concepts of birth and death into my reality and theirs as the most beauteous, harmonious and love-filled space than had been done that day. And then I left for India.

I have written of the details above with purpose to illustrate how easy it is for insignificant details of seemingly unconnected events to be lost in the welter of life's activities and yet in retrospect so much can be reviewed as having been a preparation of what is to come, can even provide a reflection of it perhaps. The family sometimes joke with me, ' Everything is significant to you, mother' and so it is, but over time I have felt a natural selective process occur whereby the most significant objects or images draw attention. It is rather like speaking to one person at a time in a crowd, impossible to hear if everyone is talking at once but usually we will be drawn to the person who has something to teach us. Listening to my inner guidance and 'reading the Universe' have begun to merge and I remain assured that there is both an inner and outer force, emanating from the same source, which have the ability to guide me safely within the central flow of life if I choose to respond. My philosophy now matches my experience that **all life is inter-connected, inter-related in intricate and amazing ways.**

On 12th February, the day that Carmella and Abel left for Lanzarote, I flew to India with Sommer, my eldest grandchild, then twelve years old. It was her first Indian journey although we are close travelling companions and there is an easy, open rapport between us. We were heading for Hyderabad in the State of Andhra Pradesh where in 1990, on a journey with my eldest daughter Sandra (Sommer's mother), we had founded MetaCentre Public School to provide education for deprived children. We were delivering eighty books, which Sommer had been collecting to inaugurate a school library, bags of clothing and other equipment. India is a training ground for me where I have undergone some of the most stringent tests of my life. Death had been a central feature on previous journeys and I could not help but wonder whether it would continue to be so on this one.

In 1977 I had been involved in research in Indian prisons, meeting and talking with men awaiting execution and had interviewed all thirty-four of the women murderesses in the Punjab, seeking to understand how culture and social circumstances affect the reasons why people kill. In India the elements so often become the instrument of death; a woman throwing her near starving children into the waters of a well rather than face a life of prostitution; abusive husbands or recalcitrant daughters-in-law set alight with kerosene; battering with rocks by those involved in land disputes; and then also there is the suddenness of natural disasters.

Our school project is run by George and Jenny Nayak, who have five children. George is a villager from Orissa State and Jenny is from Calcutta. On the last visit with Sandra we had been travelling the 1,000 kilometres to visit George's village family when we found ourselves in the path of a cyclone. I was aware that we must not take the bus as planned and insisted on hiring a taxi to travel more quickly in an attempt to beat the rising floods. Behind us 'our' bus was swept away as a bridge collapsed, drowning all seventy passengers. All telephone lines were down and we were unable to notify Jenny in Hyderabad of our safety. After many more adventures we arrived to discover we had been presumed drowned, George and Jenny's relatives had appeared for our 'wake' and the household was in a state of mourning for us! There had been amazement and celebration that day that we had come through the waters and were alive. Out of that aliveness and that joy MetaCentre Public School had been born. Water and death. Even before the journey began, the connection between the two had been revived as Sandra and I considered the hazards that Sommer and I might be brought to face.

At school Sommer had been given an exercise in drawing an Arabic calligraphy which translated into the words:

LORD GRANT ME A GOODLY ENTRANCE AND A GOODLY EXIT AND SUSTAIN ME WITH YOUR POWER

We had placed a copy of these words in the sanctuary, stuck the same picture and words on the front page of my new journal and trusted that we would be well guided.

Our arrival brought an immediate reconnection to death. George Nayak's mother, whom Sandra and I had met on our last village journey, had just died. George had tried to reach his village in time for the final ceremony but had been too late and he was in a state of deep mourning. The grief was almost tangible, hanging like a heavy veil between us. The joy of reunion after two years was overlaid by this heaviness; heavy, dull eyes, heavy limbs and speech without lift to the words. It felt like a weight bearing down on us making it hard to breathe freely, to think clearly. Realising that we would be unable to generate the inspirational thinking and planning and organise the school parents' celebration in this energy, Sommer and I changed our itinerary and decided to travel on what had intended to be the second leg of our journey, returning in about ten days time.

George's spirits rose a fraction as I showed him a photograph of his mother which accompanied an article in a magazine which I had written, published in the previous month. He knew instinctively when he saw it that the timing of her death had been correct. She had been seen by the wider world, spoken of with respect and given recognition for her life. There was an interesting connection between us as his mother was known to everyone as 'Ma', being the village elder amongst the women. I am called Ma or Maha for short by close friends. George, in the loss of his mother, said that for him I would now become 'Ma' - his mother. Sommer had not heard this comment but that night she was looking at me strangely, describing a face that she saw superimposed over my own of an old woman whose description fitted 'Ma'. She had had an unusual, distinctive face in which Benjaya had also shown an interest when looking at my photographs, stating simply "I know her" in his usual definitive way. In those first hours subtle connections were riding my mind... Ma, death, Sommer, Benjaya and myself, but I was content to scribble down these threads of thought so as not to lose them and focus on what then seemed the more important matters of how to re-route the ant colony that was marching over our beds and up the walls.

Our first stop was to meet with some of Jenny Nayak's relatives, in particular her nephew Lionel. Round the time of Benjaya's last birthday I had received a letter from Lionel's mother telling of his serious illness with renal failure. It was thought that without a kidney transplant he would die. A correspondence began between us in which we explored our relationship to death and how it can be possible for a mother to give up her son willingly, if need be. I had sent a picture of a lake, deep, calm and still and told Lionel that I would hold him there in my mind, visualising him bathing in that healing stillness. In the sanctuary we had placed Lionel's photograph together with the birth picture because of its harmonious and healing qualities and its representation of the renewal of life. Around these images a rainbow grew as each person visiting added some vibrant colour, whilst adding prayer or blessing as they connected to that scene. In those simple acts of reverence for life we had all thought it was someone else's son for whom we cared. We did not know it then but Lionel was to have his kidney transplant and to live - it was the other son who lay there who would not. On our meeting with Lionel he had a gift for us. It was a wooden model of the Taj Mahal which we carried with us for the rest of the journey.

On our way to Madras, Sommer began to explore notions of death and dying, to personalise death, to conceive of her own death. One time she asked outright:

"Who would you rather have die, Benjaya or Carmella?"

I answered:"Carmella because that is what I think she would prefer."

She then instigated discussion on the implications of the death of every member of the family, how she thought each one would affect her and also how others might be affected by her death. Our conversations were deep and real but were certainly not morbid. Sommer holds a refreshingly enlightened perception of many things and came to the resolution of death as another adventure, another of 'our kind of journeys'.

Then Sommer began to have an irresistible urge to be in water. I have never troubled to find swimming facilities in India as it is by no means easy. However, on this occasion, friends lent us a car with a driver and we set off down the magnificent coastline of the Bay of Bengal and, staying overnight in a beach bungalow, we were able to move between the swimming pool and the pounding waves, swimming until we crinkled! Then an incident occurred which brought a cold shudder.

We were out in the breakers, breathless with the exhilaration of our own laughter. The beach was deserted, fringed by a tangle of trees. At last we had escaped the constant eyes touching our whiteness and felt free to play and scream for the sheer fun of it. Then hurtling towards the sea came a dog, reddish brown, the colour of the wet sand. There was a sudden crack of a rifle shot and he dropped dead yards from the water. Our laughter stopped. Sommer looked incredulous, disbelieving that **life could be taken so swiftly, one moment a powerful driving force and the next...?**

Fear rose in me then, knowing that a rifleman must be out there, screened by the bushes. In that moment I was acutely conscious of my presentiment of death, which I had begun to wonder whether Sommer shared, and was momentarily frozen as I wondered if this was to be the moment. India is unpredictable and the death of a dog could easily be followed by the death of a tourist, both moving targets. We walked slowly out of the water. I was heading for the hotel whilst Sommer, oblivious to any potential danger, headed for the dog, words spilling out of her at the inhumanity of it all. So I turned and followed her and we said a blessing for the life of this loveless, lifeless creature. Death by the water's edge made its mark on us. We talked with amazement of its swiftness and the sensation we might have felt had we been at the end of a rifle bullet, falling... into the water. And then it was time to move on.

I was working on my inner clock which was telling me when we had to be in this place or in that and when this inner clock is working well things fall into place - cars, people, beds when hotels are full, everything appears. Sommer was amenable to move wherever the finger pointed. It is such a joy to travel with a companion who knows how to move with the flow.

Our next stop was Pondicherry, to the Ashram and Educational Centre of Sri Aurobindo and the Mother. The Ashram is a sacred space to the memory of these two lives spent in exploration into supramental consciousness and the higher potential for human evolution. We arrived during a week of birthday celebrations and the annual celebration of Supramental Day, a day when there is a focused concentration of the rising of the mind to higher mental planes. The Mother had dreamed of a city of the future to be named Auroville, which had been designed by her from visions. The central focus, which she described as 'the soul of the city', was already under construction. It is a great spherical structure called the Matrimandir, which at its central highest point holds a specially constructed chamber housing an immense crystal globe seventy centimetres in diameter, placed where the light of the sun can reflect the most powerful radiations.

Some months previously I had become aware that on this journey to India I had to travel to Auroville with the purpose of reaching the crystal, so this had been our destination and the reason for this long journey south. On arrival we discovered the crystal chamber to be closed as construction work was in progress. I could not let this go so we sought out a guardian who agreed to take us to the chamber. Then the devastating realisation came to me that to reach it I would have to walk up an immensely high, spiralling concrete parapet without any balustrade. All my life I have experienced vertigo. At the very thought of it my body began to react and even with the help offered it was impossible to ascend. Sommer was dumb-struck! She knew how much this meant to me and all I could do was to ask her to go in my place.

It was so easy for her. I watched as she walked steadily upwards. She was wearing my clothes that day for the fun of it, a flowery dress, and I experienced a weird feeling as if I was watching an image of myself ascending, yet at the same time being conscious of sitting amongst the piles of dusty rubble and worn sandals of the workmen with tears of disappointment coursing down my face. My mind was telling me I had come all this way to see this crystal and that by my own weakness I had failed. It took only a few seconds to recognise that my tears were tears of desire. What I desired was the *physical sight* of the crystal. I simply had to **let go of that desire for the pain of the moment to evaporate.** With this realisation the sense of loss immediately disappeared. I felt light headed, not with the dizziness of vertigo - this was a different lightness as I sensed my consciousness rising. Then I experienced the essential core of my 'self' moving upwards, as in a lift without sides, whilst at the same time remaining aware of being anchored in my physical body. My consciousness moved through the circular space of the Matrimandir, into the chamber and then entered the crystal itself so that I was not *seeing* it from the outside but was *experiencing* the crystal from within its centre. Whilst I was not aware of Sommer as a person, my mind knew that her presence was essential to my experience.

At the same time as this shift in consciousness was occurring, I had felt my mind filling with what I later described in my journal as 'radiant thought' which had the effect of changing my relationship to the physical world around me. **The need to 'see and understand' was being superseded by a more subtle ability, 'to be within'.** In the evening there was time to record and reflect and to listen to more of Sommer's description of the chamber from her viewpoint. I wrote a little, about experiencing the core of that radiant crystalline energy but the essential message that flowed from my pen was:

Focus must now be released from the physical body. The Light Body now takes precedence.

When guidance comes in such a way I make every attempt to follow it but in this instance was not at all sure how to do so. At the time I did not relate it consciously to the transitional process of death, for which it would have been most appropriate advice. There have been other occasions when, a few days before a death, I have experienced this amazing upliftment in some way which I have previously described as 'a journey to the stars'. The Mother of Auroville might well have described it in terms of moving into supramental consciousness. It was then Monday, 24th February - four days before Benjaya's death.

We set off on the journey back to Madras by bus. My yardstick for differentiating between imagination and mystical/supramental experience is in the test of the effects. Imagination does not hold for me an after effect, it simply colours the moment. An expansion of consciousness often brings about change and I was experiencing identifiable changes. One of the effects was felt immediately in my body. I had the sensation of having lost weight, even at times experiencing a feeling of weightlessness, not feeling the ground solidly beneath my feet.

When we arrived in Madras again we gravitated to a swimming pool and Sommer began to play a game that she was to continue throughout that week. She floated face downwards, immobile, on the surface of the pool seeing how long she could stay in this position. She asked:

"Do you think people will think I'm dead?"

"They might" I answered, "but I won't".

"Don't let them save me, will you?"

"All right" I agreed.

Our plane left Madras at 5am on 27th February. As we circled Hyderabad a rising mist prevented us from landing and we were flown back to Madras. The mist cleared and we repeated the journey. It was on this second flight, still before breakfast, that Sommer and I acknowledged to each other that we felt strange, as if events around us were unreal, that there was another reality in which we were taking part which we could neither express nor explain. We tried briefly to identify our feelings, finding we shared the sensation of disconnection to everything around us which seemed to be affecting our clarity of speech but that seemed fine to us as long as we flowed along together, laughing at the analogy of our position in circling up in the air unable to get down to Earth.

On our arrival back at MetaCentre School, all preparations were well in hand for a weekend of celebrations at which we were to be the special guests. My task of honour would be to light the lamp, a lamp not yet purchased because it had to be exactly right for the occasion. It had to be a Golden Bird. On Friday, 28th February, the day on which unbeknown to us Benjaya was taking his leave, we went out shopping for the Golden Bird lamp but it could not be found and after our hot shopping trip we stopped off at a swimming pool when, as usual, Sommer floated face downwards in the water. I experienced no particular sensations or apprehensions that day. The energy around us was one of preparation for celebration.

The following day we found the lamp and on Sunday, 1st March, it was lit to mark the anniversary of the first full year of our school. Children, parents and guests witnessed the lighting in a colourful street marquee and as the flame curled upwards I felt a sense of awesome power as if something which I described in my journal as 'The Spirit of Love' rose up from amongst us. The children played their dramas, danced and sang and speeches of unity and friendship were made. This was a love-filled space created by and for the children. Our finale that day was the song 'We Shall Overcome', led by the children as we joined in, some tearful, others with radiant smiles. On such occasions it is my habit to wear a sari. That day it was pure white, the colour of death in India, hemmed in scarlet, the colour worn by a bride. Our necks were heavy with garlands of fresh flowers as we played out our parts in one of the scenes I love best when cultures come together in a creative interplay of lives and languages. It was a historical and magical afternoon which I would not have wished to miss. At home, on that unforgettable Sunday, Sandra, Carmella and friends were also experiencing an upliftment of their spirits.

The following day was again a day of celebration in a different way as it was the Hindu festival of Shivrati, when drummers and snake charmers parade in their street pageants, and we quietly began to plan out a full week of business meetings relating to the future of the school. The heavy atmosphere of mourning which had greeted us appeared to have been transmuted by the spirit of celebration.

Tuesday, 3rd March, found Sommer and me sitting after lunch at a local hotel overlooking a lake. George and Jenny arrived together. One glance was enough to know that they were the messengers of some awesome news. George did not want to speak it out.

"Derek has just called, he is waiting for you to telephone him at home."

My heart knew then that it was death, all that I needed was the name and George, in his gentle, loving and compassionate way, was the one that I knew must say it.

"Tell me who it is George."

"It is the little one, Benjaya... drowned."

There was an infinitesimal moment when it seemed that the whole world stopped. A pause button had been pressed. My hand went out to Sommer and the first words that came were...

"My Love!"

It contained everything as my mind exploded with thoughts of Benjaya, Carmella and Abel, Sommer, Derek waiting to tell me... and then the scene in my head changed as if a switch clicked on flooding me with light and I was back in Auroville. It was an instantaneous awareness that that experience had been in preparation for this moment and for what was to come after. The teaching had already begun. I had been shown how desire for the physical, the visible connection to matter in the material world could be transcended to make way for the more subtle experience of being within'. Desire to hold onto the physical body of a boy was transcended in an instant in the absolute knowing, born of my recent experience, that **all I had to do was to let go and rise up to merge within his greater light body.** *Focus must now be released from the physical body. The Light Body now takes precedence.* These words of guidance had immense significance for me and in those first moments some fragments of understanding began to surface which didn't need to be articulated. There were no tears in me then to be released, nor grief, nor sense of separation, only a feeling of infinite compassion for Carmella and Abel and of being filled again with that vital essential crystalline energy. The overwhelming awareness was that we had been journeying together, Benjaya, Sommer and I and he had found his safe and chosen gate of exit.

The telephone call was made to Derek. He sounded strong then as he told me of the Celebration of Benjaya's life planned to take place in four days time and I knew that we must be present. He was bemused with himself as to why he had not thought to telephone me sooner but I felt convinced that all had happened to a time scale that fitted into a greater scheme of events than we could comprehend. Certainly if I had kept to my first itinerary we would have been in Auroville at that time where we would have been unreachable. The timing of events was confirmed when INTERPOL caught up with me later the same day. The immediate challenges were to find a way of travelling home in time for Benjaya's Celebration; to complete a week's business; to give consideration to Sommer's needs; and to have our own simple ceremony of acknowledgement of this most momentous event in the history of our family.

The Golden Bird had become a symbol in my mind of the soul of Benjaya, the light of his life, not extinguished but newly lit and rising up on a tide of loving celebration. On my last brief seaside holiday with him I had given him a golden-yellow towel which he had opened wide and, running naked across the sands, had flapped and swirled, darting through the beach pools calling for me to watch him being the Golden Bird. 'Land of the Golden Bird' is also an old descriptive name of India herself, the place to which I had planned to return some day with Benjaya as I felt our souls' roots were deeply intertwined in some ancient days in this extraordinary land. And so I asked for the lamp to be brought into our bedroom and lit. We placed garlands around it and as I sat quietly Benjaya was with me, his energy unmistakable as he filled me with his presence.

There was a sensation of total awareness from outside myself as if I could see this scene through 'other' eyes and the knowing was there that Benjaya was totally aware of me, the lamp and everything.

I am familiar with what is perceived to be the 'normal' process of bereavement when the mind initially reels from the shock and seems stunned, unable to think. My mind did not seem to be working to this prescribed pattern, it was directly the opposite - there was clarity. Bank managers were seen to open accounts and financial agreements were made converting accounts into rupees, which I find difficult at the best of times. Twenty-four hours later we said our goodbyes to the Nayak family, sitting with George and Jenny in the twilight of the evening as they told us Indian myths and legends in which gods and **mystical beings had been born in water, disappearing in the same way**, and we simply allowed ourselves to feel the mystery and amazement at the events of our inter-woven lives.

There was another jigsaw piece to fit in. I had an urge to ask George and Jenny whether they felt it would be appropriate to name the school-house that we hoped to build one day JAYA NIVAS (meaning the House of Victory) in memory of Benjaya. I was surprised by their reply as George, whom I had never known by any other name, told me that Jaya was his Indian name which he had used in his younger years, Jenny adding "It is the name I call him in moments of closeness". And so George who had spoken of me as Ma, his mother, upon the death of his own, revealed himself to me as Jaya and I accepted him as a new son .

It took two days to journey home, with one night sleeping on the floor of Bombay airport. Sommer was quiet, steady, waiting for the right time to let the tears flow. It was an amusement to us both that we had chosen to travel by Gulf Air whose symbol is... the Golden Bird.

Home, with only thirty-six hours to go before the Celebration. Derek and Charlotte were at the airport to meet us and as we sped homewards in the darkness it was Charlotte who told me the details that I had been waiting to hear. The family were through their first wave of shock, except for Derek, who wore his grief as a mourning cloak. How I ached to take it from him and throw it lightly over my arm. Though Derek is well used to me relating to life from a different angle, it was hard for us both to discover the contrasts we were having in this experience. Facing his pain brought home the isolation of my own position as I was still feeling myself to be in a light, clear, strong and connected space. I was not holding myself together' as some might have thought, **I simply *was***

together within an invisible supportive structure I can only describe as 'wholeness' which vibrated with life.

Everywhere I glanced around the house, symbols were speaking to me, almost calling out that the finger had pointed towards Benjaya, and in my state of protected ignorance I had been unable to read them. I would not have *wanted* to be able to read them or I would never have been able to leave. A quick glance in the sanctuary reminded me that I had placed a card bearing a picture of the Golden Bird beside the Arabic calligraphy requesting 'a goodly entrance and a goodly exit', together with other items which now also held a greater relevance. Downstairs in the lounge is a large statue of the Buddha. It is my practice to place objects in his hands from time to time. Placing anything into the Buddha's hands is similar to placing things on an altar (for alteration) which in general terms represents letting go, giving up into the hands of God. Before leaving for India I had placed in the Buddha's hands a hollow stick, the instrument that had led to Benjaya's fall.

A telephone call to Carmella at last. I could hear that she was strong in spirit and knew there would be time for much deep sharing but for the present it was simply necessary to receive her instructions and learn the part that she wanted me to play in the Celebration. Everything that had happened for others over the process of the week had, for me and Sommer, to be taken within one great stride.

CHAPTER SIXTEEN

ᗒhe Celebration

Carmella

Saturday, March 7th (Diary extract)

*The big day began at 4am when I gave up on sleep because of the nervous
excitement rushing round my body. I lay in bed feeling that a vital part of
history was about to be lived, in which I was to have a central role. How
pompous that sounds but that was how I felt.*

*We are so used to exhibitions of our material on holistic birth which
includes all Benjaya's birth photographs, but this morning the boxes which
I finished packing for the 'show' were filled with memorabilia of his life
because he has died. How wistfully peculiar that feels.*

*The Celebration of the Life of Benjaya was due to begin at 2pm but
there was much preparation work beforehand and Abel and I were first
through the doors of the village hall at 9.45am. The caretaker, not
knowing my identity, greeted me in a matter-of-fact manner which
changed abruptly to a blushing, fear-filled countenance on discovery
that I was 'the mother'. And again, when I met the tea lady, the air of
normality turned into one of hushed reverence causing me to feel like an
oddity. **Do these responses reflect the Western attitude to death I
wonder?** How can I be expected to be normal when I am now seen as
'the woman whose son has drowned'?*

The Steiner school volunteers arrived in waves and in a hive of gentle activity the plain-looking hall was transformed into a place of beauty. Coloured veils draped the walls; moss and wild flowers collected by children decorated the windowsills; and there were cards and bouquets appearing all the time. A little white silk angel made for Benjaya by his teacher hung over the centre isle and a large photograph of Benjaya with his sword and shield (which went into the coffin with him) stood on the rainbow-veiled table at the front by my spectacular celestite crystal and a vase of exquisite flowers. Soon I was thinking 'Nothing negative can happen in this sacred space' just as had been voiced about MetaCentre at the time of Benjaya's birth.

My mother and father appeared by late morning and I felt a sigh of relief surge through me. I took in their energy with a swoop and decided that they were in surprisingly good spirits, showing no sign of intense jet lag or of a hell that has been lived through. This was a time for hugs not words and I sent them home with Abel, to be with his mother and father who had also arrived.

Surrounded by half a dozen curious, loving children, I then busied myself creating the two displays that I knew intuitively were required. The first table was entitled 'Benjaya's River of Life' and consisted of a spiral display of photographs of him, from his birth photograph in the centre, to his most recent image. The second table was called 'Little Things That Mean a Lot' and was a collection of all the things that meant the most to Benj in his life. The children were transfixed by this table and memorised all the objects as if by this exercise they were embodying something of who he was.

I delegated as many tasks as I could and put local women who had volunteered their services in charge of drinks and the buffet. My closest friends I entrusted with the task of welcoming people at the door and giving candles to those who had not brought one. Time was ticking on and I was beginning to feel a bit tense. The feeling escalated when Benjaya's teacher arrived bearing a bag of his belongings, including the last paintings he did at school - brilliant splashes of colour, worthy of an artist, that looked for all the world to me like visionary pictures of the heaven world. I was choked and all my energy deserted me.

The last touches were left for others and I went home to join Abel and my parents for lunch. When I arrived it was hard to believe that we were only hours from Benjaya's funeral. My father was dressed all in yellow, as he had been at our wedding, and was in a happy mood eating Brie and French bread with a glass of wine, just as I like him best. M'haletta appeared normal - strong and centred; Abel was holding himself together well and I was the only one who was wilting and agitated. I ate a morsel of something and then went upstairs to change.

Stepping into my new ivory white top and wedding trousers of shimmering silk was like stepping into a different persona. I could feel my energy expanding by the second, and as I stood in Benjaya's room requesting his help to stay centred and strong and play my part well this afternoon, I felt more empowered than I have ever done in my life. As I walked regally down the stairs, taking the onlookers by surprise, I felt as if I could accomplish, with love, any task that the world could give me.

Off we went to the hall, where M'haletta completed her task of welcoming her grandson in his tiny wooden coffin at the gate and guiding the undertakers to the centre stage where it was to rest covered in a white lace cloth and surrounded with flowers until after the ceremony. I was amazed to see her tranquility and focused energy as she then set up a tape recorder to catch the contents of the day (a well edited transcript of which follows) and put a film in her camera to capture a visual image.

The time was here and friends and strangers and lots of children from near and far began crowding through the doors. Their love seemed to lift me higher and I was overwhelmed by the numbers of people who had come to support us. I put out 110 chairs but it was standing room only at the back and the children sat on cushions at the front.

Abel and I sat on chairs at the front facing everyone, clearly representing the two poles of energy present at this event. He, dressed in smart grey cord trousers, a black jacket, white shirt with a red belt and shoes, was filled almost to breaking point with grief whilst I, in my ivory white, stood fearless, strong and joyous at his side. Abel began.

Abel

Hello everybody. Please bear with me if my voice disappears. I want to welcome you all and apologise that I wasn't in a space to greet each of you individually. I am aware that people have come from varying distances with varying degrees of difficulty and I thank every one of you. Your presence here is appreciated, valued and important.

Today's event is a celebration of Benjaya's life on Earth and perhaps other components as well. We are not totally clear what will happen today. We have some items that we know will be contributed but we've organised this event so that there will be space for you to make contributions as and however you feel. We will all be responsible for what happens and it may be a bit disjointed or strange but it will be an expression of the way we all are now in this moment of coming together and what we create.

I believe that there are more here than we are able to see with our eyes. As you will have seen, Benj's body is here, and although I am not directly conscious of it, I am sure that his consciousness is here also.

Carmella

Abel may not be directly conscious of Benjaya but I am. The reason I am standing here so strong and confident right now is not my doing. It is because I feel blasted by the **overwhelming light and power of my son's presence which is far greater now than when he was contained in a body.** I don't have a prepared speech so please bear with me too.

I want to share with you a little about Benjaya's birth because for me his birth and death are so bound. I've been confused - is he dying or being born? I guess the answer is 'both'. He was blessed with a beautiful birth into a pool of water with twelve witnesses present who were in a high state of being. Some of these people are here now. That birth experience for me was one of being physically torn apart with excruciating pain and a kind of exquisite joy, along with a profound attitude change towards life, people and especially women. Then came the blaze of publicity as his birth photograph encircled the world via the media.

In a drama worthy of equal publicity, Benjaya slipped out of life as fast as he had entered and his body was found in a pool of water. The word 'accident' is used but **could it really be an accident?** The experience of his death has been an emotional wrenching apart with excruciating pain and, believe it or not, a joy that has been as great as the joy of his birth. There has been another deep and profound change in my attitude towards life, people and pain of any kind. So I want to say to you that there *is* life in death and the reason I am wearing this light colour is because I feel an expansion of life as well as the physical loss. **The two poles are here: birth and death, as powerful as each other.**

I am totally convinced that on some level Benjaya knew he was going to die. He talked about death and dying often, about the process of leaving his body and he even asked me who he would meet when he died. He was very matter of fact about it. He had been talking for quite a while about not going up into class one because he was going to Sherwood Forest to take from the rich and give to the poor with Will, who is here somewhere, but then about ten days before he died he changed his tune and said "Don't get your hopes up Mum, I'm not going into class one because I've got another school I have to go to". I wonder what he meant.

Our boy was a pain at times but he was also a wise old soul. I want to share with you one of the things he said to me just before going to sleep just a month ago. I wrote it in my diary:

I'm really worried about something Mum and I want you to help me. I just don't understand why there are so many ragged people about and why there isn't just one big market place where everyone can get new clothes.

We're just like puppets in a plastic world being tested to see if we're good aren't we? This world isn't real is it? I'd rather be a bull, I like galloping about.

Benjaya had three short days of totally connecting to the baby I now carry, who is due on his birthday. He was ecstatic and kissed my tummy over and over saying "welcome, welcome baby" and then he died, leaving me blasted apart and expanded into another dimension of being. What is going on? I do not know.

Now let's have some music from our friend Julian Marshall and Wiggly Lines before we open up this space for any of you to speak.

Norah McCullagh:

This is something I wrote after my own son died, I adapted it from something I read and found it very comforting. I've rewritten it for Abel and Carmella:

Close your eyes and imagine that there are three unborn beings floating before birth who have great love and concern for each other's well-being. One of these says to the others: "There is so much to be learned in a lifetime, I wonder if we can help each other? Imagine if one of us were born a man and another a woman and together they have a son. And let's say that after some years this child suddenly meets with his death, leaving the others to share the loss and the heartbreak. And they can share it in love, not shut each other out in their agony and devastation but remain there for each other to complete the learning."

The three beings between birth sit down and, with higher guidance, decide to implement the plan despite the difficulties, knowing that if they succeed their hearts will be more open than ever before.

And so they play it out - Abel, Carmella and Benjaya.

Tim Reeves

It was Saturday morning and I had woken early feeling the desire to read a book that had some substance in it. I picked up a book from my shelf called *Living with the Himalayan Masters* by Swami Rami and the chapter I looked at was called *Living and Dying*. I read for a couple of hours and then Abel phoned to tell me what had happened to Benjaya. I read it again!

Here are a few words from that chapter:

You are the architect of your destiny. Death and birth are merely two events in life. You have forgotten your essential nature and that is the cause of your suffering. When you become aware of this you are liberated...

Try to understand what death is. Don't be afraid of it...Death does not annihalate you, it only separates you from a body...

I asked: 'How does one feel existing without a physical body? He replied: 'How do you feel when you go without a shirt? It's nothing!'

Music from Jenny Quick on the electronic piano encapsulates Benjaya's character and brings tears to many eyes.

Sharon Patel

I read a piece in *The Celtic Church Speaks Today* about a little boy out fishing with his father who fell in and drowned and later came back as a vision to someone and described how it felt to drown. He said that drowning was the most beautiful experience he had had in his life, "soothing, graceful, peaceful and very enjoyable". Most of us probably imagine that Benjaya suffered but this piece suggests that perhaps he didn't. When I explained this to my son Nikhil, who's a waterbaby friend of Benjaya's, he said "I'd like to do that too!"

Rod Friend

For myself I feel it is such an opportunity to learn about life through death. Death is teaching us about our life. [He then shares words from his wife Alice who is not with us.]

Rob Henley

The year before Carmella, Abel and Benjaya joined the community in Bristol where we were living at the time, my wife drowned leaving me with five children. There are others here today who were part of that community. Will, my youngest, is five now and he and Benjaya have been close friends since they were two years old.

Will and Benjaya would sometimes stroll into my house with two or three other children and say "We're just going upstairs for a while" and I'd say "Okay, well yes," thinking, 'let's not be too negative about this'. For a while they'd jump up and down on the bed, testing it, and I just let that go on. Then it used to go quiet and after a little while I'd go upstairs and there would be two or three little boys standing there. Benjaya looked so very, very beautiful, eyes shining, skin glowing with nothing on...not a stitch. This used to go on day after day.

We were talking about this yesterday and William said "I used to do thirty things to Benjaya". I said "What! What were they?" but he wouldn't say. They had a great time being in their bodies together in the way that we hope our children do, being allowed to play without us parents getting in the way of that.

The last memory I have of Benjaya is from the early morning of that time. Sometimes he would get up early whilst Carmella and Abel were meditating or something and he would be wandering round looking for some action. And he looked for it in my house, in my bedroom! I would hear the door open and I'd open my eyes and there he'd be just standing smiling and looking at me with that smile he held so well.

Debbie Collins

I spent last Friday with a splitting headache and didn't know why until today. From Monday, when I heard about Benjaya's death, I kept getting a picture of being torn apart but what was coming out of the tear were great big creamy pearls. I offer you that image. I told somebody this and she told me of the advice given by Ram Dass to a couple whose daughter had been murdered. The story is related by Stephen Levine in *Who Dies? An Investigation into Conscious Living and Conscious Dying.*[1] I'd like to read to you the relevant passage.

> *Recently we spent some time with a couple whose eleven-year-old daughter had been abducted and murdered. It was every parent's worse nightmare. There was no way they could control the universe. There was no way they could make it go away. Their pain was so extraordinary that they simply could not hold onto it any more, and their hearts were torn open.*

> *Soon after the death they wrote a letter to Ram Dass:*

> *"We go on although we have no stomach for it. We try our best to be there for our two remaining children and that is also sometimes hard. We constantly search our own hearts and those of many friends and relatives who have opened to us, for deeper understanding and new meaning.*
> *"I see Rachel as a soul who was actively engaged in her work while on earth. Her last three years in particular showed me the flowering of a shining being - caring, loving, and reaching out to the members of her family... young and old. She was always giving little 'love' somethings to everyone. To make you smile, to help you feel good, to show she cared. She had learned somehow to bear her defeats and frustrations and not be intimidated or slowed by them. The petals were opening and reaching for the sun. She was not a clone of her parents. She was who she was. She was the best of us and the strongest of us. The wake of Rachel's death leaves the many beings who knew her and a surprising number who didn't torn open to this 'teaching'."*

> *When Ram Dass received this letter he responded:*

---

[1] Quoted with kind permission of the publishers, *Gateway Books*, Bath.

"Rachel finished her work on earth and left the stage in a manner that leaves those of us left behind with a cry of agony in our hearts as the fragile thread of our faith is dealt with so violently. Is anyone strong enough to stay conscious through such teaching as you are receiving? Probably very few, and even they would have only a whisper of equanimity and spacious peace amidst the screaming trumpets of their rage, grief, horror, and desolation.

"I can't assuage your pain with any words, nor should I. For your pain is Rachel's legacy to you. Not that she or I would inflict such pain by choice, but there it is. And it must burn its purifying way to completion... For something in you dies when you bear the unbearable. And it is only in that dark night of the soul that you are prepared to see as God sees and to love as God loves.

"Now is the time to let your grief find expression - no false strength. Now is the time to sit quietly and speak to Rachel and thank her for being with you these few years and encourage her to go on with her work, knowing that you will grow in compassion and wisdom from this experience.

"In my heart I know that you and she will meet again and again and recognise the many ways in which you have known each other. And when you meet, you will, in a flash, know what now it is not given you to know. Why this had to be the way it was.

"Our rational minds can never 'understand' what has happened. But your hearts, if you can keep them open to God, will find their own intuitive way.

"Rachel came through you to do her work on earth (which includes her manner of death). Now her soul is free and the love you can share with her is invulnerable to the winds of changing time and space."

As our friends opened to their grief, they opened to their love. They experienced Rachel at a level which they seldom touched before. Less and less, as they opened, were they so caught in the forms which always separate parent from child, loved one from loved one. Instead, the grief which spins and burns the mind begins quietly and gently to sink into the heart.

Now I want to read you a letter from Tony Concannon who was present at Benjaya's birth:

Dear Abel and Carmella,
Words cannot express how great the sadness and how deep the love I share with you in your time of loss. Ben was a wonderful light of life and it's hard to imagine him not shining with us. I remember how bright and life expressive he was at our last meeting, exuberant and full of garden curiosity and the wonder of new things growing (cabbages I think). So much seemed so outward with him, from those very outward kicks when he was inside the womb to the 'whoosh' of the birth itself.

With their all-enveloping fascination for life itself, I remember those eyes wide and beaming, always taking everything inwards to that deeper realm of childhood comprehension. I often wondered where that great enveloping expanse of seeing went to. As his eyes took everything in, out would come that beam of wonder and joy in new discovery. I remember it in those early staggering yet determined footsteps, the scaling of the sofa as adults tried to converse, proud strides through the garden, spade in hand, full with self-assurance and confidence. Even when he cried and whined (and don't they all?) those radiant eyes shone bright with Bambi tears and soft vulnerable stillness.

He knew how safe and loved he was, how nourished and cared for by both of you. I have to admit that I was jealous at times. I wish my father had carried me so proudly, securely and shared as much of himself as you did with Benj, Abel, or my mother had been so warm, tender and loving as you were with him, Carmella. Benj made a good choice of parents in you both, with impeccable taste.

I'll miss him and that universe shining in those eyes. I was thinking about him with heaviness and sadness this week on a car journey and my inner weather was reflected in the outer grey cloudiness, but as I approached Stourbridge the clouds parted and luminous rays of sunshine fell over the Clent Hills. Those 'angel's ladders' shimmered and shone bright and I felt Benj had found his stairway to the heavens, taking his light with him to join the light from which he came.

Farewell Benj. Thank you for the light you shared with us. Our world was much illuminated by your presence. Thank you Abel and Carmella for channelling that light amongst us.

Tony Concannon

Musical interlude of one of Benjaya's favourite chants which we all sing.

Spread your rainbow wings and fly into forever, into forever   x 2

And I'll be seeing you in heaven   x 2

Derek Taylor

I don't know how many of you find it difficult singing with a lump in your throat. I'm Carmella's father and I had the privilege of spending a fair amount of time with Benjaya when he was young because we all lived together. One of the things we did together was to read this book by Tolkien called *Mr. Bliss*. Those of you that know the book will know that it is about a journey. No matter how many times we read this book together he was always interested in the journey. When he came back after he'd left or when I came to Devon to visit, one of the first things I did was to read *Mr. Bliss* again and go through the journey. It really was a privilege to join him on these journeys and I'm looking forward to joining him on the next.

M'haletta

I'm the other half - I'm Carmella's mother. I've been away in India for some weeks, travelling and working. They've had INTERPOL out after me - Benjaya would have loved that. They didn't find me until Tuesday because I believe that it wasn't for me to be found before that time because on that journey I was acting as Benjaya's spiritual midwife for his exit, as I had for his entrance into the world.

I connected with that precious and magical soul before he joined us on the Earth plane. There was much preparation in our household for the coming of that soul, which became conscious as it came nearer to his birth, preparation of ourselves that we should be ready to receive him, and we were. We were ready in the topmost room of our house and we were twelve.

Benjaya joined us in a blaze of light, of life and of love that filled our house in every room. The radiance within that house is a light that will never be extinguished. **This exit, this transformation, is a magnification of that light.** This I have experienced on my journey through India, although I didn't know in the conscious mind that that was why I was feeling such magnification of consciousness and life energies.

I was on the beach in India with my grand-daughter, Sommer, who was travelling with me and we were buying shells for Benjaya because he would have loved playing with them. The shells were decorated with Hindu pictures of different aspects of God. I bought shell after shell - I just couldn't stop buying them and didn't know why. I thought what fun we'd have making up the stories. I've brought five of them here, one to depict each year of Benjaya's life, and in the centre is a plain shell.

Now Joshua is my other grandson and he is Benjaya's friend. I'd like to ask Joshua to come and take away the plain shell that represents life on Earth and leave those shells depicting aspects of God, which Benjaya, better than anyone here, will know now.

In India Benjaya spoke to me. We often spoke together without being in each other's company. He said "Now Grandma you can buy me the gold chalice," and so I did. I would like to ask Amy, his youngest cousin, if she would bring the chalice and put it in the place of the plain shell.

Benjaya and I played symbols and through speaking of symbols he taught me many things and I shared his journey with him at levels which go beyond my understanding. Benjaya loved his sword and his shield which carries a symbol of the sun and the words **Sun King**. It is because of his love for this Sun King image that Carmella has asked me to read some words I wrote before his birth which will explain more about the Sun King. I will read them as a prayer in honour of his life.

Rejoice all peoples of the Earth.
Take to the rooftops, to the mountains of your being.
For you are the dwellers upon the plains;
The builders of the way;
The guardians of the gates of the New Age of Aquarius,
Which open now before you
Through which the Sun King rides
And light streams forth upon the Earth
Into the hearts of Men.
This is the light of the world, the ninety-nine names of
The Great Living Lord
Of all realms and of names beyond naming.
And where that light does fall, none shall stay its hand
For its power is legion
And he that takes it unto himself shall be

As a mighty army
And none shall stand against him
Lest they be vanquished.
For the Sun King rides forth and the sword of truth
Lies in the scabbard of those enjoined with him.
And it may be unsheathed and lifted high
In his name only
That truth again prevails upon the Earth.
Thus will the sound of the sun be heard
Throughout the lands,
Across all oceans, in the deepest caverns
And resounding through all time and space.
Thus do you know of it; that you become One People
For the cosmic note has sounded
And the day of days has come.

And the day of days that is upon us is Jaya's day. It is a day of grace, a day of glory, a day of celebration, a day of beauty and all else will find its place within the scheme. For we are one family united in the love of child, man and spirit.

Polly Ash then sings a beautiful Sai Baba chant adapted for Benjaya.

Abel

I would like to say a few words about my relationship with Benjaya and what I am now because of him. When he was conceived we had not been planning to have a child for quite some while and I did not feel ready. I felt very strongly at the time that Benj had come through despite all our resistance and contraceptive efforts. He was intending coming and that was all there was to it.

At that stage of my life I wasn't really able to accept this and I resisted. I did nothing active about it and I allowed that resistance to turn into resentment. Benj must have felt my anger and resentment for several years. I am eternally grateful to Carmella for her wonderful mothering and often feel that if it hadn't been for her in those early years then I could have done great damage. However Benj survived that.

I sometimes think to myself that he came along with such strength because he knew it was necessary. He knew that I needed someone of that strength in my life. Another thing was that he demanded my love and he accepted me through all my shortcomings. Children are amazingly forgiving and he forgave me and continued to demand my love. And gradually I learned to love him. Quite recently I realised that despite my resistance and the fact that I felt him to be an imposition in my life, I had gained immeasurably as a result of his presence and now enjoyed him.

A few days before he died I was putting him to bed (we do a prayer every night) and he didn't want to say the prayer himself so I gave thanks for all the things of the day and I gave special thanks for him in my life. He really heard this. I had come full circle - I had finally welcomed him into my life and accepted the benefits for me of the challenges and lessons he had brought to me. It's like he had done it. He had achieved it.

When he discovered that Carmella was pregnant he was overjoyed. It was almost like he could go now. I had a conversation with him once when he said to me that he was looking forward to dying. I don't remember the details but there was an assumption made that I would die first because I was older and he said to me how lucky I was that I didn't have so long to wait as he had. He welcomed death and was ready for it because he'd achieved what he came for. He'd done so much for me that I named my business after him and having been through a very difficult period, I'm determined to see this business survive and grow.

Then he died. Our last moments together were joyful and I am so grateful that my last acts with him were acts of love. I continue to love Benj daily. He may not be here in the physical body any longer but my relationship with him has been formed and will go on for eternity. For me, the way I will live that relationship is that I will know that everything is a divine droplet, just as Benj is. What he has given me is not so much his presence, his body, or joyful things we did together - he has given me an improved ability to love. I am determined to carry that love with me and love everyone I can as an expression of my love for Benj.

I know now that life only has its meaning in death. If it wasn't for death, we wouldn't have any reason to live life with determination to grow and change and love. I recognise that it is only eight days after the death of my son and I am still in an emotional state but I make this pledge to you:

I will put one hundred per cent of my being into living every moment as if it is the last for the person or item that I am interacting with. I am willing to love as Benj has taught me.

The baby that is inside Carmella will benefit from what Benj has done for me. My ability to love that child will start from day one, from the point to which Benj has brought me after five years and four months.

I want to thank all family and friends who have supported us through this time. It has been a privilege to receive your love and I hope you will continue loving whoever you can, whenever you can, in honour of my son.

Julian is going to teach us a song now, *Jubilate Deo,* which we will sing in four parts. During the song we're going to light our candles and hold them high above our heads, creating a blaze of light to end our ceremony. This is symbolic of the magnification of light in death which is now coming into our lives.

Back to Carmella's diary

We blew out our candles after the grand finale as if they were on a birthday cake - one, two, three...blow! Then it was 'bon apétit' and everyone was free to eat, drink and be merry or sad according to their needs. Something enormous had released in me during the last couple of hours and I felt less inhibited than I have ever felt in my life. I was aware that there was the potential to have released even more during this 'harmonic convergence' as I had been actively holding back from dancing wildly during the songs and blasting out the words into the microphone in front of me. Somehow it didn't feel appropriate to express myself with such wild abandon under these circumstances. I do care deeply what others think of my behaviour.

It took me about two hours to reach the buffet but I was not hungry anyway. I was caught in embrace after embrace, tear-filled eyes meeting mine and immense love spilling over me from every angle. From the awe-inspired thanks that just kept on coming I realised that people's lives had already been irrevocably changed by this event.

Meriel (aged four) had a raging fever and slept through most of the sharings but said on waking that she had seen Benj: "There he was and we just looked at each other". Finny (aged 5) also slept and said that he saw Benj as well. Another child, known for her psychic abilities, said that she saw Benjaya standing behind my chair for most of the event.

Paul, a friend from Brighton, shared that a Steiner School teacher in Brighton had had a vision on Friday about a young boy drowning in

*Devon. He also said that other friends will be scattering rose petals on
the sea tomorrow in memory of Benj.*

*The stage curtains had been drawn to create an enclosed space and
the lid had been taken off the coffin. Benjaya was now visible -* **maybe the
counterpart to the visibility of the infant at birth** *- and I felt the pull
towards the stage that others must have felt, as if there was a new-born
child to be greeted in his crib. The children led the way and queued
excitedly at the steps of the stage just as Benj had done at Christmas to see
Father Christmas who sat where his body now lay. Children of all sizes
seemed to be eager to visit him and to take their more inhibited parents with
them the second time around. What a mind-blowing, transforming day it
has been for them.*

*Ruth, a seventeen year old, told us that she had seen a great light
filling the whole hall, especially by the ceiling, during Jubilate Deo and she
was sure that this was not simply candlelight but was Benjaya and his
friends' unbelievable power. She said that when she went up to see his body
she had a thought that maybe she should start crying but then she heard a
voice above her which said "Hey, you shouldn't think things like that!" She
said that when she looked up she saw "a spirit or something" and she
started chuckling out loud, knowing that Benjaya was saying to her that
there was nothing sad about this. She said "I felt cheeky looking at a dead
body and laughing so I moved away in case anyone saw me".*

*Just before 6pm M'haletta and I went onto the stage to anoint
Benjaya's body with Sai Baba's vibhuti and I realised with a gulp that this
would be the last time I would see my boy's physical form. On Monday
morning his body will be cremated, a thought that is too much to bear for
me. I've already been having nightmares about burning bodies and
concentration camps. Abel and I are both grateful that M'haletta has said
that she will go with him on the last leg of his journey.*

*It was difficult to get too close to the coffin as Benj was
surrounded by children, stroking his hair, arranging flowers on his
chest, tapping his legs and asking questions, fascinated by this alien
process of death. One child turned to M'haletta saying:*

"I didn't know we could turn to stone,"

as if he had learned some great secret.

"Shall I put flowers by his nose?"

said one child to another.

"He can't smell them".

"Why, where's his smell gone?"

An eleven-year-old girl asked her what was going to happen to Benjaya's body next and so they talked together beside him of funerals in different lands, of cultures and the way **we use different elements of earth, water and fire** for this important task. What wisdom in that child as she nodded in agreement that fire seemed to be the right element for Benjaya. I was watching this entrancing scene around my boy's body and thinking that death seemed such a wholesome and holy deed. And what an astounding way for a grandmother to be reunited with her grandson!

Eventually I anointed Benjaya and a little girl anointed me with the ash. Then all the children dipped their fingers in the pot sensing its magical properties and asking of its origin.

As arranged, the undertakers arrived to take the coffin back to the Chapel of Rest and the lump in my throat threatened to choke me. The remaining guests gathered flowers from the vases and formed a gauntlet through which my boy in his tiny coffin was carried by the dignified, black-suited men who showed not a flicker of emotion. Those of us with a voice sang:

'OM Benjaya, celebrate Benjaya, sing it with an open and a joyful heart...'

and threw flowers onto the coffin as it passed by. It was to this thanksgiving sound that he was driven away in a black hearse that I wished was white.

The clearing up process then began and silent servers beavered away until 7pm. M'haletta and I were the last to leave, struggling to carry the masses of flowers without causing them damage. Home again in a timeless space and a sea of flowers, we sat totally exhausted, Mum, Dad, Abel and I, discussing the day. The consensus was that we could not have created a better send off for our sweet boy.

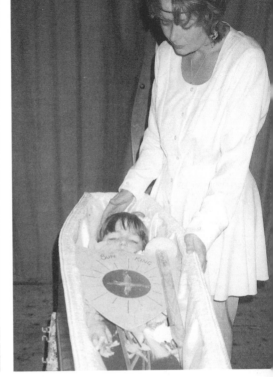

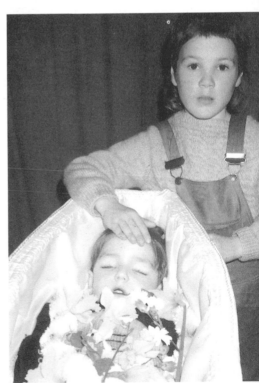

CHAPTER SEVENTEEN

Back to the Sea

M'haletta

or almost everyone, contact with Benjaya's physical form was over. One day, a Sunday, lay between the Celebration and the cremation. How do you pass the time on such a day? The two sets of grandparents had stayed overnight together with Abel's sister, Frankie, and her family and Charlotte. It was Carmella's idea that we should go to the seaside, so on that crisply cold Sunday morning we all set off for a nearby beauty spot at Bigbury-on-Sea.

Although we talked a little as we walked together up the grassy mound, there were spaces where we slipped into our reservoirs of memory, filled no doubt with a multiplicity of images of Benjaya. I found myself remembering the afternoon of his blessing ceremony, when he was six months old, which had taken place at Himley Hall in Dudley as a part of Carmella and Abel's wedding celebrations. It was a brilliantly sunny April day and all the children in their gay wedding clothes followed a piper across the lawns, waving bunches of spring flowers. His three cousins, Sommer, Joshua and Amy, had carried his blessing symbols - a chalice of water, a staff and a crown of flowers. He had been eager to grasp the chalice, tipping it up to taste 'the waters of life' from Lourdes, took a firm hold of the staff of the pilgrim, which represented commitment to walk the Earth path but wriggled uncomfortably as the circlet of flowers, our symbol of love, fell in a funny lopsided way over his ears. When all the blessings had been given and a small brass sword engraved with his name had been raised up, we formed a great circle to dance and sing his blessing song which was this:

> *The river is flowing, flowing and growing,*
> *The river is flowing down to the sea.*
> *Mother Earth carry me, a child I will always be*
> *Mother Earth carry me, back to the sea.*

Standing now, five years on, at the mouth of the Avon, the very river that had swept him towards the sea, a feeling welled in me of an infinite continuous stream of knowing. It seemed obvious that we had at some level of awareness known all that was needed to be known for Benjaya's life journey and his blessing ceremony had acknowledged the path that he would take. **A child he would always be to us in the physical image.**

It had been agreed that I would take responsibility for the last stage of Benjaya's Earth journey to his cremation and I felt confident that in those final moments I would know what else needed to be said or done. Charlotte simply determined to be with me and I was glad of it.

Sunshine poured on us both as we arrived together in the early morning of Monday, 9th March, for the first cremation service of the day. It was a jewel of a church surrounded by a horizon of Benjaya's much loved hills and we could feel ourselves riding high upon the waves of love that had rained on us all at the Celebration. The men in black were with us again bringing Benjaya in their own dignified and respectful way. What servants they had been, no-one could have wished for better, except perhaps for a dash of colour! In the gardens a young man who had been tending the flowers changed his coat and turned into the church official. There was no glimmer of surprise as we explained that Charlotte was the only congregation and I would be acting as minister and would play some music and say a few words. It was so easy, all the beliefs that there might be persuasion towards a more traditional pattern for these last rites vaporised away in the knowing that we were quite free to create our own intimate ceremony.

Our music was a tape called 'Silver Wings' by Mike Rowand, who had written Carmella and Abel's 'Wedding March' and 'Jaya's Dance' for Benjaya. I asked for the coffin to be placed directly in the sunlight that was streaming through the tall windows and that it should remain there until we left. And so Benjaya was brought to his last appointed place.

The music played as Charlotte and I sat in silence, as we had sat together at his birth. The church official disappeared and the men in black remained sitting in a distant pew. Charlotte, I felt, held the focus for all those minds and hearts that would have been with us in those moments and was 'congregating' all those energies. When the music had filled every corner of my mind, I joined Benjaya. Those words I can neither explain nor fully comprehend myself. There was a sensing that I was fully and wholly 'with' him and he with me. There was no sense of separation or division, no emotional tugging or wanting to cling, to hold onto the boy whose life walk had been most purposefully made. I moved into the beam of sunlight and stood beside him under the window, aware of his body lying there but we were also elsewhere sharing a space where words flow like a river straight from the heart and soul, words filled with mystical meaning. Later I wrote the words as well as I could recall for Abel and Carmella. This is their essence which contained all that I could ever have wished to say had Benjaya grown to manhood.

BENJAMIN JAYA, BELOVED OF HAHN
Child of the morning mists and of the Eternal Son;
Light of the World, love everlasting;
Power of the Three in One - child, man and spirit
A great work is accomplished
A beauteous life is lived.
The thread of lineage is connected between
Earth and Heaven
And a New Day dawns.
Robed in glory - blessed art thou;
Blessed are thy parents for the light they have borne
Blessed is thy family of Earth and thy family of Heaven
For the son that thou art.
And blessed is this day
Thy day of grace
When the waters and the fire do meet in thee.

Then followed the Lord's Prayer which I had re-written as a raga some years before to express the nature of our way.

Beloved Lord, who art within
The Heaven of our creation

Thy name is holy.
Thy kingdom reigns upon this Earth,
Thy will is as mine own and will be done
Below - and so above.
Thou nourish me within each day
And judge me not in my iniquities,
Thou turn my face in love towards all Men
Who never shall be called my enemies.
Mine eyes are closed to tempters
And all that is of darkness is enwrapt in light
For thine is my kingdom
All power and all glory
For ever and forever more
So shall it be.

The energy within me was spinning and spiralling as I circled to kiss the head and foot of the coffin, placing a single white rose on the gleaming polished wood with the words 'the white rose lies upon the heart through which an everlasting light is lit'... tears flowing silently now.

Charlotte then took my place strewing pink tulip petals as she walked around that small coffin... weeping... loving. From behind us a bronze butterfly[1] swooped past, dipped over the coffin and flew high into the sunlight to settle on the widow ledge. Such moments are indelible.

I had felt with such certainty that Sommer and I had, in some other indescribable dimension, travelled unknowingly but willingly with Benjaya on his exodus through the waters. Now this stage of completion of his physical life seemed to me to be a continuation of that journey and I found myself committing with an inner voice to travel with him through the transmuting flames - whatever that might mean or wherever it may lead.

A day or so later Carmella and I went together to the Chapel of Rest in Ivybridge to collect 'the ashes', a phrase that turns Benjaya into microscopic particles. How is it that we can stand and receive fragments of a life in a bronze plastic container? The urn was a square-sided plastic container of the type that might contain a gallon of oil, quite substantial, non-see-through and heavy with the volume of ashes. It must have weighed about 5lbs. Tucked in the top was a card bearing Benjaya's name, date of birth and death. It was handed over to Carmella, whose face was

---

[1]Greek *psyche* means both soul and butterfly. A butterfly is commonly used as a symbol of transition to a higher state of consciousness.

incredulous. We both tried to give the proper responses of thanks for the services rendered, then stepping outside as we turned towards the car, shaking her head saying "I cannot believe that I am holding my boy in this box!" She looked totally amazed, bemused, as if surely we were in some nightmarish game. Yet she could still drive the car steadily and chose to do so whilst I held 'the boy' carefully on my lap. There was still identity there for me in those moments and I found myself holding the container as if I was supporting a child. We talked little, Carmella reminding me of how Benjaya had commented that we live in a plastic world. In all the sequences of this death this was my saddest of moments, as it was too for Carmella as she later described in her diary:

> *The day we fetched the ashes was one of my lowest points. I wept and wept as I lived through the unthinkable - carrying the remains of my son's body in a box, his beautiful big brown eyes in white bits. But even then as I wept I heard him say: "It's just my body mum" and I remembered how I'd told him that he was not his body at all but just lived in it for now.*

We travelled to an empty house belonging to a friend which holds a special significance for us. There we had a private ceremony of release from earthly desires and longings. It was for Carmella a weeping time. We undid the cap on the container and in this lounge where Benjaya had lived for a short while we placed the unmoving urn, running our fingers through the ash. As we did so I heard myself, as if from some distant space, speaking words which guided us to an awareness of these ashes being not the residue of a body alone but representing a fusion of all that had touched upon that life.

The job of sorting out Benjaya's room, his toys, his clothes, was one which Carmella was dreading and yet at the same time she was feeling strongly that it was important to face this task straight away, so we simply got on with the job. Carmella felt that Benjaya's room should be recreated for use as a writing room where she would have some quiet space to work and which she felt would hold a strong presence of Benjaya's higher self. A few special momentos were chosen, the most significant being his last three vibrant pictures of the Heaven world which Carmella framed and hung on the wall. So Benjaya was **'lifted up' rather than 'cleared out'**.

At 9.30am on Friday, 13th March, I went with Carmella to the river behind the unit. She stood in the exact place where Benjaya had fallen in whilst I walked downstream, stopping on the stone bridge just before the mill pool. We had no pre-arranged plan. These **creative ceremonies,** great or small, were not merely a mark of respect for 'the dead', they **were deeply nourishing to us, the living.** For both of us these connections to Benjaya, played out as simple spontaneous rituals, were undoubtedly helping us to go through our inner processes as we moved towards a holistic acceptance of death. And so, on this occasion Carmella tossed Benjaya's home-made, wooden aeroplane with BENAIR written on it into the river and watched it circle round and round before catching the current to come flying through the water towards and under the bridge as Benjaya had done. Then she scattered a handful of his ashes which were taken by the air before falling and were soon lost to sight. The words that sounded in her mind then were:

'This is my beloved son in whom I am well pleased'.

A sense of stillness pervaded our river scene that morning as Carmella commited Benjaya's body back to God, releasing the last vestiges of his earthly form into the waters through which he came. She gave thanks for his life as her son and for the service he had given to others, releasing him yet again in love. In my silent introspective place downstream, I threw flowers from the bridge and watched them swirl their way towards the mill pool. There was a sense of completion in us both, described by Carmella in her diary:

It felt like the last act in my son's earthly play - the final curtain had dropped and I felt deeply sad that it was all over yet moved to applaud its perfect orchestration.

Abel had been concerned to respect the ashes but did not want to connect with them personally and so I asked him "Shall I take Benjaya home?" At last it had been said and permission was given. Benjaya, in his last Earth gown, was given into my keeping and returned home with me to Adam House, the place where he was born.

CHAPTER EIGHTEEN

A Family Rocking

M'haletta

he family had been rocked to the core yet each in their own way had also found themselves cradled and comforted. The task on arriving home was to take a snapshot of how all parts of the family were responding at different levels and in their diverse ways to the death of one of its members. If we were to work in the field of holistic death at some later time, as we believed we would, it seemed vital to learn as much as possible from every available source and family were, as always, both willing and available and the obvious place to begin. There was a personal agenda involved too as I guessed that sharing their experiences at a deeper level would help to fill in the gap that existed for me by not having shared those first days when the full shock wave had been felt. And so I asked them, one by one, to tell me how it was for them. These are their stories as they spoke them to me.

Derek's Story

I'd woken early that morning in the house by myself, looking forward to the day when I was going to play best man at Robbie's wedding, so when the phone rang early I thought it would be Robbie checking up on something, but it wasn't. I was a bit thrown to hear Carmella's voice; it didn't sound normal. I couldn't quite hear what she was trying to tell me, then I did hear but it didn't make sense. I suspect my brain simply wouldn't take in the information.

"Say that again" I remember saying, walking down the hall with the portable phone. "Benjaya's gone home"... silence... "Benjaya is dead".

"Oh my God!" I don't know if I said that out loud or not.

I asked her to tell me how it happened and she did, briefly. She told me not to come down but to wait until you got home. If she'd wanted me I would have gone, you know I would, wedding day or any other sort of day, whatever she wanted I would have done it.

The next half an hour was just emotion pouring out and sadness. I was so very, very sad walking round an empty house calling his name "Benjaya... oh Benjaya... oh Benjaya". Then I drove down the road to find Charlotte. We both cried and just held each other for what seemed like a long time, then she went to find Marc and I went back home.

I was still upset, full of tears, still calling out his name. I remember picking up his photograph, the one of him in the bluebell wood... you know the one... and a photo of you, which seemed important for some reason and I took them up to the sanctuary. I saw all the symbols on the floor - the Indian and Egyptian scene and I didn't want to disturb anything so I just put your photo and Benjaya's facing each other in the middle. Then I sat down and said to Benjaya something like "It will be okay, there's a reason for all of this and although you're in a different place I still love you... don't be frightened." I sat quietly for a bit and felt I was in communication with Benjaya.

My breakfast was still on the table and I ate it, stone cold, thinking about the wedding. I got as far as getting dressed up, and was standing in the lounge in a morning suit, all in black - and you know black's one colour I *never* wear - thinking 'I can't do this. I can't go on'. But then Marc arrived and told me that I could. He was taking charge of the practical things. He told me he had phoned Sandra and was taking Charlotte and Sandra down to Carmella's, which was a great comfort. They had united and all four children were going to be together, supporting each other. It felt good to hear that. He said I looked okay, reminded me that other people had expectations of me and that he thought going to the wedding would be the right thing to do. I needed to hear someone say that, to help me make the decision. So I phoned Robbie and told him the situation so that he would understand if I looked 'gone out'. My biggest worry then was whether I could make a funny speech at such a tragic time.

I got there and got on with it, although I couldn't eat or drink much. When the time for the speech came I managed to sublimate all the sadness I was holding and made what I thought was a funny speech and it worked I think. I told a couple of friends what had happened but all I wanted to do was to get back home.

I was very sad and not with it for days. Charlotte came to stay and Marc was at home so we formed a mutual support system but I can't remember what I did until the Tuesday when I rang through to you in India. I thought you would have been contacted by the police by then but when I reached George and found that you hadn't I realised that I would be giving you what Carmella had given me, something so painful to deal with. I was worried that you wouldn't have a support system out there - at least that was my assumption, that it would be even more difficult for you, not being at home. But it was a relief for me, something of major importance when I'd made that contact. Then there was the waiting, manning the phone twenty-four hours a day, waiting for you to call to tell us when you would be home and fetching you from the airport. The bits in between were just sad... just sadness. I was going to work and coming home but not functioning well. I just let myself be and grieve. I'd lost an important part of my life.

The Celebration was moving and I shed some more tears in a happy-sad energy together with a lot of beautiful people and after it was done I felt a lot better. I was apprehensive of seeing Benjaya but I decided to do that and found it positive. He was a shell. He had gone. Okay, I can rationalise that all this was to some good purpose but then, when I start questioning that rationalisation, questions are still left. Why? Why that child? Why, when three people lived such a good way of life and gave so much, does their reward appear so negative?

The aftermath of death affects people in such different ways. If you had needed to grieve in the same way as I had when you returned home, I might have been stronger than you by then and in a better position to support you, but that wasn't the way it was. You didn't seem to need that, you had another form of strength which didn't seem to have anything to do with time, as if you were holding something together at another level that I just wasn't experiencing. I couldn't understand what was happening for you; my grief seemed so necessary, unavoidable for me.

I haven't felt any contact with Benjaya since that first time. Now he's a memory, a vibration that can be retained in the mind but he's changed... gone... flowed away. He will remain like a photograph on the wall of my mind except that it's more like a video; it isn't and wasn't ever static. Benjaya probably made an impact on everyone he touched. He came in with an impact and he went out with an impact and there were all those bits in between.

Charlotte's Story

Early that Saturday I was snoozing away down at *Sunfields*[1] when I was woken up by a knock on the door. I looked out of the window and saw Dad's car - very strange! Then I found Dad on the doorstep in a very dishevelled state. I didn't even let him in at first, I just stood there knowing something was wrong and thinking 'Something's happened to mum'. He came in and sat on the bed and told me: "Something terrible's happened. Benjaya's died" and then we just cried. I didn't know what to say, there was nothing there in words.

Dad went back home and I found Marc at a friend's flat and told him the news pretty much in the way Dad had told me. It was a split second decision to call Sandra and get in the car and GO!

I was upset and nervous about seeing Carmella and Abe because I thought that was going to be the most awful thing, seeing them in whatever state they were in, not knowing how to deal with *that*, whatever it was but I wasn't thinking of Benjy at all! There was no sadness there for Benjy, that he had lost his life; now there's an interesting thought.

It was a good feeling when Carmella opened the door and said: "So family are here again" or words to that effect. They told us the gist of what had happened and I just let the tears flood down my face. Being there was the major thing. I just needed to be there and cry. We had about an hour crying, talking, laughing... Carmella was laughing as well. It was family humour that lifted us if only for two or three seconds.

Then Abe's parents arrived and wanted to know all the details, asking questions that would never have crossed my mind. They focused on going back over the event rather than being in what was happening now. The socialisation bit crossed my mind, the track that says 'somebody's died... it's a catastrophe... such a young boy... what a shame...' but

---

[1]*Sunfields Children's Home* where Charlotte worked and 'lived in'.

it just didn't sit with me. It was only the pain of what he had left behind for Carmella and Abe. Maybe that's because of my belief that he isn't 'lost', that he's just gone on to another place.

When we all went to the hospital. I was a bit uneasy about the children skipping along as if they were on the way to the park but we were in and out of a joking mood because we were getting nervous and apprehensive. A nurse showed us the way and asked: "Are the children going in as well?" Carmella answered "Yes". The nurse, in a bit of a snirpy way, as if she disapproved said: "If that's your wish". Carmella wouldn't let that go. She came back with "No, it's not my wish, it's *their* wish". When the nurse said "Well, I'm not sure about that" I thought, 'take a deep breath' because I might just have had to say something and that would have been a trial! She was just being a normal person, anxious about the effect it might have on the children, but she was getting in the way. Anyway, it was soon sorted out.

We each took our own time going in, doing whatever felt right for us. Abe cut a lock from Benjaya's hair and I stood looking at him and had another cry again. For the first time I think the children really realised what had happened and I was relieved that they cried then as well. I'd expected to see Benjy with his shiny hair falling forwards and rosy cheeks and I didn't like the way his hair was brushed back and he looked as if he had eye-liner on which was kind of unnatural. That took a bit of getting to grips with so I just sat on the floor with my tissues.

I cried all the way back home. Stupid things kept running through my head like 'what shall I write in my diary today?' I felt very, very sad... exhausted. Then, when I arrived home the sadness just lifted. The tears were over and I couldn't have cried if I'd wanted to. I had a drink with Marc and could tell people 'Benjaya's died'. Everybody knew him, or knew about him of course because of all the birth publicity. One friend, Isabelle, was just wonderful and she called me every day to see how I was and support me. I needed that. She talked openly, not pussyfooting around avoiding the subject. I needed to talk but not to be whispered to. We decided Benjy had most likely been taken off to do something more important.

I took a week off work and moved back home to be with Dad and Marc. I didn't want to work because I didn't want to *be* anything. I wanted to float along for a bit. I certainly couldn't concentrate and had a low tolerance level. I forgot to do the things that I do every day of the week,

like feeding my horses. I didn't even see them for two days! And I did
things like driving round the ring road three times, forgetting to get off,
going up the 'down' track in the multi-storey car park. I'm not sure how
safe it was to be driving really. It was a strange week.

Then came Benjy's Celebration and I didn't particularly want to go
but I couldn't possibly not have gone because that the way we do things,
as a family. The Celebration was similar to Abel and Carmella's wedding.
I didn't cry at all and it was fine Benjy being there. Nothing was difficult
for me because I haven't got anything to compare it to. The children all
being there was good, they just shared the celebratory atmosphere, the
chanting, the candles, it was just perfect. But I didn't think you should
handle the cremation by yourself and I thought you should have some
support and knew that I could give it, probably better than anyone else. It
was sad his little body being burnt and weird that I was the only one in the
congregation but it was a relief that all those people were not there. I was
glad it was quiet, contained, focused and special in its own way. I enjoyed
putting the petals on the coffin... the last act.

It's completed now for Benjaya and I think for me too but not for
Carmella and Abe. It's given me insight into what death is like for those
left behind. That's the main thing - insight. I am more aware. If I could
deal with every death in this way I'd be all right.

Marc's Story

I'd been out to a party and was catching a couple of hour's sleep at Phil's
flat when there was an almighty banging on the door and Charlotte came
charging straight in and said: "Something terrible's happened, Benjy's
drowned". I've got a couple of friends called Ben and it just didn't
connect who she was talking about. When it sank in it was a question of
'Oh God! What do I do now?' It was a 'do' feeling straight away -
immediate action, frantic phone calls to Sandra and Carmella. I knew I
had to get Sandra and Charlotte there and be there myself and *do*
something... *anything.*

I saw Dad first. He was dressed for his best man duties, just standing
in the lounge, immaculate as you'd imagine but with a face that said 'How
do I do this?' The only advice I could give was "Don't tell anybody, just
front the day, then you won't have to cope with anybody else".

We collected Sandra, who was bringing Josh and Amy, and it felt we were together as a unit, nobody was crumbling, crying a bit but staying with it and I know I just wasn't allowing the emotions any space. When we got there about one o'clock nobody wanted to go to the front door first. I was the worst! I snook in the back, then it was okay; well, better than I had thought it might be. There were people there already serving and I was thinking 'oh dear, there's nothing to *do* because there's people doing it and I've got to sit on this settee!' Then a car needed fetching from the workshop and I leapt up fast!

I had no intention of seeing Benjy but some doors were left open and there he was. I was standing there and he was lying there. When you've done it, you've done it... you've broken the illusion. The last mental picture you're holding, whatever it is, has gone... and this becomes the last.

I was just not working on an emotional level. It was as if I totally shut down every emotional response because I was determined to keep going. I saw my role as a worker; there were others there who were the emotional support. I would do anything, drive everybody about and get them all home again. I was thinking 'Charl can do the crying, Sandra is the mothering image, and I'll keep it all together on a practical level.' It doesn't mean my emotions don't exist. I just had them all later on when I had finished!

When we were all back home, Charl and me went to the pub and ordered two large vodkas and an ambulance in half an hour! Then we went our separate ways and about ten o'clock I totally flipped out and threw a massive tantrum, hurled a glass up the wall... shouting... yelling... I don't know what words, it was just sound really - 'it isn't fair' and so on, the sort of typical things people do and say. But there was a part of me that knew I didn't need to do this. It was really weird. A friend found me in the park and took me back home. I was relatively okay after that.

When it came close to going to Benjy's Celebration I was certain I didn't need to go for myself. I was asking myself 'what's the reason for me to go?' I was putting all these doubts out and I got the answer. Thursday afternoon an ex-girl-friend told me she had had a miscarriage with my child about a year previously, when we had been living together. She had never told me she was pregnant; there were reasons for that then but I couldn't believe she'd just let it out like that. What timing! Talking about death had triggered it, I suppose. I sat there not speaking, trying to take it in, feeling it was the worst day of my life. Now I'd got a reason for going to the funeral. It was to shed tears for a child I'd never even known existed, to give it recognition. So that's what I did and it was brilliant because I knew I was there putting out all my own feelings for that soul that might have made it here, all mixed up with trying to imagine what it might be like having a child of my own. I know that if I'd ever had any sort of ceremony for my child it could never have reached the heights that Benjy's did. I knew the energy could never have been higher no matter what had happened, so I just shared it, telling myself that I'd been able to give my child the best send off that it could ever have been given without Abel and Carmella needing to know what they were doing for me.

Time was irrelevant. I couldn't have given any recognition before because I didn't even know about it, which in a way was the hardest part to take. But I knew I couldn't have dealt with it, acknowledged it this way eighteen months ago. I wondered whether I should say something when people were making speeches but I don't think I would have handled it very well and it was a private thing. It was Benjy's day anyway, as far as people were aware. In my way it was all done and dusted, it was like clearing my conscience as well. It was tricky holding it all together, not so much on the emotional level but on a higher level, which was the state I decided was the right place to be.

What was that word we used on MetaCentre workshops? 'Bucketing', that's it! Looking back on it now, that first Saturday when I went to Carmella's, I just filled up my emotional bucket and on the night I emptied it all over the place. That's why I didn't want to go back to the Celebration because I'd thought my bucket was empty and I didn't want it filled up again. But it was totally the reverse. My bucket had suddenly got filled up... I had loads of stuff to deal with and I had to go back to empty it! I'd found an old pattern still running, the bucketing, letting out all that emotional stuff in a crazy way and I so disliked it that I decided I wasn't going to do that again, ever.

Sandra's Story

On the Wednesday after Carmella found she was pregnant, she happened to be coming to see me. Benjaya was bubbling with the secret and when we went out to the park he couldn't hold it another minute. I bent down and he whispered in my ear "Mummy's having a baby". I played out falling over in surprise and he loved it. I think he'd come that day to connect me to this new life that he already loved so much and to say 'good-bye' to us. He'd left everything neat and tidy, completed. That is my last live memory of him.

Two days later the news came in. We heard the telephone ring. Clive got up and answered it and Carmella told him. He came straight upstairs and said: "You'd better get up", putting on his clothes, which was unusual at half-past seven on a Saturday morning. When Carmella said that Benjy had gone in the river my brain just balked. I couldn't digest it, the tears started to flow and it went from there. Minutes later there was another phone call telling Clive of the death of his mother's younger sister, so all his family would be in mourning as well. We woke Josh and Amy and told them and they sat, stony faced, Amy with silent tears trickling down, no questions, no-one talked. I knew when Marc phoned that I wanted to be there and so did the children.

We travelled down to Devon more or less in silence. My heart went straight out to them. I was so aware how lovely the little house was, how warm and cocooned it was there, how safe it felt and what a right place it was to be in such a situation. Being there was an important part of the healing, of facing things and being right in the emotions of that day. Abel and Carmella were centred and communicative but we could all share the suffering and wept for one another and for our loss. We were trying to come to grips with something we knew at a mental level but it was hard to believe that Benj would not be back.

Josh and Amy wanted to go with the others to see Benjy in the hospital so I went along to be with them. After the nurse found she couldn't stop them going in she had begun to try to prepare them, telling them they were going to see a dead body but that the child wasn't inside! It was all too clumsy and obvious. I wanted to say 'they're aware, they're dealing with it, they're fine!' Their energy was being held back and it was unnecessary. Death flows. You don't need to stop, to analyse, you need to flow with it, to be with the feelings of the moment. You don't need the stilted break of stopping for other people's explanations. Yes, they did get a bit wobbly, of course they did, but they dealt with it extremely well and didn't want to leave him. They wanted to be at his side so why should I impose restrictions?

I was aware of Abel trying to put over his feelings about what he thought was happening to Benj and his beliefs about death to his sister. It was amazing that he could be so expressive of his own emotions and at the same time still want to give in that way.

The way Benjy was presented he could have been a painting or a wax model - there was no real connection to 'the boy'. It was as if a plaster cast had been made but I could stroke and touch him and speak to him easily.

We went back to Carmella's and I felt everything was under control. Carmella knew what she had to do and was doing it, passing out powerful messages through the grief. She was strong in the belief that there was a purpose to all of this. That day it felt as if the whole house was in tune with Benjaya - his little coat on the hook, things he'd collected and made, his pictures, the flowers. It was so right to be in that atmosphere that was really attuned to the vibration that he expressed.

We'd talked together about you being in India. On one level it wasn't at all surprising that you'd gone to your most sacred place, where I knew you would be in a very high space. We even thought that in some way you would 'know' what was happening before the news reached you but, because you weren't there, as the oldest I felt responsible for seeing everything was okay and in some strange way I felt that it was and we could go home.

That night I thought I'd never sleep. My eyes were sore and I'd been feeling sick all day. Clive was awake all night but I slept like a log. I felt so much for Clive and for father because they hadn't seen things face to face and I wondered how they would work through their emotions. I've been through the horrors of a mother when a child's not home when he should be, the hours and the anguish, but Benj, he's such a little flibbertigibbet I couldn't believe anything bad could happen to him. In my mind I could only see him floating off gently somewhere and couldn't get into other possibilities.

I woke up Sunday without a trace of emotion. I felt as if I'd woken like Sleeping Beauty, years later, and it was a very distant memory, a transportation through time. It had all worked through in the night. I'd transcended my emotions. There was still an aching pain for Abel and Carmella but for Benj, nothing. He was fine. I couldn't believe this had happened so quickly. I'd thought these emotions would keep rearing up, searing through everything. What is more, it was Joshua's birthday. The children didn't want to go out and we were having dinner at home. As soon as my mind was settled on the cooking, in flooded Benjaya's energy which I was absolutely unprepared for. I had been reorganising my calendar so that I would have space on Monday to sit and do a little ritual to connect to him but he wasn't going to wait that long! I was calculating 'on the third day he rose again' and had calculated from the Friday afternoon. He counted Friday in, obviously!

It's hard to explain this bit, this feeling of being flooded by a higher, radiant light. It was exactly like when I was carrying my fourth child, Luke, who miscarried. He was an exquisite light energy which made me feel radiant, really in the moment and filled with joy. I thought 'Oh no, this is just the same as Luke, how am I going to tell these two apart?' As if to answer the question, I had the distinct impression of Benjaya 'the boy' plonking himself down, elbows on the table, legs swinging, in his place where he always sat. It was extremely real to me. We sang 'Happy Birthday' to Joshua and 'Happy Birthday' to Benj and lit the 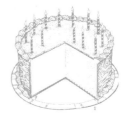 candles for both. That was just lovely and a fine thing to do and the world was beautiful. We were all at home, a splendid place and Benjaya was here with us, loving to be here as he always did and in a high radiant energy.

It was obvious to me that Benjaya had chosen to go the way that he went. The way that he was born and the way he went were so similar in pattern that it *had* to be a design. All you can do is accept it. Carmella had learnt of his death in Newton Abbot where we had lived for three years, where Luke was conceived and died. What does it all mean? I don't know but it leaves me with a feeling of a plan that was designed a long time ago.

Clive took a week off work to go down to Exeter to be with his family as he'd been close to his aunt so we were within ten miles of Carmella that following week. We spent two days together on the Wednesday and Friday and it surprised me that I could clear out Abel's car of Benj's books and lunch box with half eaten food without any effects. The day in between was the aunt's funeral, traditional, all black and there was a lot of distress around. No-one wanted to take their children and Josh and Amy had no interest in it so I looked after all the nine family children that day. On the Friday, after seeing Benjaya, I walked with Carmella along the river where we dabbed water on our heads, found a yellow ribbon lying in the grass and tied it to a tree to remember John McCarthy and Benj, things that 'should' have been painful but were not in that lighter energy. Carmella was normal, sisterly, chatting, going to the leisure centre and the market, eating choc ices. It was the day before the Celebration and I could sense the energies really rising then; from Sunday they had been rising all week and we could just step into that flow.

I'd not connected to the word 'funeral' for Benj and I'd been calling the Celebration 'the wedding'. It seemed like a slip of the tongue but I was constantly being reminded in so many ways of Carmella and Abel's wedding. No wonder we could feel so happy, it was a wedding kind of happiness and other people were getting the same feeling. Part of the union for me was of Benjaya and Luke. I had this deep feeling that they were together and would work together in some way, her son and my son. The other bigger part was that Benjaya had gone 'home' and he was uniting with all those 'people', those wonderful light beings who were there. I wasn't looking for a saying 'goodbye' event, I wanted to celebrate with him, knowing the energies would be built up to reflect his amazing new state. And they were. Family, friends, all of us were the body of that upliftment pushing the energy up to some extraordinary, greater level than usual. I felt other people's emotions drifting past but I didn't 'catch' them. During the whole of that first week I had felt that there was something like a muslin-type canopy over me, something light above my head that seemed to be protecting me from the swirling energies.

Death is not wrapped in itself and stagnated. It is a gateway that opens up to something wondrous and can take you there if you let it, if you don't allow it to stagnate you in the grief. You can build on death the same as you can build on birth and marriage and other events we celebrate. Knowing the energy that was produced by the birth, we expected that at the wedding and we got it. Knowing the pattern, because we'd experienced it, we expected it of death as well. If people want to create alternative types of ceremonies then I would support that wholeheartedly but I think they would need to be sensitive to the energy of what they are creating and to sound the right note... a high note. I've used Carmella's name all the way through but I am conscious of Abel just as much. Abel has his part to play as the rod and backbone. He is very practical and supportive and *with* Carmella but I think she is the one who knows the note, sets it running and ensures everybody else knows it!

It seems to me to be Carmella's task to act in public, part of the design for her life. She delivers big images, prototypes of birth... of marriage... of death but she is doing her own thing, not what is the norm. She did it at the birth, which is for most people a very personal time and she laid out naked across the newspapers. She had put herself out there again on the front line at death, another personal time, to demonstrate... to demonstrate what? **Death in its purest form I think.**

M'haletta

How much learning lies within the gamut of family experiences if only we take the time and care to unlock it and listen sensitively to each other. These then were some of the pieces of the jigsaw of their experiences that surfaced in the weeks following Benjaya's death. Other insights were to follow in random conversations and at the most unexpected times when triggers touched a chord in their memories. It was several months later, after I had finished compiling the contributions of dozens of people, that my mind released a memory blockage that had obviously been there for over four years.

One evening, sitting by the fireside, a memory door opened of its own accord relating to an event that had occurred in August 1987. The room where I write is called the Lotus Room. Situated on the top floor of the house, it had become my safe, creative, free space in this busy household. The memory was of three days that I had spent in the Lotus room when I had felt myself to be living in some other extraordinary reality.

The sequence of events began with a phone call to Carmella and Abel from London asking them to appear on Breakfast Television the next morning with Michel Odent, the French specialist on waterbirth. Normally I would have been sharing their excitement, helping perhaps with their fast exit, but that night I felt distanced from it all, a feeling that remained on waking. I watched the early morning programme which was live. There was Carmella, looking beautiful and composed with nine-month-old Benjaya sitting on her knee and behaving perfectly for the cameras. I listened to Carmella speaking of Benjaya's birth and in that moment I experienced his death. I could see him on the screen and knew him to be alive and well and yet my whole being was responding, reacting, as if I was receiving news of his death. A cloak of enveloping sadness overwhelmed me and a grief took hold of me like no grief I had ever known before. I was devastated, immobilised by a trauma that no-one else could see or comprehend. For three days I simply stayed in the Lotus room, often weeping uncontrollably, unable to eat, to function or communicate rationally and on the carpet I could 'see' the body of a dead child. It is one thing to have occasional flashes of foresight in writing or vision but to experience a human reaction to an event that is obviously not occurring in the present reality is a challenge to the mind's stability.

My only relief was to write and I poured out words describing my inner experiences in my journal. When that memory surfaced I was amazed to realise how deeply it had been buried in my subconscious for so long and that throughout all the period of my presentiment of impending death I had not for a moment made any conscious connection to this experience. In retrieving it I did not have to rely on memory alone, the detailed pages of journal entries made extraordinary reading four years on and sparked a wealth of questions.

Is it possible that we can experience events out of time sequence and react to those events as if they are happening in the present? If so, could that account for some forms of mental instability? Was going through this pre-reaction to Benjaya's physical death helpful to me when it eventually happened, making it easier to move into a higher state of mental functioning because I had already released a reservoir of human emotion? Did such an experience free me in some way to move with Benjaya during his transition? Why did I slip into this all-knowing reality at that particular moment when he was visible to millions of people? If all of this happened only on the screen of the mind rather than in concrete reality, does that in any way negate or diminish the reality of that experience if behaviour is changed by it, learning results from it and strength is gained from it?

I had been rocked then to the core and the agony of loss had been real within the spectrum of my experience. I have no expectation whatsoever that I will experience advance notice of any other momentous events in our family life and have no desire to do so, but if that is what the Book of the Universe offers to me then I shall read it and write a response!

CHAPTER NINETEEN

Ripples of Death

Carmella

T
he ripple effect from Benjaya's death and the Celebration/ Funeral event spread wider than we could ever have imagined, causing floods of insight to emerge from the pain and sweeping away many entrenched concepts of death. I marvel that one small boy fell into the river and countless lives have been changed, some enriched beyond measure.

No doubt death, especially unexpected death, always affects many people deeply but the question that fascinates me is: **What is the secret that allows the 'tragic' to become transformative?** It was a combination of the hundreds of letters and supportive phone calls we received, plus the in-depth interviews conducted by M'haletta, that allowed us to glimpse some answers to this question.

The children have proved to be my greatest teachers with their fresh, innocent eyes and their air of accepting grace. They seem eager and ready to absorb images and experiences presented by their surrounding world. They are usually intensely curious, highly impressionable and especially open to receiving the attitudes, fears and joys of adults whom they trust. If we, their mentors, can **courageously grasp the challenge of dealing with our own fear of death positively, then the next generation will be free of the deep-seated taboos around our earthly finale** which hinder our full expression of life. The following excerpts from interviews with parents who faced Benjaya's death with their children reveal the depth of their insight.

Juliet Crittenden (Parent at Steiner School)

I have two children, Josie 10 and Mickaela 7, who attended the school Ceremony in memory of Benjaya. On the way home in the car I overheard them talking with their friend Ondine about Carmella. They had obviously been very impressed as they were repeating what she had said word for word. They were quiet and reflective.

On the following Saturday we all went to help decorate the hall and they had lots of time to pay attention to what Carmella was doing. They were particularly drawn to a table she was creating with all Benjaya's special things and to this day they can probably tell me every single thing that was on the table. I'm so surprised at this detail of memory seven weeks on.

They were very aware that the sword and shield went in the coffin with him and thought this was a great thing to be taking on his journey. They remember all the stories from the Celebration and all the songs which they had never heard before and talk about it all so much. What impressed them most was the way Benjaya had asked his Granny for the shells with Gods on because he wanted them for his journey and they naturally assumed that he didn't have to ask her physically. It was obvious to them that he knew he was going to die and told me that of course he didn't want to go swimming on that Sunday, he wanted to die in a much more beautiful place.

My children didn't even know Benjaya but they came home after that Celebration saying: "Mummy, we feel we really know him. We know him in death." It was as if they had found a new friend, a new relationship that meant a lot to them. For weeks afterwards we sang 'Benjaya's songs' in the car going to school and the Celebration carried on and on. They even kept on repeating his name...BENJAYA...BENJAYA, as if exploring the quality of it. They discussed him with every friend that came to the house:

"Have you ever seen a dead person?"

"No"

"We have"

"What was it like?"

"Well, we saw Benjaya. We touched his hair and it was soft, he was cold and he looked as if he had blue lipstick on. He had a bump on the back of his head and was in a little coffin wearing a snowman jumper..."

Over and over they shared their memories offering images of death that were gentle and sensitive. Death is now something they can connect with as they have something tangible as a reference point. It's not something to be afraid of, it is something ordinary and at the same time extraordinary. It has become an accepted part of life.

My father died seven years ago on the operating table and although he wanted to die, he was very afraid. I could feel him sweating with the fear of death and although I did not understand it I took it on myself as if it had projected into me. Now I can build my own perceptions of death and my feelings have changed. What I witnessed at Benjaya's death Celebration rang a bell for me and I thought 'Yes, I really know this!' Death will now bring with it different triggers to that appalling fear that I might have held onto, carried with me and even passed on to my children.

Lizzie Hubbard (close friend)

My daughter Meriel, who is four, was a good friend of Benjaya's. I heard the news on the evening of his death and was absolutely horrified. I couldn't process this information and couldn't imagine how I would tell Meriel.

I told her the next morning. I just held her in my arms hoping to find the right words and she just lay there with her eyes wide open and staring. Her process has been really traumatic. What I recognise now is that she went into shock. I thought she was coping and I kept saying things to get some reaction but there wasn't any. Then she went to three different places to see good friends and at each place she suddenly went wide eyed, stopped, turned cold and got very upset.

About a week after that I began to recognise the extent of the shock. She didn't want to go out, lost all creativity, couldn't do anything for herself, didn't want to go upstairs to bed and I didn't know how to handle this process. She was vulnerable and tearful and I felt distressed and suffocated because I had Benjamin just a few weeks old and Meriel had suddenly become like an insecure two-year old. Then she started to ask some pertinent questions like "Did Benjy want to fall into the river?" I explained that Benjaya didn't need his body any more and that it was time to move on because he'd learnt all his lessons. Then I gulped because I thought 'Oh, now she's going to be afraid to learn any lessons because she'll think she has to die when she gets them right!'

She woke me up once in the middle of the night and asked: "Did Benj's body be taken to the ham shop?" I thought 'My God, this child is having to process all these macabre ideas. She doesn't even know what's sold in a butcher's and is imagining his body being chopped up.' I was astonished and wondered what else might be in her thoughts that she couldn't find words to express.

Then one morning she was smiling again and said "I'm not thinking of anything, not even Benjaya". That was the beginning of her recovery. It has been huge and what shocked me most was that she had obviously been processing this for a long time before I realised what was going on. Now she talks about him in a wistful sort of way and when Carmella asked if she would like to visit again her eyes lit up. There was so much love shared between those children in the context of play and there was a loss for her that needed to be recognised, lived with and worked through.

When Meriel went through feeling so afraid when we were out of sight and I said: "I'm only in another room," I realised that death is rather like that. I firmly believe we do go on.

Liz Giles (Parent at Steiner School)

I'm forty-two, with five children ranging between five and twelve. My youngest son Corin was in the kindergarten with Benjaya.

The explosive news was passed through a telephone tree. The class parents all phoned the next person on the list. When I heard, something between my heart and my head stopped working and I couldn't speak. Benjaya was a child I had singled out at kindergarten as an incredibly beautiful child who clearly was master of himself. I had thought that a lot of care must have gone into this child. I couldn't cry until the ceremony at the school a few days later which I found extremely moving.

Then we received the invitation to a blessing on Benjaya's life and I knew that I must take my children and go. By this time they had started to ask all kinds of practical questions about death such as: "Where's his body going? Can he see us now? Can I talk to him and will he talk back?" I had to move into intuitive answers and found myself answering: "Yes, you can talk to Benjaya and yes, he will answer if you listen carefully". This tested me because I'd never had to deal with these things before. I am so aware that we are very celebratory about birth but rather closed about death so here it seemed was a chance to face death.

We all put on smart clothes but did not feel that we had to wear the old statutory black. I found it an extraordinary event. There was a busy humming buzz when we arrived and those women for whom emotions run like a torrent were crying but I didn't feel like that. I held Corin's hand, kept the children close by and found us a row of seats near the front. The hall had been laid out with full recognition of Benjaya's life and he was so there.

The children sat for two hours, still, entranced but also eager for the moment they could see Benjaya. That was what they had been waiting for and a big test for me as for the first time in my life I was to see a dead body. It's incredible that we live in such a society where death has been so hidden. So there was a fleeting moment of dread but Corin eagerly tugged my hand saying: "Come on Mummy, we can *see* Benjaya".

So, led by Corin, I went and there was Benjaya looking totally beautiful with children tussling his hair. Again a torrent of questions began from the children which I answered intuitively and then we just gazed at him for a long time as if in meditation. I noticed that this is when the men were moved to tears - when they were faced with the reality of the loss of physical movement, the loss of the physical form. I also noticed that the parents who seemed to be afraid were transmitting that fear to their children, but if you let your children lead you and are able to be clear yourself then it is fine.

The Celebration changed my life and my understanding of my children's needs. It is so easy to get caught up in all the material things of life - mortgages, bills, cars that go wrong - and acknowledging death gives the opportunity to put things in perspective. The recognition that we are more than just a physical body is necessary for my children's education, for their future. I used to feel hollow inside but Benjaya's death has touched me with a magic wand, opening up deeper channels of my being which will not only affect my children but everyone I touch upon.

Carmella

We obviously carry a vast responsibility to set a positive behaviour pattern before the children and teach by our example - the second Education for Life principle - but as I see it that is only half of the story. The first of the principles states 'BANISH ALL THOUGHTS THAT SEPARATE ADULT FROM CHILD and put one above the other. Recognise the pure, simple and unadulterated wisdom of a child and be open to learning as much as you can teach.' **Perhaps if the children feel truly heard and**

respected they will learn to respect their own intuitive knowing and ignore our emotional wobbles that do not fit with their truth.

Sharon Patel

Just before Benjaya came to visit us two days before he died, Nikhil who's four, had been almost obsessed with water. He played in the sink and in the bath with his little wooden dolls, drowning them and then bringing them back to life. He's never played a game like that before and he's not played it since. Then a couple of days ago he started singing 'Spread your Rainbow Wings' which Girish and I sang at the Celebration and have not sung again. Nikhil wasn't there. I said to him "Where did you learn that song?" and he said "It just was".

We were really upset about Benjaya's death but Nikhil didn't pick up on our grief at all. When we told him he didn't seem that bothered and said "That's all right, it doesn't matter".

Clio Wondrausch

Two days after the Celebration I awoke and lay in bed with a clarity of consciousness that is a rare gift to me. I must have lain there for two hours or so, clearly looking at the present issues in my life. I felt I was being given very caring and wise sort of objective oversight of what I was looking at.

When I finished my meditation, Sol, who is three, and was sitting on my lap, told me that he had dreamed that Benjaya was alive again and that he came here on his own and he and I were talking and listening to each other. When I asked him what we were saying, whether is was night or day happy or sad, he just said "It was when the morning owls[1] came".

Carmella

The three most common keys that helped people shift into a constructive, loving consciousness around Benjaya's death were these:
1) The closer anyone ventured into the eye of the hurricane the more healing they received.

---

[1] If Benjaya were to pick a symbol for himself it might well be the owl. He loved owls and knew the name of every owl in our bird book by the time he could speak.

2) **A safe space to encourage expression of any rising emotion was immensely therapeutic.**
3) **Seeing the body was a vital part of the process.**

Arabella, a close friend, addressed all three in her interview and speaks for many others.

Arabella Marshall

Julian and I went to see Abel and Carmella two hours after we heard the news. Julian went in the car but I decided to walk. As I neared the front door I was feeling that I just couldn't go into that place where they were going to be with their unbearable grief. I did go in and was relieved they were in their intense grief, really crying and being in it but it *was* bearable. Carmella was even wearing something colourful. I found in those early days that I wanted to be with them almost all of the time and although I wasn't there often, every time I saw them it made the process easier for me. When I was away I was imagining what might be going on for them but confusing that with my own feelings and process of grieving. It is so easy to project our feeling onto others...

It was the most beautiful 'funeral' I have ever been to. It was different because there was a quality of giving space to everything which fulfilled all our needs. It was okay to be alone, to support, to love, to cry, to be. There was space for all of us to be there in any way we wanted to be, just as there was at their home...

I was clear that I wasn't going to go and see Benj's body but when I saw all these people going up I began to feel quite wobbly about my decision. Then Solomon, my one-year-old, yanked me up the steps onto the stage. I held somebody's hand and was just completely broken apart. He just didn't look dead, he was glowing and I hadn't expected that. I cried very deeply...but I have to recognise that this death is bringing up all I have been avoiding about death and I think that, because of this, a lot will become clearer.

Carmella

Kitty was the one who spent most time in the eye of the hurricane with us. This touching letter is a testimony to her transformative process.

Dear Carmella and Abel,

This morning I felt blessed by the circle of golden light that was coming through the curtains of my hush-darkened room. I can feel a subtle change in every cell, every molecule inside me. I feel indefinably bigger, perhaps greater. My heart holds the pain of heartache yet it is like a growing pain. My heart feels larger and my whole chest area feels dynamically re-arranged. The words 'larger than life' come to mind. My body is letting me know that I am utterly changed.

The curtains opened, the soft warm sun is streaming through opened windows. The world is an orchestra of birdsong. Jubilate Deo, Alleluia! I came home from yesterday's Celebration of Benjaya feeling completely new. I believe that death knocks you into a profound space and in the whirlwind of the Ceremony I went further into that space. I feel such deep love for you that transcends the chatter about differences between us. A love expanded with honour, respect and gratitude that I have been allowed to share something so personal and precious, just like a birth.

The last week began early on the Saturday morning for me when you invited me on a deep journey. You made an easy space for me to move in alongside you - the two of you as you dipped and soared on your own journeys. Perhaps my journey is the journey of my heart. Living this week, I have been through a drowning - I am a little afraid of using that word lightly. Some part of me that I cannot define seems gone at this moment and I am here unclothed in my newness. Thank you and thank you Benjaya from all my heart. I keep feeling that he has given us the greatest gift of all. Oh, more tears for me now.

I also realise that there are times when the notion that this event could be a gift will seem like such empty, insensitive words. How could it be a gift? Yet I feel gifted by this experience and yet would give it all up in an instant if that would bring him back. Seeing his body and touching him was a very tender offering that you gave openly to everyone. Thank you. Each person there in the village hall was there with their feelings, which feels like each were supported to give their own tender offering.

I am grateful to have been part of your support team and for you two both supporting me with the safety and freedom to give birth to whatever way the energy was flowing. Yesterday we needed some clouds

and rain as well as those bright spurts of sunlight. The liquid weather
makes easy the way of liquid emotions. And today the blessing of the
sun. Is it an ascension?
Jubilate Deo
God Bless you both
Kitty

Carmella

One of the effects of facing death head on was a sense of recognition of
our sameness. For me this feeling surfaced as I identified with all the
peoples of the world who are in pain - any pain. I cried for my own loss
but my heart felt wrenched apart by the thought of all the
millions who suffer equal or greater pain than me...daily. I began to realise
that I was lucky to have an emotional pain that was general
knowledge locally. **What about all those who look completely normal**
but whose hearts are breaking for one reason or another? Never again
will I not care because I don't know. I will treat people as if they could
have a well-spring of hidden pain.

People all around us seemed to be breaking into new levels of
awareness which lifted that which keeps us in our own separate worlds
and allowed us to reach levels of rapport hitherto untapped. Maybe the
realisation of 'There but for the Grace of God go I' had something to do
with this. Whatever the reason, I have to say that I revelled in this rare
opportunity to live in a reality free of judgements and petty behaviours
and am convinced that a great deal of **the strength Abel and I felt has**
come from opening wide to the massive inflow of love and prayers
initiated by our loss. This was no doubt increased a hundredfold by
energies streaming in from higher sources which we were consciously
invoking. I assume that had we taken the route of bitterness and self-pity,
we would have blocked receipt of this supportive force because surely **we**
cannot receive when we are closed and focused inwards.

Our friends were experiencing this state of non-separation in
different ways. Julian and Arabella Marshall share their personal
experience in this area followed by another close friend, Alice, who takes
this concept to even wider realms of possibility.

Julian Marshall

When this shocking news came through it was like a thunderbolt out of the blue and I realised I'd been in touch with superficial stuff, judgements, etc. about Benjaya which were now totally unimportant. I felt as if we all had positions, defensiveness about who we were and what we were doing in the world but very easily, through this amazing event, a whole lot which has kept us from being really close has been swept away. It feels like when the country suddenly goes to war - all the crap is cut and you get down to love, support and compassion. I am aware that Benjaya is teaching this community something very real.

Arabella

One thing that I have been aware of is that their loss is our loss because we are all parents and Benjaya is 'our son'. There is no separation between us. It came up the other day when Lizzie asked me to be Godmother to Benjamin and initially I wasn't sure. I was writing them a letter to say I didn't want to be Godmother and then I realised that actually I am committed to every being that is born but I'm normally not in touch with that commitment. If I was then life would probably be too painful.

Alice Friend

We talk about Greek and Egyptian myths but we have our own myths right now. The story of Benjaya is as important as those myths. Carmella had to be away when Benjaya died and in myths the mother has to turn her back on her sons. It is a symbol of something that the primitive people know and they go through immense rites which we have lost in our society. If Carmella had known that this was going to happen she would never have gone away, so the Gods set it up that she was turning her back.

We have to look at ourselves as women, at how we keep rescuing, keep preventing death. Now women are supposed to give birth but the shivic part of woman is death. We die when we have our period. It is a death process and there is no place in our society for those kinds of things.

I keep thinking of the image of Carmella going away on the train, leaving her son in the hands of the father and her son telling her in many ways that he was going to die but her consciousness not being able to receive that because if she did she would have been there to rescue him. Men and boys cannot be rescued any more by women. We are doing enormous harm by that. We have to let them feel their pain and give them space.

Society in general hasn't allowed itself to feel pain and so the whole of society has been built around pain being present but not allowing it to be real, to exist. So society fears the pain that is our blessing. I do not feel that around Benjaya's death which is why I am calling it a living myth. It has stretched my heart in a way that nothing else could...

There is always a sacrifice somewhere, sacrifice of the purest part so that the purest part of us can be remembered. And a sacrifice is not a tragedy. The crucifixion of Christ was not a tragedy. It was the greatest gift - 'I die so you all can live'. And Benjaya's gift? I think he drowned so that we could all drown our lower selves and live within our hearts and souls honestly.

When I saw little Benj's body I couldn't take my eyes off him, his beauty was unbelievable. I thought he would start breathing again and because of that I was more aware of my breath and then became more aware of my hearing and my voice. But my most profound experience was of him using my eyes to view the garment he had just shed. It was at this point that I knew that he would always be inside me and everybody who is ready for that experience. His soul is not separate from mine and this non-separateness is one of the greatest feelings I've had about this whole death.

To be with Benjaya, Carmella and Abel on Sunday, the third day after his death, was an honour. The way that Carmella can go between her pain and her inner joys is unbelievable. The ice-cream van came around and she said:

"Oh, Benjy wanted an ice-cream from him the other day and I didn't give it to him."

So Rod ran out and bought us all ice-creams and with much frivolity we toasted Benjy, holding our cones up to heaven. No physical gift could ever be as honouring as being in the pain and the love and in the presence of a situation where there is no veil. There was no veil there between life and death, between pain and ecstasy - no separation.

Carmella

When there is a sense of rightness about an event then there is no resistance and **resistance is a major cause of pain**. Many of us were in touch with a sense of absolute rightness about Benjaya's death and it was primarily his exit through water which confirmed this feeling. Hand in hand with this sense of fate, some of us already carried **an innate trust in the perfection of life's gifts** (some would say the Divine Plan) which serves to propel us to search for the positive and naturally leads to a sense of gratitude for the growth that ensues. It is Polly's attitude of humility, of complete openness and willingness to learn from this life event that has inspired me to include her story. It is as if this quality of being the empty chalice allows learning that would be inperceptible to those who have too many fixed opinions.

Polly Ash

I have two children, Amelia aged six and Eliot aged four. In the summer of 1991, I came to Devon to find a home, a school and a new life. I was in my camper van on a camp site and saw a boy running about in the rain - enjoying himself whatever the weather. I later discovered that was Benjaya. In a 'chance' encounter in the laundry I met a woman who for some reason brought up the subject of schooling and I discovered that our children would be going to the same school. That was Carmella and she spoke about her little boy in such a profoundly loving way that I was envious and thought 'who is this child?'

When I met Carmella again at a Sai Baba group I was low in spirits but when we talked I knew that she would be an important person in my life. I felt that she would lift me up - that I could lean on her in some way. The children played together a couple of times and then that was it. Someone came to the door and told me that they had seen Benjaya's death reported in the paper.

A wave of total grief swept over me which I couldn't understand because I have been a casualty nurse and have dealt with death a lot and seen children die in various ways but nothing has ever touched me like this. I wondered if I could have been carrying some of Carmella's grief for her because it was her with whom I was identifying.

When I went to see Abel and Carmella it felt so good. In the middle of our talking and crying I said:

"Something really profound is happening here!"

I just knew I was supposed to be there. And again when I was at the school Ceremony and saw them standing on the steps, I had the powerful feeling that everything was absolutely right. This was meant to happen to Benjaya, to them, and I was meant to be standing there. I had exactly the same feeling after Amelia was born, when they told me that she was disabled, although I cried for the difficult life she had ahead.

I've become much more spiritual, more aware, since Sai Baba entered my life. At the Celebration of Benjaya's life there was a branch decorating the table at the front of the hall which held the picture of Benjaya with a white Indian garland around it. I watched this big solid branch as it began to shake about and when I looked around no-one else seemed to be noticing it. Then it stopped shaking and Benjaya's picture fell to the floor with the garland. I remember thinking 'There he is, Benjaya is here'. Carmella tried to stand it up again but it would not stand. I've heard of falling pictures and garlands at Sai Baba events - Baba plays little jokes out of a sense of fun. It was a sign for me that made me smile, especially knowing how much Benjaya loved Sai Baba.

I stood up and sang one of Baba's bhajans 'I am the light and the light is within me'. Once you feel part of the light you feel part of everybody. I changed the words from 'Sai Baba within' to 'Benjaya within'. I felt charged with energy that night, which was so beautiful and I walked out into the darkness feeling the light within. The memory will stay with me forever. I feel myself changing every day now.

All of this has given me reassurance of what I have read and what I believe in. I need reassurance because I am alone and striving. Carmella is standing up for what she believes in, putting her life out there to be shared and I am just learning about that. I wanted to have a waterbirth with my first child but allowed myself to be manipulated by the system into something else. Amelia had spina bifida so it wasn't meant to be, and with Eliot I allowed myself to be manipulated again because of the stigma of having had one disabled child. But now my path has met up with Carmella's and I am benefiting from her confidence.

Benjaya's death has helped me to come to terms with my husband leaving me. I spoke to him about it on the phone and he said "I'm really sorry" but he didn't get the point at all. The big lesson was that he was a father who had left his children and was gambling on their understanding when they get older. I told him:

*"Benjaya was here, he had wonderful parents who loved him and now he isn't here. **We have to live our lives NOW, be really with our children NOW. We can't gamble on the future.**"*

There is a lot of learning to do but I know there's something out there for me and I am on my way.

Carmella

The belief that death is the end of life in this body, rather than the end of life itself, is one that is comforting my family immensely. There must always be a gaping physical vacuum to come to terms with and the relationship can never be the same but if we are open to the possibility of the afterlife then we are open to the experience of an ongoing relationship on a level which can be fulfilling in its own special way and in our case, at times, mind-blowing.

It is not surprising to me that Benjaya has made his presence known since his death to M'haletta, myself and close family but I am staggered that he has 'appeared' to dozens of others of whom we are aware and, who knows, maybe countless more.

It is stories like Jan Perry's which prompt us to query the **phenomenal potential for expansion of spiritual awareness offered by the death transition.** I am left questioning if my son is omnipresent, appearing to all who call or need him, offering wisdom and tricks in heaven and on Earth.

M'haletta

Three events occurred in a short space of time about two months after Benjaya's death which both challenged and expanded my notions of reality. In each instance I was acutely aware of Benjaya's familiar life energy in different ways.

To pass waiting time in a crowded hospital, I was in a happy mood scribbling a few lines of a poem on the subject of grief when suddenly I sensed Benjaya beside me on an empty chair, swinging his legs and talking in his funny, wise old riddling way. I do not see any physical form, or even outline, it is purely a recognition of a vibration of energy.

For the next two hours I sat there writing, oblivious of everyone, forgotten by the nurses, as I tried to catch the drift of our silent, hilariously happy communication. This was not a surprise in one way, as when he had been in a physical body we had many conversations when he was not physically present, but it was a delight to know that this was still possible and in such a public place!

There had been little space for relaxation since his death until Derek and I went walking in Welsh mountains. It was a crisp spring day and into my free-flowing mood skipped Benjaya's energy again. It was the same exhilarating, darting vibration as it had been on our last outing together, when we had followed the course of his peat-brown river Avon on Dartmoor. His energy was almost tangible. I could tell where it was - moving ahead of me with a bubbling infectious joy. I was simply out for a walk with Derek ...and Benjaya. Derek was way ahead and my inner ear heard Benjaya calling

"Follow me...follow ME"

as he had done in his insistent way so many times before. My awareness was sharp and clear and was in no way the hazy longings of past memories.

Songs began to flow through my head that I had never heard before and I joined in, singing, striding and laughing, so aware of the orchestration of nature all around me. The rocks and rivers, grasses and trees all had sound. I felt myself flowing into this expansive inter-connected experience of being one with the natural world more completely than ever before. **Was *this* how Benjaya, how many of our children, experience Earth's reality** I wondered. I had a momentary understanding of how Nikhil could have known Benjaya's song...because 'it just was'.

The third experience that month was when I returned to Carmella's for a few days to record more interviews. On entering the house this time I had a strange feeling. A brown toy bear was sitting on the floor and I was conscious of myself thinking 'Oh, there's my Albie!' A rush of warmth went through my body at the pleasure of what seemed to be a reconnection. Next I wanted to sit on 'my' chair, eat from 'my' egg cup and so on. There was a sense of possessiveness about this which bore no relevance to my own needs or feeling, then the sensation was gone.

On the day I was due to return home I found myself becoming more and more restless, walking up and down the stairs frequently. Then, without any rational reason I felt myself on the verge of tears and in an effort to calm myself I sat down on the couch. I then became aware that my face felt smaller, my legs were short and swinging above the floor and I was angry. Carmella was cooking in the kitchen and I wanted her to be there with me, to talk to me, play with me, *see* me. Then the room began to feel small, too small for me and I had to get out.

"I want to go home. I have to go home NOW"

I called out, to Carmella and Abel's surprise as I was due to leave in an hour or so anyway.

As soon as I had spoken, other words began to tumble out. I found it acutely difficult to express the vision and expansion of consciousness that I was experiencing so intensely. I could not understand how anyone could not see what I could see, could not be aware of the light drenching the room, pouring in, upon and around the house. I spoke in breathless words of its power and of how it was being absorbed into the Earth and the natural objects in the room such as the baskets of stones, crystals and branches which hang on the wall. I was in anguish that **people could not absorb the light in any great measure due to the dense blanketing of human thoughts.**

I refused to eat the lunch that Carmella had cooked, feeling thoroughly upset by the focus on the process of eating which seemed to have no relevance to me and I made quite a speech about it. I chose to go out for a walk instead and my steps took me to the river where I sat to reflect on a rather strange morning and to return to a more normal state. It was easy then for me to understand what Alice Friend had meant by her description of feeling Benjaya viewing his body through her eyes.

Jan Perry

I never saw Benjaya in his lifetime. I am one of the millions who heard of his death on television and radio. A boy who lived in Devon - what did it have to do with me? Where did this indescribable, immense grief come from that lasted for days? I felt as if *I* had lost a child, as if he was *my* child but he wasn't even local and I knew nothing of his family.

A few weeks later I met Marael Robertson, who told me she knew the family well and the grief welled up again. I knew then that I was involved in something extraordinary. I discovered through Marael that M'haletta was running an Easter event at Adam House and that Benjaya's parents would be there. I *had* to go. When I walked in I felt an immense whoosh of love - sudden and overwhelming, just like the grief had been. The house radiated with love.

I cannot share all the amazing things that happened there for me but my most profound experience was around the birthing pool. We had been raising our consciousness and working with the meaning of the chakras

and had reached the eighth chakra, I think, when we all came together around the pool. No-one was told or asked to do anything, they all knew what was right for them in the moment. I began to see a great light which...well for me was the light of Jesus. I simply knew I had to submerge my head in the water and go under as Benjaya had. I put my head into the warm water, I've no idea for how long, and when I emerged such a serenity enfolded me that I felt completely cleansed and reborn. I felt such a bond with Benjaya and a longing to be close to him, to know more of him.

Marael became a friend and I was staying at her cottage shortly after this event. We were sitting quietly together when suddenly I felt a fantastic, vibrant energy enter the room. I called out "I'm sure this is Benjaya". And there he was. I had an image of a little boy so clearly and then I felt active, alive and buzzing with energy fit to burst. He was alert, full of laughter - a wonderful showman holding up a wooden sword calling:

"Victory...victory".[2]

Then Benjaya began speaking through me to Marael about what he used to do when he visited her - playing on the swings and talking to George.

"Who's George?" said Marael.

"You know, ginger George, your *cat*. He's here with me now," he said.

Then Marael laughed at her assumption that it was a person and remembered her dear cat George who had died. There was lots more, small things all significant to him. At 4am the buzzing energy was still scurrying around the cottage and I suggested we both get some sleep. I had wanted to be close to him and how much closer can you get than that?

Then there were the drawings. I've no talent in that direction but the energy returned again and I suddenly had the urge to make colourful vibrant

[2]At Benjaya's blessing ceremony, when he was six months, old M'haletta held up her gift to him of a golden brass sword engraved with his name and called "Victory...victory".

patterns which I am told were Benjaya style. He told me to give M'haletta a wooden tulip with pale pink petals and then I learned that pink tulip petals were the last offerings put onto his coffin. And there was the penny that miraculously appeared on my mat which I was told to give her and discovered that a song called 'Magic Penny' was his favourite.

A few months later I found myself slipping into an awareness of myself as a different person in a previous life. I explained to Marael what I was hearing - "Just water," I said, then sobbed and sobbed for ages. The whole story then began to rise to the surface of my mind. I knew that once, long ago, as a poor unmarried girl I had become pregnant and I'd prayed that the child would not live. I had a little boy and he was born dead. The grief and guilt were terrible. I'd wrapped his little body in a cloth and put him in the river to float away but I'd wanted him to come back so much.

In this life events have repeated themselves. I was married but when I became pregnant I was told that a pregnancy would be dangerous for me and I had an abortion. The guilt and desolation have been the same, wanting the baby back ...the terrible hurt. Benjaya's death has brought these vital memories back to me, helping me to understand so much. Also, experiencing the vibrant continuance of his life has released something that was blocking the joy in my life.

I take Divine Service on Sundays at local churches and one day, standing on the platform of a church, I suddenly found myself speaking of Benjaya. This turned into a flow of wonderful philosophy which I gave as it came to me and found myself radiating with pure love. So much vibrance and light coming into the world and those present were absorbed in it. Afterwards people spoke to me about feeling able to talk about love and death in a different way.

Benjaya in his spirit form has had a profound effect on me and I think on humankind. He's moving people on who never even came into contact with him. People are having experiences of release and re-awakening of their souls. What could have been just one more tragedy is releasing joy and love in people at all different levels. The people I spoke to will go home and talk about him, spreading that energy further and further. There's no end to all these ripples.

CHAPTER TWENTY

Stepping into the Stream

Carmella

A bel and I have been asked teems of questions since Benjaya's death most of which we feel we have been unable to answer in the fullness they deserve due to time limitations or other circumstances. There are also questions that have gone unheard but which our senses have received and now I have the chance to set the record straight.

A Question of Courage

Time and time again we have been described as courageous in the way we handled Benjaya's death, the implication being that the speaker would not have the ability to do likewise and has made us special in some way. In many respects 'courageous' is not a suitable label. Speaking for myself, of course I can be courageous and have sometimes been so during the time of Benjaya's death but, in the main, I have not. The way that I have behaved is a way that has come naturally due to years of hard work focusing on changing my victim-conscious attitude, seeing things in a different light, seeking and applying tools for living that work for me and integrating them into my way of being. In this time of crisis what I have been doing is applying these integrated tools.

The meaning of courage for me is drawing upon great depths of inner strength to face that which appears to be difficult and at times unsurmountable. The more difficult something appears to be, the more courage one needs to face it.

Where I acknowledge my courage is in facing and exploring the relationship to my son's dead body (an area from which I recoiled), dealing with the tiny bits of his body in a plastic urn, and seeing his body disappear for the last time. I think it took courage to simply avoid collapsing uselessly into the depths which were calling at these times.

It concerns me that we are sometimes seen as being 'special' because we have managed to successfully apply our philosophy to some areas of our lives. Once we are on a pedestal, the only way we can go is down and down we will go when it is discovered that we are still riddled with faults with which we wrestle.

I firmly believe that **anyone with a similar training and philosophy to ours could face the death of their child in the same way... or better.** All of my immediate family, who hold a similar attitude to mine, responded with loving strength.

A Question of Escapism

Our friend Lizzie voiced a question which we discovered many people to be holding in relation to our behaviour but she at least was sure of the answer:

> *"I just sat there at the Celebration in awe of Carmella and Abel, wondering 'Is this really for real? Are they being an amazing example or is this them escaping somewhere?' Yet I'd seen them dealing with their grief and knew that they weren't trying to escape the reality of it and wouldn't have to come down with a bump. Even so it was hard to believe they were so together. Carmella seemed on a high connected to something beyond herself."*

I don't know about being an amazing example, that was not an aim of ours, but I am one hundred per cent clear that we were not hiding or suppressing anything from anyone at any time. We have both felt excruciatingly painful emotions daily but it was not our way to show them by falling into black depressions, being angry or losing control as may be natural for some.

There is a big difference between being real and allowing oneself to wallow in self-pity and I watch myself carefully in this area because I have a natural tendency towards self-pity. I dare to call our experience 'holistic grief' because I think we manage to allow ourselves to feel and express whatever is bubbling within us, however painful, whilst at the same time remembering that **What you Nourish Grows** and preventing ourselves from consciously nourishing that which would increase the anguish and induce self-pity. I can see how it would be very **easy to keep ourselves in a totally useless space for years to come by simply focusing our minds on those parts of the experience that fill us with disabling horror.** I am sure that at any time I could reduce myself to an absolute wreck within seconds if I chose to do so but that is not constructive for anyone, especially Benjaya, who I believe would be **held back by grief that is out of balance and has no respite.**

I personally choose to nourish that which makes me feel good about Benjaya's life and death, such as focusing on the gifts he gave us, opening to him in his newly expanded form, and giving recognition to his birth into spirit life - just as I gave recognition to the death aspect of his physical birth. The pain for me feels like a natural and necessary *part* of the whole but not *the* whole and I am not suppressing the grief and escaping when I am expressing the joy. What happens is that the two exist within me at the same time and whichever is the more powerful emotion of the moment rises for its expression.

A Question of Convention

We were admired by many and frowned upon by a few for our choice to avoid a conventional funeral but it was a matter of making conscious choices rather than avoidance of anything else. Abel and I were born unconventional, as Aquarians often are, but at the same time our shared philosophy gave us the added confidence to go ahead and follow our own inner promptings. We had no qualms about what other people might think. That was irrelevant to us because of the power of knowing what must be done. We believe that if anyone was taken aback or felt threatened in any way it has to be their responsibility, not ours. How could we jeopardise the beauty and full expression of the celebration of our son's life and passing into a new life because someone, somewhere, might think it a bit 'off ' that his body was displayed on the stage of the village hall?

We were not saying 'We will do what we like and blow everybody else and what they think'. It wasn't like that at all. It was a knowing of the importance of what had to be done and being sensitive as far as we were able. For instance, we kept the lid on the coffin for the whole of the service and then drew the stage curtains afterwards so that no-one would be faced with a body unless they chose voluntarily to 'pay their respects'.

Following what we felt was the right thing to do for us and for Benjaya struck a chord in many people, so much more than if we had exercised restraint and compromised ourselves for the sake of the few. I think that **because we were so clear in our stream others were pulled into it and felt the celebratory flow that moved together with the tides of grief.**

At Benjaya's birth the midwives actually said that they felt 'drawn into the stream'. At the outset of the birth the 'system' strongly resisted the stream and midwives were not sent until the last minute. We carried on regardless in our clear flow and the midwives eventually fell into the stream. That is all we can do - hold our stream steady and invite people in to test the waters.

Making a stream takes a lot of work and accepting the status quo is much easier...but then you have to live with the consequences. If I had stayed in the hospital to give birth I would have either had to give away my power and accept the flow on offer or to find a source within me to create a stream which would run contra-flow to the existent one. The MetaCentre stream, into which I could flow without any effort, had been built up over many years and positive energy seemed to pulsate from the walls. I wonder what was pulsating from the hospital walls, or for that matter, the walls of the Crematorium that was our conventional alternative for the funeral service?

A Question of the Children

One of the questions so often asked of me is 'How can you be so open and loving with the children? I couldn't do it, I'd close down.' The answer is this. Not only do I feel that I have more love to give because of being cracked open by the death experience but I also have an enormous residue of love which was directed towards one little boy for five years and now seeks different outlets. **Because I have 'lost' my child I can appreciate to an enormous degree the beauty and precious nature of children.** It's as simple as that. Anyway, **how do you know what you could or**

could not do if you haven't experienced this situation?

This question comes from the common mind-set that the natural response to loss is to close down and stop giving out, which isn't true for everyone.

I do feel more protective towards children in general and sometimes I have the urge to chastise mothers who are berating or abusing their children in some way. I cannot help but think that **they would not behave in that way if they knew their child would not be there tomorrow.** They would not take anything for granted any more.

A Question of Others' Grief

How was I able to spend so many hours supporting others through their grieving process? For many years I have carried a desire to work with death and M'haletta and I had discussed how we would go about running workshops on the subject. Here was my opportunity and I found myself deeply interested in other people's experience of grief despite my personal connection to the source of their pain.

It was an extremely useful experience for a while and I felt uplifted by my ability to give a little comfort here and there. It gave me the opportunity to tap into my own strength and to share the highest perspective I could reach, as well as recognising the inevitable depths. However, this strengthening did not continue after about the third week because of the momentous amount of energy it took to keep on facing forces in need of lifting up.

Some people were easy to be with and I gained energy and others were draining simply because their belief systems were so different from my own. There were times when I became immensely irritated with the pervading 'tragedy-consciousness' around death in general. It grates on me, it is not my truth and to be congruent within myself I cannot collude with it even to save the energy of explaining myself.

From the first moment of hearing about Benjaya's exit in water I have believed that it was no accident but a perfectly orchestrated finale. When a leaf falls off the tree before it's old and wrinkled we see it as a natural event - **some leaves must fall first.** When a child leaves this world it is more often than not seen as 'a waste', something dreadfully wrong. This is the stance that drains me because with all of my being I believe the opposite to be true. Gut-wrenchingly painful it may be to lose a child but does that make it wrong and that life wasted? What an insult to suggest it! Do we only lovingly parent our children so that they may live to the age we expect them to and become productive adults, or **might a five-year-old have lived five precious, fulfilling years and have no need of living more?**

I do understand that people are well-meaning and often totally thrown into confusion as to what is appropriate to say to the bereaved but I think it **is important to start looking at and changing the way we face death NOW.** I want to beg people not to say to me - You must be feeling... this or that, but to ask me how I am feeling. Mis-reading my reality and making negative suggestions as to how I must be makes uncomfortable dialogue, which is sad considering the opposite is intended. I've spent a lot of time saying: "No, actually, no I don't feel that...no, no and no". **It takes a lot less energy to agree "Yes, life is bloody awful".**

What has also been difficult is people finding out further down the line. Here is an example of a situation that has occurred frequently. I was out shopping happily when I met a woman who had known Benj.

"And where's your boy today, at school?"

she says innocently in the course of conversation. Oh God she doesn't know!

"No, I'm so sorry to have to tell you but Benjaya is no longer with us, he died six months ago."

A scream in the high street followed by tears coursing through the pallor of shock on her face. Shopping shelved, I then have to move into the role of comforter and answer sensitively the 'Oh, how absolutely dreadful' comments.

Sometimes it's not actually possible to function normally even when I'm feeling fine because the external world makes it impossible to do so. Just a simple common question from a stranger such as 'Do you have any children?' throws me into a space of having to be discerning and having to deal sensitively with both my own reply and their response to it. However, the up-side of this is that deep and meaningful conversation that cuts through all the time-passing pleasantries is a regular and enriching occurrence in my life.

A Question of Avoidance

Someone once said **'There's only one thing worse than speaking ill of the dead - and that is not speaking of the dead at all.'** How true for me. Despite having heard that people will go to great lengths to avoid someone who is experiencing trauma in their life, I was shocked when it happened to me and curious to know why people do it. I have only been conscious of two people crossing the street at the sight of me but have been in numerous bizarre conversations where I have been acutely aware that the other person knows of Benjaya's death but is avoiding mentioning it at all costs, leaving me feeling unloved and unconnected.

The avoidance strategy makes rapport almost impossible. I have been taught that to gain rapport one needs to match the space which the other person is in and only then, if appropriate, move the communication in another direction. You cannot avoid what is hanging in the air, pretend it doesn't exist and expect to talk in a real way about something else. I'm not suggesting for a minute that all one should talk about to the bereaved is the one who has died. I'm saying that losing a loved one can have as much impact on daily living as giving birth and nurturing a new-born child. And would we, when meeting a mother who has just given birth, avoid all mention of the birth and the baby? No. So what is the difference?

Perhaps fear of pain is the difference. Pain in our society is generally perceived as a threatening enemy to be obliterated immediately. Whatever the apparent motive for avoiding pain, be it a sincere belief that you are being kind to the other person, or maybe a subconscious fear of activating your own fear, ignoring the source of pain will automatically increase the discomfort. It is well worth bearing the minor shock waves of emotion in order to have a real and heartfelt communication - albeit bitter/sweet.

It doesn't take many words to connect. About 90% of the cards and letters we received after Benjaya's death said something like 'I don't know how to express what I feel...' This is all that is needed to gain rapport. It is because of this pattern of avoidance in so many that I have found it **refreshing to meet people who say 'I'm sorry about your son'** and I thank them for mentioning it because it feels like a gift to me that he has been recognised as a vital part of my life.

I want to encourage those whose natural instinct is to avoid looking at death to do as Beauty did in *Beauty and the Beast*. She was frightened but she dared to look the beast in the face and to be open to who he really was rather than what he looked like or what other people said about him. And when she gave herself the chance to understand his true nature he turned into a handsome prince, they fell in love and lived happily ever after!

A Question of Beliefs

The mind is a very powerful tool. 'It's all a matter of belief' was an answer to many questions.

When I was three-and-a-half months pregnant with the baby that was due on Benjaya's next birthday I began to bleed. This baby was our only connection left to parenthood. I had never ceased being a mother and I felt as if Benjaya had connected to this soul and blessed it. Abel's need to be in control had evaporated immediately after Benjaya's death and this baby was wanted with all our hearts.

Blood in pregnancy is not always something to fret about but the heartbeat had not yet been heard and this was not a good sign. I had two days of not knowing whether the baby was alive or dead, would stay or go and it was horrific. My higher self said 'What will be will be' whilst my other self screamed 'My God, I cannot go through another death. I can't lose another child, I will fall into an emotional pit. I haven't enough strength left.' All these limiting beliefs were rising to the surface and I was very scared about the possibility of having to face, not only the loss of the baby, but actually seeing this quite well-formed foetus coming out of me and dealing with the blood and everything else.

I went to the hospital for a scan because the blood was continuing and the baby was not releasing naturally. The nurse looked at the screen, looked at me and shook her head saying:

"I'm sorry, this baby has been dead for about three weeks".

I went into shock and it was arranged that I would have a D. and C. operation later that day to suck the baby out. I expected that when I came round from the operation I would feel distraught. How else could I possibly feel on the total death of motherhood?

I was too groggy to think after the operation and went in and out of consciousness until the following morning. Then the sea of emotional despair began to loom, threatening to envelop me. I knew that part of this monstrous wave was to do with the tragedy-conscious thoughts that I was carrying and I wanted to release them and feel at least a little easier. I had my homeopathic remedies, my crystals and special objects in a little cupboard by the bed making a personal altar where others kept their Lucozade and toothbrushes. I opened the cupboard doors and with all the strength I could muster I sat up on the bed, cross legged and in view of the whole ward began to meditate and call upon help. A familiar voice entered my head almost immediately and said:

"Mum, it's simple. You have a choice. If you think about things that make you sad like losing me and the baby you'll get small and turned in on yourself but if you think of things that make you happy like God's perfect plan and Sai Baba and things you love, then you will get bigger and shining like a sun."

This was such a powerful experience, which included an intense sensing of Benjaya's presence, that in the blinking of an eye I realised the truth in his simple statement on a very deep level. The rest of that morning I spent humming 'My Favourite Things' from *The Sound of Music* and from that moment on did not feel any grief about losing that baby. It did not arise to be released. I simply gave thanks to the tiny being for the time s/he had been with me and for the life-force s/he had offered to help me through the death experience.

As I left the hospital, the woman in the next bed, whose face was a picture of perplexity said:

"Whatever has happened to you? I thought you'd just had a miscarriage but your face is shining?"

I said **"Everything's all right now; I've just changed some beliefs"**

The perplexity remained firmly in place!

A few months later I became pregnant again. It was a beautiful conception - a conscious conception which felt absolutely perfect as it was an expression of love between Abel and myself. Abel was very happy, was talking to the being who had chosen us - wanting a baby to receive his new-found love borne of so much pain.

A month later I began to bleed heavily and the baby was gone. I fell into a pit of despair which I had little desire to leave. I held some strong beliefs which I could not find the strength to change once I had fallen into the pit and which kept me firmly stuck into the side of grief that I hadn't yet experienced. They said 'This cannot be fair. God has deserted us. Three deaths is too much to bear.' And it was. I railed against God, I felt powerless, desolate, angry and a total victim of circumstance.

Now I had doubts that I would ever be able to carry a baby to full-term. Perhaps we would never be parents again. I grieved for this possibility as well and wished for death to come and take me to the place where those I loved were growing in number. I was angry with those who made assumptions that because the baby was here for such a short time I must feel less grief. **Time is irrelevant. It is what you believe about the situation that makes or breaks grief.**

Abel was sad and silent, carrying his heavy load with dignity and vulnerability. I looked at him and thought 'For God's sake how much more cracking open does he need?' I wanted him to be protected and I wanted to be protected from any more anguish and life lessons and pleaded for at least a break in the intensity. No-one could protect us except our own attitudes which, given a few months to surface, did win the day. We both finally found a place of acceptance within ourselves, a place where having a child would be fine and not having a child would be fine, a place that said with sincerity 'May the will of God be done'.

A Question of Understanding

'Why do you think this happened to you?' has been frequently asked by others and by ourselves. The 'why'? within me has arisen from my inherent need to understand rather than the space of 'why *me*?' I have thought and said on many occasions 'Thank God it *was* me rather than someone who has no supportive beliefs from which to draw strength'.

The whole scenario of the entwined lives of our family trio seems like a giant unfinished jigsaw puzzle to me. Some pieces show recognisable parts of the picture and the logical mind can say 'these are all flowers and they fit together' or 'this yellow bit fits with this yellow bit'. Likewise I can say that the water birth fits with the water death; Benjaya's intense interest in death fits with his early departure; and my early study of the subject and my continued desire to work with death fit with experiencing it at first hand.

I could say it is my understanding that Benjaya's task was to help start a trend in waterbirth, to teach us about birth, love and death, and to balance and integrate his two main character traits of Fearless Warrior and Tibetan Monk. And I could say that the next baby came so that I held life within me when facing death and could hold the lifeline of motherhood, or even that the second miscarriage occurred because I simply didn't get the messages offered by the first two deaths. Some jigsaw pieces, however, are deceptive. They seem to match perfectly at the time but then another part of the picture just won't fit so you have to concede that this piece doesn't fit there after all and remove it.

And what about the vast expanse of blue sky that boggles the mind with its challenging subtle sameness? We can only go so far with our powers of understanding and then we have to recognise that **to attempt to understand everything is futile.** So most of my sky came with the second miscarriage - I simply couldn't work it out, which caused me pain and consternation. Well, if my life is a jigsaw puzzle, from experience I should know that the best way to complete the picture is to let go of the struggle, get on with life and either someone else will do it for me or when I get back to it with a different attitude then the pieces will miraculously drop into place.

$\mathcal{A}$ Question of Divine Design

Why do I feel so strongly that Benjaya's death was not an accident but a perfectly orchestrated finale? There are many different issues that rise for me in response to this question. My first response is to share that on hearing of Benjaya's death there was an instant and inexplicable knowing within me that this was right - catastrophic to my senses - but right. It was not a reasoned strategy for coping but **a resonance on some deep level with the drama that was playing itself out.** Polly describes that same profound feeling of rightness that defies all logic in her interview. It is, however, true that I am firmly convinced that **nothing ever happens by chance,** which no doubt helps to underpin this sense of rightness.

Our story is littered with synchronistic happenings which to us are examples of the Divine Law that operates the Universe, that oversees the pattern of nature, working its natural way in our lives. We believe that the material we need for our next stage of growth will be placed before us as we need it and all that we must do is respond to it constructively, but not necessarily with conscious understanding. If we do not, then **the same lesson will return time and time again until we hear the message being offered.**

Could it possibly have been chance that in pregnancy I was kicked for the first time at the very moment I had asked for a kick if my wombchild wanted a waterbirth? Was it chance that Persh captured on film, in dim light, an image described by the press as 'One in a million...the kind of picture you only see once in a lifetime' that proceeded to circle the world - the image of a harmonious birth in water? Was it chance that Abel, Benjaya and I lived for two years with a family whose mother had drowned? Or chance that I met a woman called Polly in a campsite laundry? Was it coincidence that a group of students made a tableau representing birth and death using the photograph of Benjaya's birth, the Taj Mahal with its pool in front and a blue ribbon as a flowing river? If there is no Divine Design, why on Earth was M'haletta, by not being able to reach the Auroville crystal, given the lesson of transcending desire for physical matter in favour of experiencing the light body - just days before she needed that teaching more than any other? And of all the names available in the world, how come the man to bear her the news of Benjaya's death is also known as Jaya? Of all the ways for a child to die why did this child, son of parents who work with the healing power of water, happen to have a water death?

If Benjaya's death was not meant to be, then what sense can we make of premonitions? Accidents and premonitions surely do not mix or are we supposed to clearly comprehend every predictive sign and focus our energy on blocking and preventing that which looks likely to occur? The premonitions were many, although I feel that we were protected from the specifics that would have been agonising to know. M'haletta was almost waiting for the death of someone, half expecting to be gunned down with the unfortunate dog in the water. Sommer was 'playing' at drowning, coming to terms with its effect on the family and Nikhil drowned his dolls repeatedly. Benjaya himself made a flag with a skull and crossbones on it and played at drowning his pirates, not to mention all the more direct talk about death and whom he would choose to return to.

I knew on some level but not the level that would render me suicidal with fear. I have never dared to admit it before but I did feel an unsettling and incongruent sense of relief around Benjaya's death, as if the worst had come, I was facing it at last and surviving. One mother of a child in Benjaya's kindergarten shared with M'haletta:

"After the Celebration I began to understand why, when I had first seen Carmella walking up to kindergarten and looked into her eyes, I had seen a huge sadness. It seemed to me that she was crying inside.

Now I believe that she had known that this beautiful child was going to leave her. That haunting sadness has left her now."

Countless clues to Benjaya's impending death have arisen over time but one of the most astounding accounts of a premonition came in a letter from a man we had never met who was living in Brighton when Benjaya died:

Dear Abel and Carmella,

What I experienced before your son's death was so strong that I felt impelled to write and tell you about it.

The Friday before the weekend on pre-conceptual care at Dove's Nest at which you were to speak Carmella, my partner Penny and I both felt a great heaviness. We couldn't make up our minds whether to go to the event or not. I woke that day with a great, dark cloud and as the day progressed my feelings became darker. Penny went out for the afternoon and I stayed at home with our son Krysten. I felt so tired that I propped myself up with cushions on the settee and fell into a half sleep, keeping an eye on Krysten playing happily alone.

I remember the heaviness becoming overwhelming and having a pain in my chest and a picture coming to me of a little boy trying to clamber down a river bank. I wanted to help him but I saw him slip into the deep waters. I came round from my strange state sobbing, feeling my heart would burst and I reached for Krysten and hugged him tightly. I felt so frightened and anxious. What had I seen? Was this a presentiment of something that would happen to Krysten in the future?

I had applied for a job in Devon at the Steiner School and was waiting to hear if I had been successful. We were thinking of moving to the Totnes area and wondering where we might live. The only way I could make sense of what I had experienced was to see it as a warning that we shouldn't live near water. When Penny returned I said nothing to her as I found it too upsetting to talk about.

That night the image of a child slipping into water came back over and over again. I prayed, said the Lord's Prayer and begged the picture to go away.

The next day, unrefreshed by sleep and still feeling heavy, we did go to Dove's Nest only to sense a heavy atmosphere and stuckness there. The first speaker, Maya, uncomfortable at having to unexpectedly carry the beginning, explained that there had been a tragedy in the B'Hahn family and that you were unable to come. Only at the end of the day, just as we were about to leave, did Penny and I discover what had happened to your family.

In a flash I saw the little boy slip into the river once again and with it a great rush of warm light which bathed me and took away all the pain and heaviness I had still been feeling. I told Penny and Maya what I had experienced and wondered why I had felt such a great sense of loss. Later, when I realised that Benjaya was about to go into class 1, the class I was being considered to teach, I could understand why it had touched me so profoundly.

We prayed for you all and sent you love and strength to cope with those first days and have felt that Ben has been very close to us since, helping us in our work.

> *Much love to you*
> **Tim Coombs**

I think it is unlikely that anyone could have 'saved' Benjaya from his river exit, but if perchance he had been pulled out alive from the river, then my guess is that he would have drowned in the swimming pool on the following Sunday and Divine Design would not have been thwarted.

Does that mean then that I believe that we should not act to save life? No. It means that I believe that **we cannot and should not always attempt to be in control over the play of destiny.** Just as I would counsel a couple facing birth to plan and discuss their ideal birth, the highest and most beautiful entry they can imagine for their child and then release it and accept that there may be another agenda that it is necessary to face, I would say something similar about the ideal death: **'Do what you believe to be the highest, most supportive action in the moment but do not become attached to the outcome because there is a force that may know better.'**

A Question of Time

It is said that time heals and I'm sure it does - given enough of it! I want to share about the first twelve months of my grieving process in order to show that life does not necessarily become easier as the **time ticks by and** friends succeed in returning to the normality of their family lives.

At first there was a kind of dazed numbness, as if **the shock brought with it protective veils which prevented the brutal truth from fully entering consciousness.** The veils blew in the wind from time to time and a gust of the physical finality of death would hit home, bringing immediate anguish and unstoppable waves of tears. **As time passed the veils thinned and the truth sank in to deeper levels.** Words that hadn't computed before, such as 'Never will I see him again' would suddenly sink in - Oh my God, that means never, **NEVER EVER.** The veils were both a blessing and a curse as the process took its course.

There was in those first months an overwhelming sensation of some-thing vital missing from my life, as if I had lost a limb. The flesh and blood that I had borne was gone, never to be re-created. Part of my future was gone, the bit of me that was to take the B'Hahn name forward was gone. I would walk to the village and notice a puzzling sensation in my right hand and then I'd realise that it didn't feel right because I had never walked to this village without a small boy's hand in mine.

The lack screamed from almost every corner of life: no small shoes in the line next to mine; no crumbs in the bed on Sundays; no place at the table; just a space where the car seat used to be; and silence where chatter once filled the air. Space...silence...gaps...holes ...everywhere. **Rehabilitation was needed.** I did not focus on the lack but directed my thoughts to where he is now, but the impact of the physical loss I could not avoid.

The first year brought the first set of cycles to be lived without our child. Easter without eggs, a summer holiday without buckets or spades, conkers underfoot without the incentive to collect them, Advent with no calendar, his birthday without him, and Christmas with no stocking to fill. We are still waiting for time to weave its healing magic.

Tides of Healing

Restless waves engulf me
Sleep illusive, thoughts confused
The sea is calling
Offering healing
As if by water I've been abused

Seven weeks now
Since the river took
My son's body from the Earth
But water does not wound me
It reminds me of his birth

I sit now on the stony beach
The vast sea all about me
What power
What a truly awesome place
To set the spirit free

And I wonder at our language
Which speaks with fear of death
Why is it that we're
So utterly sure
That life on Earth is best?

I dare to question
Are we not dead
To the joys that re-birth brings?
Let's open our eyes
To the possible truth
That at death our hearts will sing!

CHAPTER TWENTY-ONE

ᏧheᎡeturn

Carmella

here was never a moment when I believed that my son was dead in the dictionary defintion of the word, i.e. not alive, extinguished, obsolete. For me **there is no doubt that life is indestructible and that birth and death are both merely transitions upon our journey.** Therefore, I automatically continued speaking with Benjaya after he had left his body just as I had done six years earlier before he had fully entered it.

Although talking to Benj and sending him love was a natural and easy process for both Abel and me, listening and hearing his communication with us was an entirely different matter. My greatest fear in those first months after his death was that we would lose contact with him due to our own insensitivity. We so wanted to continue our close relationship with him and knew that in theory this was possible; therefore our initial inability to create a hotline to heaven was a cause of much distress. We both felt that he was knocking on our door and that we were failing him by not being able to pull that door open more than a crack to let him in.

We had snippets of connection with him which helped and uplifted us greatly, but sometimes 'doubt' would be lurking nearby asking 'Did you really hear that? Was it memory? Wishful thinking?' Most experiences with him have come when we were least expecting them - a sudden feeling of being hugged tightly; a silly joke popping into mind in the supermarket; the television switching itself on when we are feeling down.

There was no doubt in me about an experience I had one day at home. I felt such a powerful impression that Benj had brought a friend called Jo to lunch that I pulled up an extra chair and felt compelled to be sociable. Part of me felt ridiculous talking out loud into the 'empty' space but I simply could not risk ignoring my intuition and appearing exceedingly rude. After lunch I sensed that Benj was excitedly showing Jo all around his 'old' house.

I've also felt waves of high energy, beginning on the Sunday after his death, as if **my spirits are being lifted by an invisible source.** A burst of happiness will suddenly enter my sad or tired state and I sense a bubbling, happy gremlin about. I joined the Global Harmony singers shortly after his death as a conscious act of healing but I did not expect Benjaya to join up too! Sometimes it felt as if he was singing through me and at times I was acutely aware of acting quite out of character for a newly bereaved mother.

A few months after his death I sat down with excitement and a surety that if I put pen to paper the happy gremlin would speak to me. I could feel him tapping inside my head, urging me to listen. And so I wrote a question and the following flowed out in a rapid stream with which I could hardly keep up, especially as my body seemed to be involuntarily bouncing about!

What was dying like for you Benj?

Quite nice really after the shock of the cold and the water going up my nose. I knew I had died because there was a lady there with me, kind of in my head, and she told me it was time to go now and leave my body behind. I didn't really think about you then and what it would all mean for you, I just held the lady's hand and left my body there in the water. I knew it wouldn't come up and breathe again 'cause I was not there in it.

*I went with the lady and I was a bit shocked but I remembered you said that **I wasn't my body** and now I understood. **It wasn't painful dying like that,** not at all, just very cold and bubbly up my nose before it went fuzzy and then clear when the lady took my hand.*

*Daddy was the first to feel sad and I knew he was so sad but I couldn't help him and the lady kept saying that it was painful for Daddy now but that it was a good thing really because **he would learn to love people so much more.** So I was kind of happy and sad then. Sometimes I was in the new place and sometimes I was in the world close to Daddy, trying to tell him that it was all right. I wasn't worried about myself because the lady was kind to me.*

Then I had to come to you and it was strange to suddenly be able to come to you on a train. The lady was leading me. We just loved you. I couldn't do anything else and I knew you would be so sad to lose your boy. But **I am not lost you see and what is most difficult for me is when you think I am lost because you can't see or hear me.**

Do you know if it was it planned in advance that you would die at five years old?

Well yes I do. The timing wasn't absolutely fixed and I could have stayed longer if my teachers and me thought it best for everyone. There was still a lot I could have learnt about being still and gentle and not so big-headed but I'm learning that here. Sometimes I get so big that I become all the people I've ever been and all the learning I've ever had. Then I get smaller and have to learn simple lessons about myself that I didn't learn as Benjaya.

So when I chose you and the waterbirth before I was born, I did know that I might not stay a big life but I didn't know how long I had. I didn't worry about death at all did I? I was just interested in it. Some-times in that little body I did feel sad for you and wanted to love you so much to make up for having to leave you - that's why I hugged you so tightly so often.

The teachers told me that this was a good time to go because of lots of reasons:

1) *It was easy to fall in that river right by the workshop and I had to die in water.*
2) *There would be time for you and Daddy to heal and have another baby.*
3) *So many lots of people would learn about death - people I wouldn't know later.*
4) *Daddy and you could learn so much faster if I went sooner.*
5) *The planets were right. I don't understand that but I will.*

What did you think of your funeral?

I loved it and was very happy apart from a teeny bit of sadness when some people cried. I was allowed to go as my big beautiful self, although I showed my boyself to some people, and I was so, so bright.

*Lots and lots of beautiful beings, teachers and friends were there too
and we had a good, good time. Lots of people who knew people present
were there to add their light together and we know you felt us. Most
people felt us, even Pops who won't ever admit he did - not until he dies
anyway. I was especially happy that you felt me there in my big body
and were a happy mummy. I wanted the people to see you shine with
light so that they could feel some happiness about me dying. We were all
above you kind of shining and receiving your love and giving ours. The
children felt us and they knew that death is all right.*

*It was so good to have my friends there but you know, in my big
body, I didn't look at Will as a little boy because I could see him as a
kind of soul light in a little body who was my friend. And **the soul light
didn't have an age,** wasn't young and sweet, but equal to my big light.*

*Daddy was sad I know and we all loved him so much that day. Part
of his sadness was being overwhelmed with so much love and not having
learnt what to do with it. He needed then to open to his emotions and
allow tears and tears to flow out. Until he opened his channel wide the
love just couldn't come out. So his tears were healing for me to see
because I knew he had to do it.*

*But Mummy, your tears are a bit different. You didn't need to make
a channel for love because your tears have been making a channel for a
long, long time. I know you have to cry when you get full up with pain
but sometimes they are not healing and it would help you to know the
difference. I know you miss me and I miss you too and sometimes get
sad, but there's so much here to do that's good and I want you to get on
with the so much that's good for you to do in your life. You'll always be
my snodscumber beauty [private endearment] wherever you are because
we love each other so much don't we?*

It was sheer delight to talk with Benjaya as if there was no separating veil
between his world and mine but unfortunately I was unable to maintain
the delight and my emotions roller-coastered from the heights to the depths
for many months to come. I wanted to feel secure in the knowledge of
how and where my boy was as time progressed but every time I thought
I'd grasped a clear glimpse of understanding things would change and I
was left floundering in a state of unknowing.

In April when I was still pregnant with the first baby I was sitting in
bed resting when I had a sudden flash of knowing that Benjaya would

return in the next child - not the one I carried, the following one. I felt shocked, surprised and excited all at once as this seemed to have come out of the blue, certainly not from my own thought process. I wrote in my diary:

I'm scared because I'd love this to happen. I don't dare trust this message because I'll be so hurt if it's wrong. I'm not going to tell anyone about this except Abel.

A few weeks later, as I was waking up one morning, I had a clear image flash into my mind of a baby being sick and simultaneously I heard Benjaya's voice say:

"I'm going to be like that Mum."

I wanted to believe it so much but knew that these two incidents were not necessarily the voice of truth although they felt like it at the time.

In June 1992, a few weeks after I had miscarried, I flew to Italy to see a spiritual master. This had been made possible by my friend Alice who, on hearing me say that all I wanted to do was to sit at the feet of love, had arranged the whole trip. Benjaya most definitely went with me.

In a question and answer session with the master I was going to ask him if he knew how and where my son was now but I managed to get out only two words "My son..." before being interrupted with:

"AH, BEN. He left for you to all learn lessons but he is urgent to return".

He then placed his hands on my womb in an act of healing and blessing saying:

"He will return in you."

I was both stunned and elated and was now totally convinced that our boy's spirit would reincarnate in me when the timing was right.

Back in England shortly after my trip, I was sitting in a cafe in Totnes sharing with friends about this encounter with the master when I noticed that a woman on the same table, whom I had met briefly once before, was looking somewhat disturbed. When my friends had left she moved closer and said:

"I'm rather shaken because I couldn't help but overhear what you were saying and as you spoke about your son returning in you I saw a young boy sitting at the end of the table with a big grin on his face nodding, his head. I hope you don't mind me telling you. I don't usually tell people of my visions as I'm unsure how they might react."

Needless to say I did not mind.

I have to say that although I chose to share my convictions with care I was very excited by the thought of the potential of Benjaya coming back so soon. I began imagining not only the comfort that his return could bring us but also the amazing evidence of life after death that might present itself. After all, if Tibetan masters make a habit of fast reincarnations and their ongoing consciousness is identified despite the different bodies that host it, then why should it not happen in the West with our boy who, as a baby, was the image of a Tibetan monk?

When Abel and I conceived again in July, I felt Benjaya's presence strongly and was convinced that I could sense his excitement about the possibility of coming again in my womb. We were delighted with the prospect of all that lay ahead, despite knowing the challenges of pregnancy, birth and parenting full well. It was therefore devastating when this baby also died. We were not just losing a baby but also losing the hope that our boy would be with us physically again. Had I not been told that Benjaya would return in the second baby? Had we now lost the chance? Could my own visions and even the words of a spiritual master have been created by my own powerful subconscious desires? I couldn't rule out this possibility.

Gradually, after floundering in unthinkable despair, the light could be seen at the end of this dark tunnel and Abel and I both managed to let go to a point where it did not matter any more if Benjaya returned or not. As we released our attachment to parenting, our trust in the perfection of life's unfolding pattern returned.

However there was now a more subtle loss emerging for us to contend with, which presented us with another precious gift. Can there ever be a dark cloud without a silver lining I wonder, or **is there a law of polarity that states that the negative cannot exist without the positive?**

We were becoming increasingly aware that Benjaya was learning and changing at a rapid rate that was out of step with Earth time. In meditation one day I heard him say with great pride in his voice:

"I'm growing fast now Mum, it's like I'm almost seven".

A few months later, through a sensitive friend of ours he said:

"I'm still growing and I'm this big now".

No longer did we have a visual image of our son that matched the present reality and we felt that to hold him continually in our minds as the beloved five-year-old we knew might trap him in the past. We began to feel as if we were losing him on yet another level and my feeling of loss increased to a crescendo after an event that was soon to come, blinding me somewhat to the gift on offer.

It was almost twelve months after Benjaya's death when M'haletta and I met with two friends, Marael and Jan, in Marael's cottage where Benjaya had made his vibrant presence felt before. Jan especially wanted to share her life-changing encounters with Benjaya with me and after her loving speach about him it was no surprise that we felt him there in the room. It was Jan who heard him speak and she relayed clear messages of his boyish memories, including things known only to me. There was then some confusion and crossed wires and finally, when we found clarity, we understood that Benjaya had now **moved completely from boy-consciousness into his Greater Self** and it was from this space, new to us, that he was now attempting to communicate.

The atmosphere seemed to be electrified with the power of this Greater Self as he now spoke through Marael, introducing himself as Ben-el-eth and asking us to release all desire for the boy-consciousness with which we were so familiar. With my inner sight I saw in that moment a vast and magnificent eagle with wings outstretched which proceeded to descend into me so that I felt transfigured by its form. I could not move a muscle as I felt the power of the talons and breadth of the wingspan dwarfing this tiny room. Confidence, strength and capacity for love seemed to be throbbing through my feathered body and I knew that this power would be at my fingertips from now onwards if I sought it. It was the power of my son in his present form and the words of the Italian master echoed in my head 'He will come back in you'. Is this what he meant? It certainly seemed unlikely that Ben-el-eth was preparing to reincarnate.

My heart almost broke in the following two weeks because I interpreted the request to release desire for boy-consciousness to mean not just in the moment, but forever, which meant that my little boy was now truly gone. There was only one thing I wanted more than the magnificence of that eagle power, confidence and love and that was to retain the connection with the familiar, cheeky clown-boy with whom my life had been so interwoven even through the veil of death. Now, a year down the line, I was facing a similar desolation to that of the bereaved non-believer who must come to terms with death being the end of contact with their loved one. It was a nightmare which, thank goodness, was short lived because Benjaya the boy came bouncing straight back into our lives a couple of weeks later, causing an explosion of relief.

It was February 23rd, 1993, when Abel and I finally had a session with a locally-renowned medium for which we had waited seven months due to the level of demand. Abel and I are not in the habit of visiting mediums because we believe that there are certain risks involved. **It is so easy to give away our power by believing that a 'professional' knows better** than our own inner source of wisdom and thereby limiting the unfoldment of our innate abilities. Also, if a medium is given visual images or vague impressions, there is a necessary process of interpretation involved which may be correct or way off beam. **Interpretation is a minefield.** So why did we choose to pay to see this particular woman? The appointment was made at the time when we knew Benjaya was trying to communicate and we were struggling to raise our energy high enough to hear him. We wanted to give him the best possible opportunity to tell us anything he felt needed to be said, with no interference, and this woman's name was given to us from all angles. She has a reputation as a very pure channel coupled with personal humility and integrity. Also, she did not know us or anything about our situation which seemed an important criterion to us.

I spoke excitedly to Benjaya before the session, telling him that we would be going to see a woman who had the ability to hear and relay his words and to be prepared if he wanted to use the opportunity. I also attempted to raise my consciousness as high as possible, believing that **the higher the vibrations in the room, the clearer the communication is likely to be -** a little like tuning in a radio to a particular frequency.

Abel and I entered the pleasant room in the little bungalow and took our seats by the window overlooking green valleys and a river to the sea. The elegantly dressed, middle-aged woman with sparkling eyes began by explaining that she would say a prayer and then sit and listen for whatever presented itself for our learning. The tape recorder was switched on and she began:

D.C: *There's a child around you with big eyes. That's the first thing that people will notice about him - his eyes. He's a beautiful child, a special child. Who's Ben? There's someone calling out "Hello, I'm Ben".*

Carmella: *He calls himself Ben but no-one else does.*

D.C: *I thought Benjamin at first but he said "I'm Ben". I have to work out if he's in spirit or on Earth as they all look the same to me. He seemed not to know where he was, there seemed to be a jolt with him. Is he in spirit?*

Abel: *Yes.*

D.C: *He's telling me off saying "I was here, it's your confusion!" I'm telling him to speak slowly. He's so happy, so full of life. I'm having trouble making him stand still to talk as he's so fidgety. He's telling me you knew he wouldn't be here for long, Carmella. He said he communicated this to you early on. It's like he was too precious to stay.*

*He's saying "Don't be sad, **I was a gift**". This one's never left you and he says "You heard me, it was me - not imagination and I do hear you when you speak to me". He will move things and make a noise to let you know he's heard you and you'll find things go missing because he's mischievous. He's producing flowers now for the anniversary that is around [his death anniversary].*

He'll become your teacher - both of you - you're learning about each other through him. He changed your life in the short time that he was here but he says "The teachers become the students now". I'm going up four levels with him which is where our guides are. He's saying "They're writing a book you know and I'm helping them write". It's your healing book Carmella and it will help others.

The pain of parting was for you great but for him - none! He's so happy although he's telling me that his death was quite sudden. He gave me a thud but he's telling me "no pain" and showing me a little silver slide. He seemed to go from one side to the other and is saying " You did the right things, no guilt is needed. I love you Mum. I love you Dad".

He often gives you hugs at night and seems to touch your face a lot Carmella. He touches and strokes your hands Abel. With your face it will feel like a hair grazing your cheek and then you will begin to recognise what it's like. He stands beside your bed as you go to sleep.

He says "You used to touch my face and now I touch yours".
He says "Tell her how she's a medium". He won't work through
you as a medium, he'll work around you. There are mediums of all
kinds. He will come through writing, that's how he'll come. Remember
that I'm talking to a child who's back in spirit and has great knowledge.
You are going to have direct contact with him always. Just talk to him -
they hear our thoughts stronger than our words because thoughts are a
stronger vibration and that's what they answer.

Carmella: *I'm unsure how to relate to Benjaya now as I understand that*
he has moved into his Greater Self and is no longer the five-year-old
boy we knew.

D.C: *Yes, he went to the higher level quite quickly, but remember in your*
time he's your little boy. Relate to the little boy, don't try to let him go
yet. We really have no understanding of spirit - with them there's no
judgement and he understands that you need the little boy to hold onto
still. He comforts you being five years old - well he's older now, he's
nudging me, telling me. Let him grow with you and you'll not stop his
progress. He has an expanded mind now, an intelligence far beyond
ours which we all have and he will awaken it in both of you. He'll give
you greater spiritual knowledge and help your mediumship so he can
come through.
You've got another child waiting to come and this child can't wait.
Ben will be a part of this child and you'll see a spirit that you'll recog-
nise. You see this is another thing that we don't understand, we are all
part of the whole and our spirit can be in many places at the same time.
Ben does not weigh heavily on you two, he came in very light and
loving and it feels as if the two of you have dealt with his passing. Some
spirits come in and they're so heavy but he just wandered around as was
his wont. He's no different, his character does not change but it grows
much more rapidly than we ever grow.
*He's blowing you kisses.[1] **XXXXX***

Oh he's given me one too. Children are so refreshing to work with. He's
together with the first child you lost, who wasn't born.
Get on with the book. There'll be another one. God Bless you

---

[1]Benjaya usually blew us kisses as we left his bedroom last thing at night.

The following morning, greatly encouraged by Benj telling me that it is him I hear, I sat awaiting his communication. Again I could feel his excitement and again I could hardly scribble the words down fast enough.

Well I said I'd come didn't I?
Here I am and I'm still a trickster. I can feel that you want me to say
something about Ben-el-eth because you need your confusion sorting
out. It's like this you see - I am Ben-el-eth, far bigger than just Ben and I
can call upon so much you wouldn't believe. That's how I can be so
much help to you because I can expand my boyself to give almost
whatever you need. Actually, that's a bit confusing too because it's not
like I am a boyself who can get bigger and wiser - that's how it was
*when I first came here - now **I am the whole wiser self and can still***
come to you as my boyself because that's what you draw from me like
***a magnet that attracts certain metals.** You attract Benjaya and give me*
a chance to play the trickster. I think I'll come as both Benjaya the
trickster and Ben-el-eth the teacher because you and Daddy would love
both I am sure. And it doesn't matter if you mix us up because we are
mixed up anyhow aren't we! (laughter)
I'm still a joker and do you know why? Because I make myself
laugh a lot and that's so funny. I suppose I'm a bit excited now because
you're hearing me so clearly. About time you washed your ears out and
noticed my jumping tricks! Why didn't you think of me when your socks
disappeared and the troll kept falling over? I thought you were a bit dim
not to notice me jiggling about and doing funny things. It was me who
knocked the bag of sugar over too.[2] I thought that was a good one! I
won't do anything naughty though, I'm just trying to show you that I'm
around and that you can still have your boy in your life.
Oh Mum, I love you and Daddy and I don't want to lose you so I
won't. I don't have to and I'm so happy that I've been allowed to come
and be with you and help you. It makes me laugh that one day you're
putting my socks on me and then WHAM, BANG I'm supposed to be
dead but I'm not, I'm hiding your socks and feeding you bits of wisdom!
You'll catch my happiness, just wait and see, then you'll know why I
can't keep still because happiness makes your legs bubble and run.
Nice walk we had with Tim wasn't it? And you didn't even notice

---

[2] I was on a diet and in a moment of weakness was ogling the chocolate in a shop when a bag of sugar leapt off a nearby shelf and landed at my feet.

me. Seven miles by the river and sea and do you think anyone so much as helped me over a stile. No! Never mind, I didn't need to go over the stile with heavy legs like yours anyway and I know you were thinking of me even if you didn't know I was there.

Whenever you think of me I know about it and often I come instantly to be with you. It's so easy you wouldn't believe and it's taken me a while to understand how **part of me can be clowning around Higher Green and another part is teaching or learning somewhere else.** God's amazing you know. He must be because I'm amazed! Everywhere's so beautiful where I live that I just can't help being bubbly. I tried to learn to be still but I haven't managed that one yet. 'Still' is not my cup of tea. You love a nice cup of tea, don't you Mum? You like stillness too and that's why I was a bit of a trouble wasn't it?

I still go and play with my friends - not because I need to, I don't, but they call me with their thoughts and I go. I've been to see Will, Meriel, Josh and even Phoebe who I didn't play with much before I died. They all want me now though don't they? Now I'm dead I got to be important.

I think I've said enough because I'm worried about my big head saying the wrong things.

Tell EVERYBODY I love them (specially Daddy)
Your boy

PS. What do you think of Charlotte's new baby then? She's a friend of mine of course.

A couple of days later he was with me again, his familiar energy skipping around me, prompting me to catch his wordflow.

Hello Mum,
Get yourself comfy because you don't feel comfy. That's better. Sometimes I'll be here as large as life and sometimes not so obvious and d'you know why? Because **you** can't settle down and catch me. **I can come to you any time you think of me without disturbing anything I am doing at the time.** I know it's hard to understand but I can just carry on doing that thing as well. If I couldn't I'd be as limited as you are in your body - or at least as limited as you think you are. Sai Baba doesn't let his body stop him from going anywhere he likes does he? Every day people see him in different places at the same time.

At first I found it difficult to be all about the place because my thoughts were caught up in my boyself, as if my way of thinking of myself as a boy was like a net from which I had to free myself to grow in this new world. Now I know I'd hate to be a fish wriggling in a net trying to find the freedom it once had. Even when I was a boy in my body I recognised the holes in the net and slipped through sometimes to talk to you from a place of freedom. At night it was usually, or out **in nature where God seemed to flow about more freely.**

I think that when I came into my body I felt more trapped than most children do. I often felt like I wanted to throw myself through that annoying net, to blast to the freedom on the other side. I know I had no patience and even said I wanted to be a bull, but I want you to understand that what lay behind that impatient charging nature was a free spirit enthusiastically seeking expression in a restricting world. I think you always knew that, Mum, even when others judged me harshly.

But don't you or Dad feel bad (that rhymes) about your hard work with me because **I came to express myself as spirit as fully and wholly as possible and it was my job to do that within the net of life's restrictions.** I wouldn't have chosen Dad would I if I didn't feel the need to face restrictions! Now Dad, that does not mean that with the next child you behave the same - oh no! We both learnt from the way we were then and we must move on mustn't we? The net for the next child will be a little less knotty I hope.

Thank you Dad for all my swords, pity I didn't get a gun though. Even now I think it would have helped me blast my way through the net. The next child will have a gun, right? And I'll pull the trigger! I know what's a game and what's not. It is the motive that matters. If I'm a poor kid whose Mamma's been shot in the street somewhere and I want a gun then perhaps then it's best I don't have it to shoot revenge and hate into people, but for me it would have been a tool to shoot my exploding power out and relieve the jumping tension in my body. Don't worry about me though because when I am teaching or healing now I can channel energy without a gun.

I can feel you noticing the big words I am using and wondering 'is this my boy?' **Don't box me into boy-consciousness.** I'm using bigger words because I am pushing you a little bit to move towards where I am now. I'll not go too fast but it's easier for me to use a more adult way of speaking to explain some things. Don't forget that you'll always be my

Mum but I will always be much more than your son. You can choose which part of me you're ready for.
I think that's enough. This book will be a long one if I keep talking and you want to quote me!

Goodbye. I love you.

Benjaya/Ben-el-eth continues to make his presence known, expressing different aspects of himself in accordance with our needs. The Trickster is held responsible for many a trick - including hiding countless items, dematerialising a watch, playing with the computer and regularly turning on the television.

I began to recognise a presence in the bedroom, mainly at night, standing by my side of the bed. I could sense the gentle, fun-loving energy with which Benjaya expressed his love to us, but in vastly greater measure. The sensation of my head being stroked was as real as if the hands were physical, and always the healing energy was accompanied by a wafting breeze.

Ben-el-eth, with eagle wisdom, gradually took over the task of teaching me through the pen, and no doubt in many other ways. And life's events, as they have done for us all, continue to provide the illustrations on which our learning is based, offering us the challege of sculpting new scripts.[3]

There is no end. Benjaya the boy is now history, and yet -

My son/sun is shining still
as he did upon the Earth;
Breaking the mourning with his light.

---

[3]Currently in production -
Heaven to Earth by Carmella . The sequel to *Benjaya's Gifts* written in intimate diary-form. Has Benjaya returned as it has been predicted?
The Cloak of India by M'haletta. A Probation Officer's Transformational Journeys.

Gifts for your Learning

Ben-el-eth (through Carmella)

There is that which is to be said here and it is entrusted to me to say it.

The concept of separation - that which keeps humanity bound in an isolated state of 'I' importance - **must be abolished** as your time quickens into a new era. It is now scientifically proven that all in existence is interconnected energy of varying frequency/density. Therefore no-one, nothing, ever can be separate. All is of the same substance.

The wisdom seen in the eyes of a babe at birth is not his or her personal wisdom but is one and the same wisdom that is veiled within you all. It is **the** wisdom, the communal ocean of knowing of the soul.

It is the erroneous belief in solidity that allows the belief in separation and makes a mockery of the transitions of birth and death. If the eye did not perceive matter but the moving, dynamic particles which form the illusion, then would humanity's consciousness move mountains in an instant. It is this that is the revelation of death; for death is but a dance of freedom from the body's earthly thought.

The 'I' that speaks to you now is not a son but a sun - the sun. I am one with all that is. I am light. I am Benjaya, Ben-el-eth and beyond. I can see through the eyes of those on Earth and enlighten the thoughts of the mind. So give me your minds that I may play my tune of infinite light amongst their limitations. Entrust to me your fears that I may bask in the love that lies beyond them. Offer me your pain that I may return to you the value of its gifts. **For all that is, is gifted for your learning.**

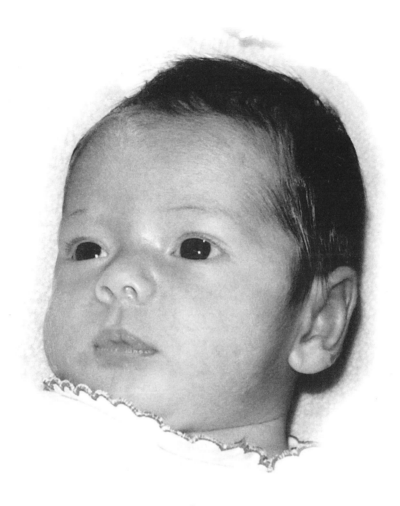

Asher Sai
Second Born Son
of
Carmella and Abel B'Hahn

Entered life through water
1st December, 1993

His dark, magnetic, Tibetan-shaped eyes spoke a thousand words.

Further Information

BirthWorks

Carmella B'Hahn
Heartwood, Bowden House
Totnes, Devon TQ9 7PW
Carmella@HeartofRelating.com
www.HeartofRelating.com

3F Brent Mill Estate, South . Tel:01364 72802.
Contact for hire or purchas ubs, baptistries &
flotation tanks. Also beautiful, ecological nappies for sale.
Training booklets on: *Holistic Birth and the Spiritual Midwife*
The First Breath
Water, Birth and Culture
£2.50 each + 50p p&p or £7 + £1.20 p&p the set
Evolution of MetaCentre - A Light Centre Handbook
£3 + £1.50 p+p
All by Carmella and M'haletta

Holistic/Waterbirth & Shedding Light on Death workshops on demand.

Hazelwood House (home of Hazelwood Press)

A beautiful place which offers bed and breakfast, family holidays, rest and recuperation for all people, including those from war-torn countries, alongside a programme of concerts, lectures, art weekends and exhibitions. Benjaya's river runs through its wild valley.
For further details ring **01548 821232**
Hazelwood Press has been set up expressly to publish books such as *Benjaya's Gifts,* which is its second publication.

Jaya Nivas, the educational project in India, is progressing well. The land has been bought and money is presently being raised to erect the buildings. Contact M'haletta, MetaCentre International, Adam House, Adams Hill, Clent, West Midlands DY9 9PS, England. Tel: **01562 883297**

Rod Friend, artist of the stained glass memorial illustrated on the front cover, is committed to raising energy through art. Enquiries about commissions welcome. Starlight Studio. Tel: **01453 75091**